British and Commonwealth Armies 1939-43

Helion Order of Battle
Volume 1

Mark Bevis

HELION & COMPANY

This book is dedicated to Tim Kohler, who, in 1984, introduced me to TOEs in the first place

Helion & Company
26 Willow Road
Solihull
West Midlands
B91 1UE
England
Tel. 0121 705 3393
Fax 0121 711 4075
Email: publishing@helion.co.uk
Website: http://www.helion.co.uk

Published by Helion and Company, 2001

Designed and typeset by Bookcraft Ltd, Stroud, Gloucestershire
Printed by The Cromwell Press, Trowbridge, Wiltshire

© Helion and Company 2001

ISBN 1 874622 80 9

British Library Cataloguing-in-Publication Data.

A catalogue record for this book is available from the British Library.
All rights reserved. No part of this publication may be reproduced, stored in a retrieval system, or transmitted, in any form, or by any means, electronic, mechanical, photocopying, recording or otherwise, without the express written consent of Helion & Company.

For details of other military history titles published by Helion & Company contact the above address, or visit our website: http://www.helion.co.uk.

We always welcome receiving book proposals from prospective authors.

Front cover photograph – a M3 Stuart light tank, probably belonging to the 8th King's Royal Irish Hussars, photographed in Libya, 1941/2 (RAC Tank Museum, Bovington).

CONTENTS

Introduction — vi
Note on abbreviations and nomenclature — vii

PART 1 NORTH-WEST EUROPEAN THEATRE 1939–43

1.1	British 1st Armoured Division, May 1940, France	1
1.2	British 1st Armoured Division, June 1940, France	1
1.3	British 1st Infantry Tank Brigade, BEF, 1940, France	2
1.4	British Independent Armoured Units, BEF, October 1939–40, France	3
1.5	British Infantry Division, 1939–40, Britain/France	3
1.6	British Territorial and Line of Communication Divisions, 1940, Britain/France	4
1.7	British 30th Brigade, Calais Garrison, June 1940, France	4
1.8	British Infantry Brigades, April–June 1940, Norway	5
1.9	British Home Defence Infantry Forces, June–December 1940, Britain	6
1.10	Canadian 1st Infantry Division, 1940, France/Britain	7
1.11	Canadian 2nd Infantry Division, 1941–43, Britain/Dieppe	8
1.12	British Parachute Brigade, 1941–42, Britain	9
1.13	British 1st Airborne Division, 1942–May 1943, NW Europe	10
1.14	British Anti-Aircraft Divisions, 1939–October 1942, Britain	11
1.15	BEF Corps and Army Support Units, October 1939–June 1940, France	11
1.16	British Corps and Army Support Units, Home Defence, 1939–40, Britain	12

PART 2 NORTH AFRICAN THEATRE 1938–43

2.1	British 7th Armoured Division, March–September 1940, North Africa	14
2.2	British 7th Armoured Division, October 1940–February 1941, North Africa	15
2.3	British 2nd Armoured Division, March–April 1941, North Africa	16
2.4	British 7th Armoured Division, April–May 1941, North Africa	17
2.5	British 7th Armoured Division, June–August 1941, North Africa	18
2.6	British 7th Armoured Division, September–December 1941, North Africa	19
2.7	British 1st Armoured Division, December 1941–February 1942, North Africa	21
2.8	British Armoured Divisions, March–July 1942, North Africa	22
2.9	British 1st Armoured Division, August 1942–May 1943, North Africa	23
2.10	British 7th Armoured Division, August 1942–May 1943, North Africa	25
2.11	British 10th Armoured Division, September–November 1942 North Africa	26
2.12	British 6th Armoured Division, November 1942–May 1943, Tunisia	28
2.13	British Blade Force, 6th Armoured Division, November 1942, Tunisia	29
2.14	British 4th Light Armoured Brigade, mid-1942–May 1943, North Africa	29
2.15	British Army Tank Brigade, October 1940–February 1942, North Africa	30
2.16	British Army Tank Brigade, March–July 1942, North Africa	31
2.17	British 23rd Armoured Brigade, August 1942–January 1943, North Africa	31
2.18	British Army Tank Brigade, January–May 1943, Tunisia	31
2.19	Independent Armoured Units, 1940–May 1943, North Africa	32
2.20	Indian 3rd Motorised Brigade, February–April 1941, North Africa	32
2.21	Indian 3rd Motorised Brigade, January–May 1942, North Africa	33
2.22	British and Commonwealth Infantry Divisions, June 1941–43, North Africa	33
2.23	Australian Infantry Division, 1940–41, North Africa	34
2.24	Australian Infantry Division, mid-1942–43, North Africa	35
2.25	New Zealand 2nd Division, mid-1942–43, North Africa	36

2.26	Indian Infantry Division, 1940–41, North Africa	37
2.27	Indian Infantry Division, early 1942–43, North Africa	38
2.28	British Parachute Brigade, November 1942–May 1943, Tunisia	39
2.29	British Corps Support, 1938–40, Egypt	39
2.30	British Corps and Army Support, October 1940–April 1941, North Africa	40
2.31	British Corps and Army Support, April 1941–February 1942, North Africa	40
2.32	British Corps and Army Support, February–July 1942, North Africa	41
2.33	British Corps and Army Support, August 1942–May 1943, North Africa	41

PART 3   MIDDLE EAST, CENTRAL AND WEST AFRICAN THEATRES   1938–43

3.1	Indian 1st/31st Armoured Division, April–December 1941, Iraq/Persia	43
3.2	Indian 2nd Armoured Brigade, August 1941, Persia	44
3.3	South African 7th Armoured Brigade, September–November 1942, Madagascar	44
3.4	African Infantry Division, July–November 1940, East Africa	45
3.5	African Infantry Division, November 1940–November 1941, East Africa	45
3.6	Indian Infantry Division, October 1940–November 1941, East Africa	46
3.7	Indian Infantry Division, 1940–41, Iraq/Persia	47
3.8	South African 1st Infantry Division, October 1940–February 1941, East Africa	48
3.9	Australian Infantry Division, 1941, Syria	49
3.10	East African 22nd Brigade, September–November 1942, Madagascar	50
3.11	British Cavalry Division, July 1940–March 1942, Palestine	50
3.12	Sudanese Home Defence Forces, 1939–September 1940, Sudan	51
3.13	British Garrison Forces, 1939–August 1940, British Somaliland	52
3.14	Kenyan Home Defence Forces, 1939–November 1940, Kenya, S. Abyssinia	52
3.15	Gideon Force, December 1940–May 1941, W. Sudan, W. Abyssinia	53
3.16	British Garrison Forces, 1940–41, Habbiniya Airbase, Iraq	53
3.17	British Habforce, May–July 1941, Iraq/Syria	54
3.18	British Force 121, May–September 1942, Madagascar	55

PART 4   MEDITERRANEAN THEATRE   1939–43

4.1	British 2nd Armoured Brigade, April 1941, Greece	56
4.2	Australian and New Zealand Infantry Divisions, March–April 1941, Greece	56
4.3	Commonwealth Infantry Divisions, 1943, Sicily	57
4.4	British 231st Infantry Brigade, July 1943, Sicily	58
4.5	British 1st Airborne Division, July 1943, Sicily	59
4.6	Crete Garrison, November 1940–April 1941	60
4.7	Crete Garrison, May 1941	60

PART 5   FAR EAST, AUSTRALASIAN AND INDIAN THEATRES   1939–LATE 1943

5.1	British 7th Armoured Brigade, 1942, Burma	62
5.2	British and Commonwealth Independent Armoured Units, 1942–43, various theatres	62
5.3	Indian Infantry Division, 1937–42, India/Burma/Malaya	63
5.4	British Infantry Division, 1942–43, Asia	64
5.5	Australian Militia Division, 1939–September 1942, Australia	65
5.6	Australian Infantry Division, August 1942 onwards, New Guinea, New Britain, Bougainville, Borneo	66
5.7	Indian 50th Airborne Brigade, October 1941–September 1943, India/Burma	67
5.8	Indian Cavalry Brigade, 1937–42, India	67
5.9	British China Command, 1939, Hong Kong/Shanghai/Singapore	68
5.10	British Hong Kong Garrison, 1940–41	68
5.11	Commonwealth Units in Burma, December 1941–42, Burma	68

5.12	Malaya and Singapore Garrisons, 1942	70
5.13	Java Garrison, February–March 1942	73
5.14	New Zealand Garrisons, 1939–45, Pacific Islands	73
5.15	Pacific Islands Native Forces, 1941–43	74

PART 6 SPECIAL FORCES (ALL THEATRES)

6.1	British Independent Companies, April 1940–41, NW Europe	75
6.2	British Commando Forces 1940–43:	75

    Special Service Brigade, late 1940–March 1941
    Raid on Lofeten Islands, Norway, early 1941
    Commandos 1–12, 1941–42
    30 Commando (Special Engineering Unit), mid-1941–43
    Raid on Vaasgo, Norway, December 1941
    Raid on Dieppe, France, August 1942
    Special Service Brigade, 1943
    Lay Force, March–September 1941, Middle East
    Middle East Commandos, 1941
    Royal Marine Commandos, February 1942–43
    Army Commandos in Tunisia, November 1942–43
    10th Inter-Allied Commando, July 1942–43

6.3	Miscellaneous Royal Marine Units:	77

    7th RM Battalion/No.31 Brick, January–July 1943, Egypt
    Royal Marine Boom Patrol Detachment, 1942 ("Cockleshell Heroes")
    11th RM Battalion, Crete/Tobruk raids, April–October 1942
    Force Henry, April 1940, Norway
    Primrose Force, April 1940, Norway
    Hook of Holland Marine Company A, May 12th 1940, Holland
    RM Siege Battery, 1940–August 1942, Kent, England
    32nd RM Howitzer Battery, 1941, Shetlands
    19th RM Battalion, May 1940–43, Scapa Flow

6.4	Royal Marine Naval Base Defence Organisation 1 (MNBD01), June 1940–February 1941, Britain	78
6.5	Royal Marine Naval Base Defence Organisation 2 (MNBD02), April 1943–44, Egypt/Sicily	79
6.6	Royal Navy Commando 1942–43	80
6.7	Royal Navy Combined Operations Assault Pilotage Parties, (COPP Teams), 1942–43, Mediterranean	80
6.8	British Special Operations Executive (SOE)	80
6.9	Long Range Desert Group 1940–43	80
6.10	Special Air Service (SAS), 1941–43	83
6.11	Special Boat Service/Squadrons 1940–43	83
6.12	Special Service Squadrons, Royal Armoured Corps, mid-1941–mid-1942	83
6.13	British and Commonwealth Special Forces 1942–43, Far East, including	83

    RM Force Viper, February–April 1942, Burma
    Burma II Commando, February–April 1942, Burma
    204th Mission Battalion, 1942–43, China
    Australian Independent Companies, late 1941 onwards
    1st Indian Independent Company, April 1941 onwards, Malaya
    1st and 2nd Fijian Commando, 1943, Pacific Islands
    Southern and Eastern Independent Commandos, Guadalcanal, December 1942–June 1943
    Royal Marine Rose Force, December 28th 1941–January 1942, Malaya

Notes for wargamers	85
Bibliography	87

INTRODUCTION

This is the first volume in a series dedicated to tables of organisation and equipment (TOE). A companion, covering British and Commonwealth armies 1944–45, is already in preparation, and supplement volumes are also planned.

I was first introduced to the concept of accurate TOEs when wargaming at polytechnic during the 1980s. It soon became apparent that existing TOE charts produced for wargamers were incomplete and riddled with errors, or were produced for certain rules; these lists are a result of my frustration with publications then in existence. At the time much TOE data was only accessible in academic literature and archives, beyond the reach of most wargamers and military enthusiasts. Whilst this situation has changed since 1990, much of what has been produced recently relies on contemporary handbooks (not the most reliable of sources) or German archives. In addition, much data is presented in a top-down format, depicting the number of brigades, regiments and companies within a division. When TOE information for companies and platoons has been presented, it has often been within text, and displays inconsistencies between authors and publishers.

The approach for this book has been manifestly different. Because the TOE charts depicted here were originally designed for wargamers, who are most interested in unit organisation at 'the sharp end', the reader will find plenty of information on this element of a formation. Organisation within a battalion is presented in a standard user-friendly format, which allows for instant comparison between opposing forces, and quick access to a particular level of units. No unfamiliar symbols or box diagrams to learn! Brigade, divisional and corps support units are all detailed, presenting a clear view of those formations available to divisional commanders at a given time. Throughout, the emphasis is placed on the combat elements of a formation.

In addition, it is worth noting that a separate section on so-called "Special Forces" is to be included in each volume. In many cases this will be the first published attempt to draw together the unit organisation of all special forces. This is particularly so for British and Commonwealth formations.

Within each list, the chief combat units are listed under the heading 'Main Combat Elements', with brigade and divisional support units under their own headings. Accompanying notes remark on the allocation of radios, infantry anti-tank weapons, weapon in service dates (IOC – initial operational capability), morale and training ratings, variations and other miscellaneous notes. The issue of radios, and training levels, are overlooked in many publications, and yet these factors can alter the combat ability of a unit drastically, regardless of how well equipped a unit is in weapons. Such considerations are given priority here.

All the various non-combat elements of headquarters units are grouped together as rifle sections per HQ for ease – these usually represent signallers, intelligence staff, service personnel, batmen, cooks, artillery survey units, etc., who, in an emergency, could be used as extra riflemen. Similarly, vehicles are assumed to have a crew in addition to any troops noted – lorry drivers are not included in manpower totals. Supply trucks, wagons, tankers, bread vans, etc, are also not noted, as they were not direct combat elements. See the 'Note on Abbreviations and Nomenclature' and 'Notes for Wargamers' for further assistance when using the lists.

It is intended that each volume in this series will be sub-divided into theatres of operation; within each theatre, a broadly standard order of content is planned – Armoured Divisions; Armoured Brigades; Independent Armoured and Armoured Recce units; Mechanised Divisions and Brigades; Motorised Divisions and Brigades; Infantry Divisions; Infantry Brigades; Airborne Brigades/Divisions; Horsed Cavalry formations; Corps support units; Army support units; Special Forces; Miscellaneous/Garrison forces.

The format of these charts allows for updates and corrections, and it is intended that such information will be incorporated into future volumes. Additional information and corrections would be welcomed, and should be sent care of the publishers.

NOTE ON ABBREVIATIONS AND NOMENCLATURE

ABBREVIATIONS

AA	anti-aircraft	H/T	halftrack
AALMG	LMG mounted on tripod for AA purposes	HVAP	see APCR
A/C	armoured car	IP	Indian Pattern
ACV	armoured command vehicle	LAD	Light Aid Detachment
AFV	armoured fighting vehicle	LCA	Landing Craft Assault
AP	armour piercing shell, or solid shot, no explosive burst	LCM	Landing Craft, Mechanised
		LMG	light machine gun (Bren, etc)
APC	armour piercing, capped (solid shot with piercing cap)	LP	Local Pattern
APCBC	armour piercing with cap and ballistic cap	LSI	Landing Ship Infantry
APCNR	armour piercing composite non-rigid	MMG	medium machine gun on tripod of rifle calibre, e.g. Vickers
APCR	armour piercing, composite rigid (HVAP in American parlance) – tungsten core	MNBDO	Royal Marine Naval Base Defence Organisation
		NZ	New Zealand
APDS	armour piercing discarding sabot	OP	Observation Post, also known as FOO
ARV	armoured recovery vehicle	PHQ	Platoon headquarters
A/T	anti-tank	Pl HQ	Platoon headquarters
AVLB	armoured bridge layer	RCL	Recoilless Rifle (also RR)
BAR	Browning Automatic Rifle	RHQ	regimental headquarters
BHQ	Battlegroup headquarters	RTR	Royal Tank Regiment
Boys	Boys anti-tank rifle	S/C	scout car
Btn HQ	Battalion headquarters	sec	section
Btn	Battalion	SHQ	squadron headquarters
CBW	Chemical, Biological Warfare (usually recce/detection units)	S/L	searchlight
		SMG	sub-machine gun
CHQ	company headquarters	smk	smoke
COPP	Combined Operations Assault Pilotage Parties	SP	self-propelled
CS	close-support	SPG	self-propelled gun
demo	demolition	sqd	squad or section of about 10 men
DHQ	Division headquarters	sqdn	squadron
ECM	Electronic Counter Measures	Trp HQ	troop headquarters truck w/LMG this was the most common Commonwealth tank in 1940–41, and was usually a 15cwt truck with closed cab and open-backed cargo body, with a pintle-mounted Bren gun just behind the cab. Crew would be a driver and passenger in the front cab with rifles, and one or two men in the back manning the Bren gun and carrying rifles. The prime purpose of the vehicle would be to teach driving skills and group manoeuvring, this being important when it is considered that most people at that time could not drive.
EW	Electronic Warfare		
FC	fire control (see 'Notes for wargamers' section)		
flamegun	flamethrower		
FOO	see OP		
HE	high explosive		
HEAT	high explosive anti-tank (hollow charge anti-tank round)		
HKSA	Hong Kong Singapore Artillery		
HMC	howitzer motor carriage		
HMG	heavy machine gun on tripod, 12.7mm or similar class of calibre		
HQ	headquarters	WP	White Phosphorous

ARTILLERY FIRE CONTROL

Artillery batteries are described as having one of three types of fire control, these being Obsolete, Assigned, and Flexible. All are Flexible type unless stated otherwise. For descriptions please see the appendix 'Notes for Wargamers'.

MORALE AND TRAINING VALUES

These are very important in judging the ability of the force in question, and take the form of a descriptive grading. Training includes fieldcraft ability (i.e. the ability or lack thereof to use cover when advancing and hiding), accuracy of firing, and the knowledge of modern combined arms tactics. The latter is significant when trying to form mixed battlegroups tasked to achieve certain objectives. The following criteria are used:

Excellent Training Specialists with over 6 months training in their specialism – e.g. Commandos, Paratroops. Very good levels of initiative, whereby units will continue to operate even with major officer/NCO losses, or where local commanders can improvise new plans on the spot, and carry them out. Good fire discipline with high levels of marksmanship, and extra training in melee combat. Very good fieldcraft skills, with an ability to use cover and concealment for advancing. Have the ingenuity and perseverance to use captured weapons immediately.

Good Training Usually combat veterans with at least 3 months effective training or 6 months combat experience, or with effective combined arms training. Capable of responding to order changes effectively and improvisation under combat stress even with some leader losses. Good fieldcraft skills or experience, able to use terrain instinctively to aid defence and attack. Above-average firing accuracy or good melee skills, and able to use captured weapons with some effect.

Average Training The bulk of British and Commonwealth troops, typically about 8–10 weeks training in basic combat skills. Very much reliant on officers and NCOs in order to function effectively. Capable of following an initial battle plan, and also of combined arms actions, but with limited ability to respond quickly to circumstance, especially when under combat stress and suffering casualties. Average shooting skills and limited fieldcraft skills; would be able to carry out ambushes and create interlocking earthworks for defence given a few hours.

Poor Training Conscripts with rushed training, 6 weeks or less (told how to march and shoot and little else), with inexperienced officers and NCOs. Very often troops being used for something other than they were trained for, e.g. using pioneers, trained to dig, as infantry. Totally incapable of using terrain to aid an advance, and usually indifferent or poor shooting skills. Poor camouflage skills. No enthusiasm for melee combat. Very reliant on officers and NCOs to keep semblance of order, will be poor at changing orders once in combat, and will have little or no training in combined arms combat.

Bad Training Not common in British and Commonwealth armies, basically civilians shown how to use a rifle and told to get on with it! Alternatively, native volunteers with more enthusiasm/bravado than skill, such as Arab tribesmen. Although particular individuals may have military ability, the unit will have no fire discipline, no knowledge of use of cover, and no training in battle planning. Attempting to change orders once under fire or expecting the use of initiative would be disastrous.

Morale is a much more subjective statement, but here it is seen primarily as the ability of a unit to withstand casualties before suffering a morale reverse (i.e. halts if advancing under fire, breaks off and withdraws if defending), and is based loosely on the following:

Excellent Morale Elite troops with high motivation and disregard for casualties, will typically sustain 70% casualties before collapsing. Very capable of continuing to function even with heavy officer/NCO losses. However, will suffer a major drop in enthusiasm if not used in action. Usually highly or well-trained.

Good Morale Veteran troops or troops with well known "warrior" status, can typically take 50% casualties before failing, especially in defence. Capable of continuing to function despite some officer/NCO losses. Typical of many non-English British and Commonwealth units, which were noted for their above-average valour. Indeed, one observer in the Far East commented that an infantry brigade with a Gurkha battalion and an Australian battalion either side of a British battalion, would be capable of dealing with anything.

Average Morale The vast bulk of conscript regular infantry of the period, with sufficient training and motivation to carry out orders at first, but will often halt at 10–15% casualties, and may break at 30% losses, especially if suffering significant officer/NCO losses.

Poor Morale Troops that have had less than 4 weeks training, or have not had any time to co-ordinate with other units, or where motivation is lacking, or the troops are unwilling to advance. Will often halt whilst under fire, even with very light losses. Can still be acceptable in defence, but will break on 15–30% losses.

Bad Morale Not common in British and Commonwealth armies, usually untrained militia, unenthusiastic troops and civilians. Will often break and run even if only receiving ineffective fire. Completely unmotivated troops, such as some of the Australians at Singapore, might be classed thus.

Note that a unit can be described as poor in training but good in morale. Very often troops with indifferent or poor skills would still have high motivation, especially in defence. In certain cultures (especially outside Europe) losses have less effect on unit morale even in poorly trained units or armies – many Soviet and Japanese units would take enormous losses and still try to carry out their orders.

AMMUNITION

Whilst it has been emphasised that troop quality, doctrine and radio allocation are just as important as equipment quality, there is another equipment factor that is often overlooked, i.e. ammunition type issued to anti-tank weapons. Much criticism has been directed towards the 2pdr anti-tank gun and tank gun, especially for the early-war period, yet when its stated penetration figures are examined it can be seen that for its calibre of 40mm, it had an excellent penetration performance, especially when issued with later types of ammunition. It should also be noted that the British 2pdr and 6pdr did have high explosive rounds available to them, although these were rarely issued due to doctrine, and production delays. Here then is a general guide to the various types of anti-tank ammunition issued at different dates:

   2pdr 40mm – AP (1938); APC (May 1942); APCBC (September 1942); HE (November 1942).
   2pdr Littlejohn – from early 1943, any 2pdr-equipped vehicle could have the Littlejohn adaptor fitted, firing APCNR (armour piercing composite non-rigid) squeezebore rounds.
   6pdr 57mm – AP (1941); APC (1941); APCBC (September 1942); HE (January 1943); APCR (October 1943); APDS (May 1944).
   17pdr 76.2mm – AP, APC, APCBC (January 1943); HE (June 1944); APDS (August 1944).
   25pdr field gun – HE, smoke, mustard gas (1938); AP (early 1942).
   37mm M6 tank gun – AP, HE (1938); APC (May 1941); APCBC (September 1942); canister (only Far East, 1944+, when in British/Commonwealth service).
   75mm QF tank gun – APC, HE (1942); APCBC (February 1943).
   75mm M2, M3 tank guns – APC, HE (1942); APCBC (late 1942).
   76mm M1, 3" M7 tank guns – APC, APCBC, HE (1942); HVAP (October 1944).

During the first three months following its introduction, the newer ammunition would be rare and would be used alongside the older standard round, perhaps at the rate of 3–6 rounds per tank or gun. Thus, for example, it can be assumed that British tanks in June 1942 would primarily have 2pdr AP, with a few APC rounds; by August they would mainly have APC, with a few rounds of APCBC available from September 1942. Late 1944 Fireflies would only have 2–3 rounds of APDS, the rest being APCBC and some HE, although by 1945 the allocation was probably greater. Initially there were a lot of problems with the APDS round, as it suffered from grave dispersal problems over 600 metres. These problems were more or less sorted out by 1945, when the Comet came into service.

   Note that the 25pdr field gun, often used as an anti-tank gun in the desert, did not have an AP shot until 1942; up until then it had to use plain HE with impact fuses, which, being of 25lb (11kg) weight, would have been quite effective against tanks if a direct hit was scored. The Close Support tanks with 3.7" and 3" howitzers never had an anti-tank round, relying on HE and smoke rounds only.

PART 1
NORTH-WEST EUROPEAN THEATRE 1939–43

1.1 BRITISH 1ST ARMOURED DIVISION, MAY 1940, FRANCE

The Division's main combat elements were:
- 2 Armoured Brigades (2nd – The Queen's Bays, 9th Queen's Royal Lancers, 10th Royal Hussars; 3rd– 2nd RTR, 3rd RTR, 5th RTR)
- 2 Divisional Motor Infantry Battalions (2nd Btn, King's Royal Rifle Corps, 1st Btn, Rifle Brigade)

During the campaign, the Divisional Motor Infantry Battalions, and one Armoured Regiment (3rd RTR) were detached to Calais. The Division fought in France after Dunkirk, and was not part of the BEF. The Division is rated at average training and average morale.

SUPPORT UNITS

Divisional Support
Included:
- 2 A/T Batteries, each: Battery HQ (1 rifle sec, 1 truck)
  - 3 Troops, each: 4 × 2pdr, 4 trucks, 2 LMG
- 2 AA Batteries, each: Battery HQ (1 rifle sec, 1 truck)
  - 3 troops, each: 16 × Lewis AALMG, 4 trucks
- 1 Engineer Squadron: Sqdn HQ (2 rifle secs, 1 lorry, 1 motorcycle)
  - 4 Troops, each: 4 × (12 man) rifle/engineer secs, 3 LMG, 2 trucks
- 1 Field Park Troop: stores, workshop sections

Brigade Support
Armoured Brigade HQ (10 × tanks and/or Vickers VIB, 3 × staff cars or Daimler S/C, 1 × mock-up 4x4 ACV with mild steel/wood body)

MAIN COMBAT ELEMENTS

Armoured Regiment
RHQ (3 × Vickers VIC, 0–2 × A–13 Mk.2)
- 3 Squadrons, each: Sqdn HQ (1–2 × Cruiser, 1 × CS-tank)
  - 2 Troops, each: 3 × Vickers VIB
  - 2 Troops, each: 3 × A–9 or A–10 or A–13 Mk.1 or A–13 Mk.2
  - 1 Recce/Liaison Troop: Trp HQ (1 × Daimler S/C or Scout Carrier)
    - 3 Sections, each: 3 × Daimler S/C
    - or 2 Sections, each: 2 × Scout Carrier

Divisional Motor Battalion
Btn HQ (2 trucks, 1 lorry, 2 rifle secs, 2 LMG)
- 4 Companies, each: Coy HQ (1 rifle sec, 1 × 2" mortar, 1 Boys A/T Rifle, 2 MMG, 2 trucks)
  - 3 Platoons, each: 4 rifle secs, 4 Boys, 1 × 2" mortar, 3 LMG, 4 trucks
  - 1 Platoon: Pl HQ (1 × Scout Carrier, 1 × staff car, 1 LMG)
    - 3 Sections, each: 3 × Bren Carrier, 3 LMG, 3 Boys, 1 (6 man) rifle sec
- 1 Battery: 4 × 3" mortars, 1 Boys, 4 trucks, radio truck

Notes
1. Radios were in all AFV and other Coy HQs, when working.
2. Infantry sections had No.68 rifle A/T grenades or No.73 or No.74 A/T grenades.
3. Proposed Armoured Regiment (not formed) was as follows:
RHQ (4 × tanks, 3 × Scammel Wreckers)
- 3 Squadrons, each: Sqdn HQ (2 × tanks, 2 × CS-tanks)
  - 4 Troops, each: 3 × tanks

1.2 BRITISH 1ST ARMOURED DIVISION, JUNE 1940, FRANCE

The Division's main combat elements were:
- 2 Armoured Brigades (2nd and 3rd) (each of 1 converged Armoured Regiment)
- 1 Divisional Infantry Battalion (initially 4th Borders, later 2/6th East Surrey Regiment)

The Division fought using this formation for a brief time. The Division is rated at average training and average morale.

SUPPORT UNITS

Divisional Support
Included:
- 2 A/T Batteries, each: Battery HQ (1 rifle sec, 1 truck)

3 Troops, each: 4 × 2pdr, 4 trucks, 2 LMG
2 AA Batteries, each: Battery HQ (1 rifle sec, 1 truck)
   2 Troops, each: 16 × Lewis AALMG, 4 trucks
   1 Troop: 5 × 40mmL60 Bofors, 5 trucks
1 Engineer Squadron: Sqdn HQ (2 rifle secs, 1 lorry)
   4 Troops, each: 4 × rifle/engineer secs, 3 LMG, 2 lorries

Brigade Support
Armoured Brigade HQ (2 × tanks, 1 × Vickers VIB, 3 × staff cars or Daimler S/C, 1 × mock-up ACV)

MAIN COMBAT ELEMENTS
Armoured Regiment
RHQ (2 × Vickers VIC, 0–1 × A–13 Mk.2)
   3 Squadrons, each: Sqdn HQ (1 × Cruiser, 1 × CS-tank)
      2 Troops, each: 3 × Vickers VIB
      2 Troops, each: 2 × A–9 or A–10 or A–13 Mk.1 or A–13 Mk.2
   1 Squadron:[1] Sqdn HQ (1 × Matilda I)
      2 Troops, each: 3 × Matilda I
   1 Recce/Liaison Troop: Trp HQ (1 × Daimler S/C or Scout Carrier)
      2 Sections, each: 3 × Daimler Scout Car
      or 1 Section: 2 × Scout Carrier

Divisional Infantry Battalion
Btn HQ (2 rifle secs, 1 staff car, 2 trucks, 5 motorcycles)
   4 Companies, each: Coy HQ (1 (13 man) rifle sec)
      3 Platoons, each: 1 (7 man) Pl HQ rifle sec, 1 × 2" mortar, 1 Boys, 3 (10 man) rifle secs, 3 LMG, 2 lorries
   1 Support Company: Coy HQ (1 rifle sec, 1 truck)
      1 Platoon: 2 × 3" mortars, 2–3 trucks, radio truck
      1 Platoon: 4 × Twin AALMG, 4 Boys, 4 trucks
      1 Platoon: 2 × rifle/engineer secs, 1 lorry, 1 LMG
      1 Platoon: Pl HQ (1 × Carrier, 1 × Daimler S/C, 1 LMG)
         3 Sections, each: 3 × Bren Carrier, 3 LMG, 1 (6 man) rifle sec

Notes
1 Radios were in all AFV and other Coy HQs, when working.
2 Infantry sections have No.68 A/T grenades or No.73 or No.74 A/T grenades.
3 In June 1940, survivors transferred to England possessed fourteen A–13 Cruiser tanks and twelve Vickers Mk.VI.

1.3 BRITISH 1ST INFANTRY TANK BRIGADE, BEF, 1940, FRANCE
The Brigade's main combat elements were:
   2 Infantry Tank Battalions (4th and 7th RTR)
The Brigade is rated at average training and good morale.

SUPPORT UNITS
Brigade Support
1st Tank Brigade HQ (4 × Matilda II, 6 × staff cars, 2 × radio vans)

MAIN COMBAT ELEMENTS
4th Tank Infantry Battalion
Btn HQ (2 × Matilda II, 4 × Vickers VIB, 2 × staff cars)
   3 Companies, each: Coy HQ (1 × Matilda I, 1 × Vickers VIC, 2 × staff cars)
      5 Platoons, each: 2 × Matilda I (MG), 1 × Matilda I (HMG)

7th Tank Infantry Battalion
Btn HQ (2 × Matilda I, 4 × Vickers VIB, 2 × staff cars)
   1 Company: Coy HQ (1 × Matilda I, 1 × Vickers VIB, 1 × staff car)
      5 Platoons, each: 2 × Matilda I (MG), 1 × Matilda I (HMG)
   1 Company: Coy HQ (1 × Matilda II, 1 × Vickers VIB, 1 × staff car)
      5 Platoons, each: 3 × Matilda II
   1 Company: Coy HQ (1 × Matilda II, 1 × Vickers VIB, 1 × staff car)
      2 Platoons, each: 3 × Matilda II
      3 Platoons, each: 2 × Matilda I (MG), 1 × Matilda I (HMG)

Notes
1 Radios were in all AFVs.
2 For wargames purposes, from March 1940 up to half of any Matilda I platoons fielded can be fitted with mine-ploughs.
3 This unit could be classed as Army Support for BEF forces in France.

---

1 This squadron was only present in one of the armoured regiments.

British and Commonwealth Armies, 1939–43

1.4 BRITISH INDEPENDENT ARMOURED UNITS, BEF, OCTOBER 1939–40, FRANCE

All were army-level assets. There were seven armoured recce and cavalry regiments available 1939–40. Four were cavalry, these usually being assigned to infantry divisions. The Phantom Squadron reported directly to GHQ on enemy and friendly unit locations. These units are rated at average training and average morale.

ARMOURED RECCE AND CAVALRY REGIMENTS:
Each:
RHQ (4 × Vickers VIc, 2 × Scout Carriers, 41 motorcycle couriers)
   3 Squadrons, each: Sqdn HQ (2 × Vickers VIc, 2 × Scout Carriers)
      2 Troops, each: 3 × Vickers VIB
      4 Troops, each: 3 × Scout Carriers, 1 rifle sec, 3 Boys, 3 LMG

RECCE REGIMENT (12TH LANCERS)
RHQ (2 × Morris CS9 A/C, 5 × Leyland radio lorries)
   4 Scout Sections, each: 3 × Daimler Scout Cars
   3 Squadrons, each: Sqdn HQ (3 × Morris CS9 A/C, 3 × staff cars or 3 × Daimler S/C
      3 Troops, each: 3 × Morris CS9 A/C

NUMBER 3 AIR MISSION PHANTOM SQUADRON
      2 Troops, each: 3 × Guy Mk.1 A/C

Notes
1   Radios were in all AFVs and other Coy HQs.
2   Infantry sections had No.68 rifle A/T grenades or No.73 or No.74 A/T grenades.

1.5 BRITISH INFANTRY DIVISION, 1939–40, BRITAIN/FRANCE

The Division's main combat elements were:
   2–3 Infantry Brigades (each of 3 Infantry Battalions)
   1 Divisional Recce Battalion

This list should be used for Regular Infantry Divisions and Brigades used mainly in the BEF, and in France after Dunkirk. The Divisional Recce Battalion was not always present, and, in effect, was a unit attached from Corps. Five Divisions were Motor Divisions, theoretically fully motorised and possessing 2 Brigades, 2 Field Artillery Regiments, and 2 Engineer Companies, although in practise they were little more than reduced strength Infantry Divisions.[2] Troops are rated at average training and average morale, or at average training and good morale if Guards or Highland units.

SUPPORT UNITS

Divisional Support
Included:
   4 A/T Companies, each: Coy HQ (1 rifle sec, 1 truck)
      3 Troops, each: 4 × 2pdr, 2 × LMG, 4 trucks or Dragon IID
   3 Field Artillery Regiments, each:
      2 Artillery Batteries, each: Battery HQ (1 radio van, 4 trucks, 4 rifle secs, 2 Boys, 2 AALMG)
      3 Troops, each: 4 × 25pdr Mk.1, 5 trucks, radio van, 2 AALMG, 1 Boys
      or 1 Troop: 4 × 18pdr, 4 × Light Dragon III, radio truck, 2 AALMG, 1 Boys and 1 Troop: 4 × 4.5" L15 infantry howitzers, 4 × Light Dragon III, radio truck, 2 LMG
   3 Engineer Companies, each: Coy HQ (1 rifle sec, 1 truck, 2 Boys, 2 LMG)
      3 Platoons, each: 4 (12 man) rifle/engineer secs, 1 Boys, 1 LMG, 2 lorries
   1 Engineer Stores Company: explosives, tools, bridges, 1 bulldozer

Brigade Support
Included:
   Infantry Brigade HQ (4 rifle secs, 2 staff cars, 3 lorries)
   1 HQ Defence Platoon: 4 rifle secs, 3 LMG, 1 × 2", 1 Boys, 4 trucks
   1 A/T Company: Coy HQ (1 rifle sec, 1 truck)
      3 Platoons, each: 3 × 25mmL73 portée on trucks

MAIN COMBAT ELEMENTS

Infantry Battalion
Btn HQ (2 rifle secs, 1 staff car, 2 trucks, 5 motorcycles)
   4 Companies, each: Coy HQ (1 (13 man) rifle sec, 1 lorry)
      3 Platoons, each: 1 (7 man) Pl HQ rifle sec, 1 × 2" mortar, 1 Boys,
      3 (10 man) rifle secs, 3 LMG, 2 lorries
   1 Support Company: Coy HQ (1 rifle sec, 1 truck)
      1 Platoon: 2 or 6 × 3" mortars, 2–3 trucks, radio truck
      1 Platoon: 4 × Twin AALMG, 4 Boys, 4 trucks

---

2   The five divisions nominated as Motor Divisions were: 1st London, 2nd London, 50th (Northumbrian), 55th (West Lancashire) and 59th (Staffordshire).

1 Platoon: 2 rifle/engineer secs, 1 lorry
1 Platoon: Pl HQ (1 × Carrier, 1 × Daimler S/C, 1 LMG)
3 Sections, each: 3 × Bren Carrier, 3 LMG, 1 (6 man) rifle sec.

Divisional Recce Battalion

Btn HQ (2 rifle secs, 4 trucks, 1 car, 6 motorcycles)
3 Companies, each: Coy HQ (3 rifle secs, 2 Boys, 2 trucks, 10 motorcycles)
3 Platoons, each: 3 rifle secs, 3 LMG, 1 Boys, 1 × 2", 11 × M/C Combinations
2 Platoons, each: Pl HQ (2 × Daimler S/C w/LMG)
3 Sections, each: 1 × Daimler S/C (Boys), 2 × Daimler S/C (LMG)

Notes
1. Radios were in all Coy HQs and AFV Platoon HQs. The Divisional Recce Battalion possessed 16 radios in total. All artillery is rated as Assigned FC.
2. Infantry squads had No.68 rifle A/T grenades.
3. For wargames purposes, there is a 10% chance of one brigade per division being Guards.
4. Daimler S/C not available in 1939, only staff cars.

1.6 BRITISH TERRITORIAL AND LINE OF COMMUNICATION DIVISIONS, 1940, BRITAIN/FRANCE

The Division's main combat elements were:
2–3 Infantry Brigades (each of 3 Battalions)
Line Of Communication (LoC) divisions were originally assigned to the BEF to guard supply dumps, harbours, etc, but became combat units after Dunkirk. Territorial units fought in Norway, and in France following Dunkirk. Troops are rated at poor training with good or average morale.

SUPPORT UNITS

Brigade Support
Infantry Brigade HQ (6 rifle secs)

MAIN COMBAT ELEMENTS

Infantry Battalion
Btn HQ (2–6 rifle secs, 2 LMG, 3 Boys)
4 Companies, each: Coy HQ (2 rifle secs, 2 LMG)
3 Platoons, each: 4 rifle secs, 0–1 × 2" mortar
0–1 Battery: 2–4 × 3" mortars (Obsolete FC)

Notes
1. No radios at all. No divisional support.
2. Infantry sections had no A/T grenades. The LMG and Boys in Battalion HQs and Coy HQs could be distributed amongst the rifle platoons. Typically any Boys A/T had only 20–30 rounds each available.

1.7 BRITISH 30TH BRIGADE, CALAIS GARRISON, JUNE 1940, FRANCE

The Brigade's main combat elements were:
2 Motor Battalions (2nd Battalion, King's Royal Rifle Corps, 1st Battalion, Rifle Brigade)
1 Territorial Motorcycle Battalion (1st Battalion, Queen Victoria's Rifles)
3rd RTR

The garrison fought against 10th Panzer Division in defence of Calais. Where not given, units are rated at average training and average morale.

SUPPORT UNITS

Brigade Support
Included:
British 30th Brigade HQ (4 British rifle secs, 2 French rifle secs, 6 British lorries (poor training, average morale)
1 French Infantry Company: Coy HQ (2 rifle secs) (poor training, good morale)
4 Platoons, each: 4 rifle secs, 1 LMG
1 Platoon: 2 × 60mm M35 mortars
2 French Infantry Platoons, each: 4 rifle secs, 1 LMG (poor training, average morale)
1 French MG Platoon: 4 MMG (poor training, good morale)
1 French Artillery Battery: 4 × 75mm M1897 (poor training, good morale)
2 British A/T Troops, 229th A/T Battery, each: 4 × 2pdr, 4 trucks
1 British Heavy AA Battery: Coy HQ (1 rifle sec, 1 lorry)
2 Troops, each: 4 × 3" 20cwt AA, 4 lorries
1 British Light AA Battery: Coy HQ (1 rifle sec, 1 lorry)
3 Troops, each: 4 × 40mmL60 Bofors, 4 trucks
1 Royal Marine Company (ship detachments): Coy HQ (1 (9 man) rifle sec, radio (good training and morale)
2 Platoons, each: 30 men
1 MG Section: 2 × Vickers MMG, 16 men
5 French Militia Platoons, each: 4–5 rifle secs (poor training, poor morale)
3 Naval Batteries, each: 4 × 4.7" or 4" guns from RN destroyers (Obsolete FC)

MAIN COMBAT ELEMENTS

British Motor Battalion (average training, good morale)
Btn HQ (2 rifle secs, 2 LMG, 1 car)
    4 Companies, each: Coy HQ (1 pistol sec, 1 × 2" mortar, 1 Boys, 2 MMG)
        3 Platoons, each: 2 rifle secs, 2 pistol secs, 4 Boys, 1 × 2" mortar, 3 LMG, 4 trucks)
        1 Platoon: Pl HQ (1 × Scout Carrier, 1 × staff car, 1 LMG)
            3 Sections, each: 3 × Bren Carrier, 3 LMG, 3 Boys, 1 (6 man) rifle sec
    1 Battery: 2–4 × 3" mortars, 1 Boys

3rd Royal Tank Regiment, 1st Armoured Division
RHQ (2 × A–13 Mk2, 1 × Scammel Wrecker)
    2 Squadrons, each: Sqdn HQ (1 × A–13 Mk2, 2 × A–10 CS)
        2 Troops, each: 3 × A–9
        1 Troop: 3 × Vickers VIB
    1 Squadron: Sqdn HQ (3 × Vickers VIC)
        4 Troops, each: 3 × Vickers VIB

1st Battalion, Queen Victoria's Rifles, Motorcycle Battalion
Btn HQ (2 rifle secs, 4 trucks, 1 car, 6 motorcycles)
    3 Companies, each Coy HQ (3 rifle secs, 2 Boys, 2 trucks, 10 motorcycles)
        3 Platoons, each: 3 rifle secs, 3 LMG, 1 Boys, 1 × 2", 11 × M/C combinations)
        1 Platoon: Pl HQ (2 × Daimler S/C w/LMG)
            3 Sections, each: 1 × Daimler S/C (Boys), 2 × Daimler S/C (LMG)

Notes
1   Radios were in all Btn HQs and all tanks, and all Motorcycle Btn Coy HQs and Scout Cars.
2   Infantry had no A/T grenades.
3   The French Militia platoons represent various Pioneers, Customs Guards and sailors.
4   The Motor Battalions appear to have had no trucks and up to half the men had pistols only.

1.8 BRITISH INFANTRY BRIGADES, APRIL–JUNE 1940, NORWAY

Four infantry brigades served in Norway –
    15th Infantry Brigade[3] (1st Btn Green Howards, 1st Btn King's Own Yorkshire Light Infantry, 1st Btn York and Lancaster Regiment)
    24th Guards Infantry Brigade (1st Btn Scots Guards, 1st Btn Irish Guards, 2nd Btn South Wales Borderers)
    146th Infantry Brigade[4] (1/4th Btn Lincolnshire Regiment, 1/4th Btn King's Own Yorkshire Light Infantry, Hallamshire Btn York and Lancaster Regiment)
    148th Infantry Brigade[4] (1/5th Btn Leicestershire Regiment, 1/8th Btn Sherwood Foresters)

Only the 15th Infantry Brigade had any Brigade support. The Guards are rated at average training and good morale; Regulars are rated at average training and average morale; Territorials are rated at poor training and average morale. Independent companies are rated at good training and good morale.

SUPPORT UNITS

Corps-Level Units Assigned As Support (mid-May 1940 onwards, Narvik operation only)
Included:
    12 AA Troops, each: 4 × 3.7" AA guns, 6 lorries
    15 AA Troops, each: 4 × 40mmL60 Bofors, 4 trucks
    1+ Artillery Batteries, each: Battery HQ (1 radio van, 4 trucks, 4 rifle secs, 2 AALMG)
        2 Troops, each: 4 × 25pdr Mk.1, 5 trucks, radio van, 2 AALMG, 1 Boys
    5 Independent Companies, each: 289 men (Commando units operating behind enemy lines)
    5 Armoured Landing Craft, each: 1 tank or 1 company of infantry
    9 Destroyers, 1 Battleship (4 × twin 15" guns), 2 Light Cruisers (Assigned FC)
    1 Battalion Sailors/Marine Battalion "Primrose Force": 725 troops (see List 6.3)

BRIGADE SUPPORT
Included:
    Infantry Brigade HQ (4 rifle secs, 2 staff cars, 3 lorries) with up to:[5]
        1 HQ Defence Platoon: 4 rifle secs, 3 LMG, 1 × 2", 1 Boys, 4 trucks
        1 A/T Company: Coy HQ (1 rifle sec, 1 truck)
            3 Platoons, each: 3 × 25mmL73 portée on trucks
        1 Light AA Battery: Battery HQ (1 rifle sec, 1 truck)
            3 Troops, each: 4 × 40mmL60 Bofors, 4 trucks
        1 Royal Marine Searchlight unit

---

3   Regular infantry.
4   Territorials.
5   15th Brigade only.

MAIN COMBAT ELEMENTS

Regular Infantry Battalion (15th Brigade)
Btn HQ (2 rifle secs, 1 staff car, 2 trucks, 5 motorcycles)
    4 Companies, each: Coy HQ (1 (13 man) rifle sec)
        3 Platoons, each: 1 (7 man) Pl HQ rifle sec, 1 × 2" mortar, 1 Boys, 3 (10 man) rifle secs, 3 LMG
    1 Support Company: Coy HQ (1 rifle sec)
        1 Platoon: 4 × 3" mortars, 2–3 trucks, radio truck
        1 Platoon: 4 × Twin AALMG, 4 Boys
        1 Platoon: 2 rifle/engineer secs
        1 Platoon: Pl HQ (1 × Carrier, 1 × Daimler S/C, 1 LMG)
            3 Sections, each: 3 × Bren Carrier, 3 LMG, 1 (6 man) rifle sec

Guards Infantry Battalion (24th Brigade)
Btn HQ (2 rifle secs, 1 staff car)
    4 Companies, each: Coy HQ (1 (13 man) rifle sec)
        3 Platoons, each: 1(7 man) Pl HQ rifle sec, 1 × 2" mortar, 1 Boys, 3 (10 man) rifle secs, 3 LMG
    1 Support Company: Coy HQ (1 rifle sec, 1 truck)
        1 Platoon: 4 × 3" mortars (no ammunition available initially)
        1 Platoon: 2 rifle/engineer secs, 1 lorry

Territorial Infantry Battalion (146th, 148th Brigades)
Btn HQ (4 rifle secs, 1 LMG, staff car)
    4 Companies, each: Coy HQ (2 rifle secs, 1 Boys)
        3 Platoons, each: 4 rifle secs, 0–1 × 2" mortar, 3 LMG

Notes
1. Radios were in all Coy HQ and AFV Pl HQs. All artillery is rated as Assigned FC.
2. Infantry sections have no A/T grenades.
3. Troops were hampered by lack of skis, no winter training, no translators and little AA protection or artillery until later in the campaign.

1.9 BRITISH HOME DEFENCE INFANTRY FORCES, JUNE–DECEMBER 1940, BRITAIN

Regular and Territorial divisions had 2–3 brigades, each of 2–3 battalions. Home Guard units operated in independent units. Regulars are rated at good or average training and morale, Home Guard units poor to bad training and poor to average morale, and Territorials poor training and average morale.

SUPPORT UNITS

Divisional Support
Included:
    3 Artillery Batteries, each: Battery HQ (1 radio van, 1 lorry, 4 rifle secs, 2 AALMG)
        2 Troops, each: 4 × 25pdr Mk.1 or 18pdr or 75mm M1897A4, 5 trucks
    2 A/T Troops, each: 2–3 × 2pdr, 3 trucks (Regulars only)
    0–1 A/T Troop: 2 × 3t Bedford/3pdr M1890, 2 × 10t lorry/12pdr M1900 AA
    1 Engineer Company: Coy HQ (1 rifle sec)
        3 Platoons, each: 4 rifle/engineer secs
    0–3 Attached Recce Squadrons, each: (poor training, average morale)
        Sqdn HQ (2 × Beaverette II, 2 × Scout Carrier or 2 trucks, 1 Boys, 2 rifle secs)
        3 Troops, each: 3 × Bren Carriers, 1 (6 man) sec, 1 LMG, 3 × Beaverette II or 3 × Bedford OXA A/T Lorries

Brigade Support
Infantry Brigade HQ (6 rifle secs, 4 buses or lorries, 1 car) with:
    1 Recce Company: Coy HQ (1 rifle sec, 1 truck) (average morale, poor training)
        0–1 Platoon: 3 × 2pdr or 3" Smith Gun, 6 × Bren Carriers
        0–2 A/T Platoons, each: 3 (8 man) rifle secs, cycles, 3 Boys, Molotovs
        0–2 Platoons, each: 3 (8 man) rifle secs, 3 light trucks
        0–2 Platoons, each: 3 (9 man) rifle secs, 9 × M/C combinations
        (maximum of 3 platoons)
    OR 1 Recce Squadron: Sqdn HQ (2 (9 man) rifle secs, 2 trucks, 2 LMG) (Regulars only)
        4 Troops, each: 1 (12 man) Rifle Pl HQ sec, 3 LMG, 1 truck
            4 (9 man) rifle secs, 12 × M/C combos w/LMG

MAIN COMBAT ELEMENTS

Regular Infantry Battalion
Btn HQ (2 rifle secs, 2 LMG)
    4 Companies, each: Coy HQ (1 rifle sec)
        3 Platoons, each: 3 rifle secs, 1 LMG, 1 × 2" mortar, 1 Boys anti-tank rifle
    1 Support Company: Coy HQ (1 rifle sec)
        0–1 Platoon: 4 × 3" mortars
        1 Platoon: 2 × Twin AALMG
        1 Platoon: 2 rifle/engineer secs
        1 Platoon: Pl HQ (1 × Bren Carrier, 1 LMG)
            2 Sections, each: 3 × Bren Carrier, 3 LMG, 1 Boys, 1 (6 man) rifle sec

Home Guard Battalion
    Btn HQ (4 rifle secs, 0–1 Boys)
        1 Scout Platoon: 2 rifle or shotgun secs, 5 civilian cars or horses
        4 Companies, each: Coy HQ (1 rifle sec, 1 Lewis LMG or BAR)
            4 Platoons, each: 3 (12–18 man) rifle secs
            1 Platoon: 3 × Northover Projector
            1 AA Platoon: 2 × AALMG

Territorial Infantry Battalion
    Btn HQ (4 rifle secs, 1 LMG)
        4 Companies, each: Coy HQ (1 rifle sec, 1 Boys, 2 LMG)
            3 Platoons, each: 3 rifle secs

Notes
1. Few radios were available, mostly down to Btn HQ level. Artillery rated as Assigned FC.
2. Infantry sections had No.68 rifle A/T grenades, WP grenades, Molotovs or No.73 A/T grenades.
3. Home Guard battalions varied from 640–1,600 men in strength.
4. Regular and Territorials could be motorised in civilian buses and lorries.
5. Divisional batteries were limited to 200 rounds per gun on average.
6. Brigade Recce Companies were in Regular Divisions only, and converted from Brigade Anti-Tank Companies that had been disbanded in June 1940.
7. At least one Regular Battalion was a Mountain Troop unit in the north of Britain, with mortars on pack horses, probably the Lovat Scouts Cavalry Regiment.
8. For wargames purposes, infantry type by proportion is: 1–29%: Territorial, 30–67%: Regular, 68–00%: Home Guard. Home Guard units can replace 1 in 4 squads with shotguns or other civilian rifles, and any or all can be rearmed with improvised melee weapons such as pitchforks, scythes and pikes. Up to 1 Home Guard Battalion can be motorised in 12 AEC armoured buses. Scout platoons can only be on horses if in outlying rural areas like Dartmoor or Scotland.

1.10 CANADIAN 1ST INFANTRY DIVISION, 1940, FRANCE/BRITAIN

The Division's main combat elements were:
    3 Infantry Brigades (1st – Royal Canadian Regiment, Hastings and Prince Edward Regiment, 48th Highlanders of Canada, 1 Infantry Battalion each; 2nd – Princess Patricia's Canadian Light Infantry, Loyal Edmonton Regiment, Seaforth Highlanders of Canada, 1 Infantry Battalion each; 3rd – Royal 22e Regiment, Carleton and York Regiment, West Nova Scotia Regiment, 1 Infantry Battalion each)
    Divisional Recce Regiment (1st Mechanised Cavalry Regiment, August–September 1940 only)

In June 1940 one Brigade plus supports was deployed briefly in France then returned to England via Cherbourg. By October a full Corps of two Infantry Divisions was deployed in England. Troops are rated at average training and good morale.

SUPPORT UNITS

Divisional Support
Included:
    1 Engineer Battalion: Btn HQ (2 rifle secs, 2 trucks)
        3 Engineer Companies, each: Coy HQ (1 rifle sec, 1 truck, 2 Boys, 2 LMG)
            3 Platoons, each: 4 (12 man) rifle/engineer secs, 1 Boys, 1 LMG, 2 lorries
        1 Engineer Stores Company: explosives, tools, bridges
    1 Machine Gun Battalion: Btn HQ (2 rifle secs, 2 trucks)
        4 Companies, each: Coy HQ (1 rifle sec, 1 truck)
            3 Platoons, each: 4 Vickers MMG teams, 2 trucks, 1 Boys, 1 LMG
    4 A/T Companies, each: Coy HQ (1 rifle sec, 1 truck) (October 1939 onwards)
        3 Platoons, each: 4 × 2pdr A/T guns, 4 trucks
    1 Field Artillery Brigade: Brigade HQ (4 rifle secs, 6 trucks) (1939–May 1940)
        4 Batteries, each: 4 × 25pdr or 18pdr field guns, 6 trucks
        1 Battery: 4 × 4.5"L15 Mk.2 QF howitzers, 4 trucks
    1 Field Artillery Brigade: Brigade HQ (4 rifle secs, 6 trucks) (1939–May 1940)
        4 Batteries, each: 4 × 25pdr or 18pdr field guns, 6 trucks
        1 Battery: 4 × 25pdr or 18pdr field guns, 6 trucks (up to Nov 1939)
    1 Field Artillery Brigade: Brigade HQ (4 rifle secs, 6 trucks) (1939–May 1940)
        3 Horse Batteries, each: 4 × 18pdr field guns, 6 trucks
        1 Battery: 4 × 4.5"L15 Mk.2 QF howitzers, 4 trucks
    3 Artillery Regiments, each: (June 1940 onwards)
        2–3 Artillery Batteries, each: Battery HQ (1 radio van, 4 trucks, 4 rifle secs) 2 Troops, each: 4 × 25pdr Mk.1, 5 trucks, radio van, 2 AALMG, 1 Boys

Brigade Support
    Infantry Brigade HQ (4 rifle secs, 2 staff cars, 3 lorries) with up to:
        1 HQ Defence Platoon: 4 rifle/pioneer secs, 3 LMG, 1 × 2", 1 Boys, 4 trucks
        1 Infantry A/T Company: Coy HQ (1 rifle sec, 1 truck)
            3 Platoons, each: 4 × 2pdr, 4 trucks
        1 Recce Squadron: Sqdn HQ (1 (6 man) rifle sec, 3 × M/C combinations, 2 Boys, 1 LMG)
            2 Troops, each: 3 × M/C combinations, 1 (9 man) rifle crew sec, 1 LMG

MAIN COMBAT ELEMENTS

Infantry Battalion
Btn HQ (2 rifle secs, 1 staff car, 2 trucks, 5 motorcycles)
    4 Companies, each: Coy HQ (1 (13 man) rifle sec, 1 lorry)
        3 Platoons, each: 1 (7 man) Pl HQ rifle sec, 1 × 2" mortar, 1 Boys, 3 (10 man) rifle secs, 3 LMG, 2 lorries
    1 Support Company: Coy HQ (1 rifle sec, 1 truck)
        1 Platoon: 2 × 3" mortars, 1 truck, radio truck
        1 Platoon: 4 × Twin AALMG, 4 Boys, 4 trucks
        1 Platoon: 2 (6 man) rifle/engineer secs, 1 lorry
        1 Platoon: Pl HQ (1 × Bren Carrier, 1 × Daimler S/C, 1 LMG
           3 Sections, each: 3 × Bren Carrier, 3 LMG, 1 (6 man) rifle sec

Divisional 1st Mechanised Cavalry Regiment (August–September 1940)
RHQ (2 rifle secs, 3 LMG, 2 Boys, 2 trucks)
    1 Troop: 3 × Guy Mk.1 armoured cars
    3 Squadrons, each: Sqdn HQ (1 truck, 1 car, 1 rifle sec)
        3 Platoons, each:
           2 Sections, each: 2 × Carrier or improvised armoured car, 2 LMG
           2 Sections, each: 3 (4 man) rifle secs, 3 cars or 6 M/C combos
           1 Section: 3 (9 man) rifle secs, 3 LMG, 3 trucks or 1 lorry

Notes
1. Radios were in all Coy HQ and AFV Pl HQs. All artillery rated as Assigned FC.
2. Infantry sections had no A/T grenades.
3. From June 1940, divisional artillery consisted of three Field Regiments each of 2 Batteries until January 1941, when a third Battery was added to each Regiment.
4. Organisation of Divisional Recce Squadrons is provisional.

1.11 CANADIAN 2ND INFANTRY DIVISION, 1941–43, BRITAIN/DIEPPE RAID

The Division's main combat elements were:
    3 Infantry Brigades (4th – Royal Regiment of Canada, Royal Hamilton Light Infantry, Essex Scottish Regiment, 1 Infantry Battalion each; 5th – Black Watch of Canada (Royal Highland Regiment), Le Regiment Maisonneuve, Calgary Highlanders, 1 Infantry Battalion each; 6th – Queen's Own Cameron Highlanders of Canada, South Saskatchewan Regiment, les Fusiliers Mont-Royal, 1 Infantry Battalion each)
    Divisional Recce Regiment (8th Reconnaissance Regiment/4th Hussars)
    14th Army Tank Battalion (attached for Dieppe operation)
Troops are rated at average training and good morale.

SUPPORT UNITS

Divisional Support
Included:
    2–3 Engineer Companies, each: Coy HQ (1 rifle sec, 1 truck)
        3 Platoons, each: 4 (12 man) rifle/engineer secs, 3 LMG
    OR (in 1943): 2–3 Engineer Companies: Coy HQ (4 (11 man) rifle secs, 1 LMG, 1 Boys, 2 lorries)
        3 Platoons, each: 1 (17 man) rifle/engineer Pl HQ sec
           4 (12 man) rifle/engineer secs, 4 LMG, 2 lorries
    1 Field Park Company: Coy HQ (3 rifle/engineer secs, 2 lorries)
        1 Workshop Section: 4 rifle/engineer secs, workshop lorries, gantry cranes
        1 Stores Section: 3 rifle/engineer secs, explosives, tools, etc
        1 Bridging Section: 5 rifle/engineer secs, pontoon bridges, etc
    3 AA Batteries, each: Battery HQ (1 rifle sec, 1 truck)
        3 Troops, each: 4 or (1943+) 6 × 40mm Bofors, 6 trucks
    4 A/T Batteries, each: Battery HQ (1 rifle sec, 1 truck)
        3 Troops, each: 4 × 2pdr or 6pdr, 4 truck portées, 2 LMG
    3 Field Artillery Regiments, each:
        3 Artillery Batteries, each: Battery HQ (1 radio van, 5 trucks, 4 rifle secs, 2 Boys, 4 AALMG)
           2 Troops, each: 4 × 25pdr, 5 trucks, radio van, 1 Boys, 2 AALMG, OP Team
    1 Machine Gun Battalion: Btn HQ (4 rifle secs, 4 trucks)
        1 AA Platoon: 4 × twin AALMG, 4 trucks
        4 MG Companies, each: Coy HQ (1 rifle sec)
           3 Platoons, each: 4 Vickers MMG, 1 Boys A/T rifle, 1 LMG, 4 rifle crew secs
    1 MP Company: 6 Sections

Brigade Support
Infantry Brigade HQ (6 rifle secs, 4 lorries) with:
    1 Defence Platoon: 4 rifle secs, 3 LMG, 1 × 2" mortar, 1 Boys

MAIN COMBAT ELEMENTS

Infantry Battalion
Btn HQ (5 rifle secs, 1 LMG)
    4 Companies, each: Coy HQ (1 rifle sec)

3 Platoons, each: 1 (7 man) rifle Pl HQ sec, 1 × 2" mortar, 1 Boys, 3 (10 man) rifle secs, 3 LMG
1 Support Company: Coy HQ (1 rifle sec)
    1 Platoon: 4 or 6 × 3" mortars, 4 or 6 Carriers, 1 × Carrier Pl HQ
    1 Platoon: 2 rifle/engineer secs, 1 lorry
    1 Platoon: Pl HQ (1 × Carrier, 1 × Daimler S/C, 1 LMG)
        4 Sections, each: 3 × Carrier, 3 LMG, 1 Boys, 1 × 2", 1 rifle sec
    1 Platoon: 4 × twin AALMG, 4 Boys, in 2 rifle crew secs

8th Reconnaissance Regiment/4th Hussars Divisional Recce Regiment, 1941

Btn HQ (4 rifle secs, 4 trucks, 3 LMG, 2 Boys)
    1 AA Platoon: 4 × twin AALMG, 4 Boys, 4 trucks
    1 Signals Platoon
    1 Battery: 2 × 3" mortars, 2 trucks (Assigned FC)
    1 Anti-Tank Platoon: 8 × Boys in trucks or Bedford OXA anti-tank lorries
    3 Companies, each: Coy HQ (3 rifle secs, 1 LMG, 3 trucks)
        3 Platoons, each: Pl HQ (1 × Carrier, 1 LMG, 1 Boys, 1 × 2", 1 × Light Recce Car)
            1 Section: 2 × Light Recce Cars
            2 Sections, each: 3 × Carrier, 1 Boys, 3 LMG, 1 × 2", 1 rifle sec
    1 Platoon: 4 (8 man) rifle secs, 4 trucks, 1 Boys, 4 LMG

8th Reconnaissance Regiment/4th Hussars Divisional Recce Regiment, April 1942–43

Btn HQ (3 rifle secs, 3 LMG, 2 Boys, 3 × Light Recce Car)
    3 Companies, each: Coy HQ (3 rifle secs, 1 LMG, 3 trucks, 1 Light Recce Car)
        3 Platoons, each: Pl HQ (1 × Carrier, 1 LMG, 1 Boys, 1 × 2", 1 × Light Recce Car)
            1 Section: 2 × Light Recce Car OR 1 × A/C, 1 × Daimler S/C
            2 Sections, each: 3 × Carrier, 1 Boys, 3 LMG, 1 × 2", 1 rifle sec
    1 Platoon: 4 (9 man) rifle secs, 4 trucks, 1 Boys, 4 LMG
    1 Mortar Battery: 4–6 × 3" mortars, 5–7 × Universal Carriers
    1 A/T Platoon: 4 × 2pdr A/T guns, 4 trucks, 2 LMG
    1 AA Platoon: 4 × twin AALMG on trucks, 4 Boys

14th Army Tank Battalion, Dieppe 1942

Btn HQ (2 × Churchill III)
    2 Squadrons, each: Sqdn HQ (2 × Churchill III)
        5 Troops, each: 3 × Churchill III
    1 Squadron: Sqdn HQ (2 × Churchill III)
        2 Troops, each: 3 × Churchill III Bobbin (early prototype carpet layers)
        1 Troop: 3 × Churchill II Oke (early prototype flamethrower tanks)
    1 Scout Troop: Troop HQ (1 × Daimler Scout Car or Lynx Scout Car)
        3 Sections, each: 3 × Daimler or Lynx Scout Car

Notes

1   Radios were in all Coy HQs and AFVs. All artillery is rated as Assigned FC up to July 1942. After that treat as Flexible FC, with OP teams in truck or Daimler S/C.
2   Infantry sections had No.74 or No.75 Hawkins A/T grenades. Boys A/T Rifle can be replaced with PIATs from June 1943.
3   Divisional A/T Batteries did not have 6pdr until July 1942, with other units receiving them later.
4   In 1942 25pdr can have AP. From May 1942 the 2pdr has APC, with APCBC available from August 1942.
5   Armoured Car is Humber III, was planned to have been Daimler II or Humber IV, but none materialised. Light Recce Car is Beaverette I or II, or Humber Mk1 Ironsides from mid 1941, or Otter Mk.1. From 1942 could be Humber MK.II, III or IIIA, or Morris Light Recce Mk.I or Mk.II.
6   The 2nd Division had the 14th Army Tank Battalion (Calgary Armoured Regiment) assigned during July–August 1942 for the Dieppe raid.
7   The 3rd Canadian Infantry Division arrived in Britain in August 1941, with same organisation as above but with three Engineer Companies.
8   For wargames purposes, may replace Daimler S/C with Humber Light Recce Mk.II or III.

1.12 BRITISH PARACHUTE BRIGADE, 1941–42, BRITAIN

The Brigade's main combat element consisted of 3–4 Parachute Battalions. By November 1942 there were three brigades in existence, as follows:
    1st Parachute Brigade (1st, 2nd, 3rd and 4th[6] Parachute Battalions)
    2nd Parachute Brigade (4th,[7] 5th and 6th Parachute Battalions)
    3rd Parachute Brigade (7th, 8th and 9th Parachute Battalions)
The units are rated at good training and excellent morale.

SUPPORT UNITS

Brigade Support

Airborne Brigade HQ (6 rifle/SMG secs) with:
    1 HQ Defence Platoon: 4 rifle/SMG secs, 3 LMG, 1 × 2" mortar

---

6   Only until July 1942.
7   Only after August 1942.

MAIN COMBAT ELEMENTS
Parachute Battalion
    Btn HQ: 2 rifle/SMG secs
        3 Companies, each: Coy HQ (2 (8 man) rifle secs)
            3 Platoons, each: 1 (6 man) rifle/SMG Pl HQ sec, 3 rifle/SMG secs, 3 LMG, 1 × 2"
        1 Battery: 4 × 3" mortars (Assigned FC)
        1 MG Platoon: 4 × Vickers MMG, 1 Boys

Notes
1   Radios were at Coy HQ and above.
2   Infantry had Type 74 or Type 75 anti-tank grenades.

1.13 BRITISH 1ST AIRBORNE DIVISION, 1942–MAY 1943, NORTH-WEST EUROPE

By May 1943, the Division's main combat elements were:
    2 Airborne Brigades (1st – 1st, 2nd and 3rd Parachute Battalions; 2nd – 4th, 5th and 6th Parachute Battalions)
    1 Air Landing Brigade (1st – 1st Border Regiment, 2nd South Staffordshire Regiment, 1 Battalion each)
In practise, most of the 1st Airborne Division was still forming during this period. During 1943 the 6th Airborne Division was also raised. Paratroopers are rated at good training and excellent morale, Pathfinders as excellent training and excellent morale.

SUPPORT UNITS
Division Support
Included:
    1 Pathfinder Company
    1 OP Team
    1 MP Company
    1 Defence and Employment Platoon: 4 rifle/SMG secs, 3 LMG, 1 × 2" mortar, 4 trucks
    1 Field Security Section: intelligence and rear security officers, Jeeps
    1 Engineer Stores Squadron: explosives, tools
    1 Artillery Regiment: RHQ (4 SMG secs, 2 LMG, 16 Jeeps or 6 trucks)
        3 Batteries, each: 6 × 3.7" howitzers, 6 trucks, 2 Jeeps, OP Team
        OR 3 Batteries, each: 6 × 75mm M1 pack howitzers, 12 Jeeps, 3 trailers, OP Team
    2 A/Tank Batteries, each: Battery HQ (1 rifle sec, 1 truck)
        3 Platoons, each: 4 × 6pdr, 4 Jeeps
    1 AA Battery: Battery HQ (1 rifle sec, 1 truck)
        1–2 Troops, each: 6 × 40mmL60 Bofors, 6 trucks
        0–1 Troop: 6 × 20mm Oerlikon, 6 Jeeps
    0–1 Recce Squadron: Scout Cars
    0–1 Recce Squadron: Sqdn HQ (2 × Tetrarch, 2 × Tetrarch-CS)
        4 Troops, each: 4 × Tetrarch
    0–1 Recce Squadron: Jeeps, motorcycles

Brigade Support
    Airborne Brigade HQ (6 rifle/SMG secs) with:
        1 HQ Defence Platoon: 4 rifle/SMG secs, 3 LMG, 1 × 2" mortar
        1 Attached Engineer Squadron: Sqdn HQ (2 rifle/SMG secs)
            3 Platoons, each: 4 (12 man) rifle/engineer secs, 3 LMG, 4 flamethrowers
    Air Landing Brigade HQ (6 rifle/SMG squads) with:
        1 HQ Defence Platoon: 4 rifle/SMG secs, 3 LMG, 1 × 2" mortar
        1 Light Battery: 4 × 4.2" mortars, 4 trucks, 1 radio Jeep
        1 Attached Field Engineer Company: Coy HQ (1 rifle sec)
            3 Platoons, each: 4 (12 man) rifle/engineer secs, 3 LMG, 4 flamethrowers
        1 A/T Battery: Battery HQ (1 rifle sec, 1 truck)
        3 Platoons, each: 4 × 2pdr, 4 Jeeps, 2 LMG
        1 Recce Company: Jeeps, motorcycles

MAIN COMBAT ELEMENTS
Parachute Battalion
    Btn HQ (4 rifle/SMG secs)
        3 Companies, each: Coy HQ (2 (8 man) rifle secs)
            3 Platoons, each: 1 (6 man) rifle/SMG Pl HQ sec, 3 rifle/SMG secs, 3 LMG, 1 × 2"
        1 Battery: 4 × 3" mortars
        1 A/T Platoon: 4 × 6pdr, 4 × Jeeps
        1 MG Platoon: 4 × Vickers MMG
        1 Pioneer Platoon: 2 rifle/SMG/engineer secs, 2 LMG

Air Landing Infantry Battalion
    Btn HQ (2 rifle/SMG secs)
        HQ Defence Platoon: 1(8 man) rifle/SMG Pl HQ sec, 3 rifle secs, 3 LMG
        4 Companies, each: Coy HQ (2 (8 man) rifle secs)

British and Commonwealth Armies, 1939–43

                4 Platoons, each: 1 (8 man) rifle/SMG Pl HQ sec, 3 rifle secs, 3 LMG, 1 × 2" mortar
        1 Support Company: Coy HQ (1 rifle sec)
           1 Battery: 8 × 3" mortars, 10 Jeeps, 42 crew
           1 A/T Platoon: 4 × 2pdr A/T guns, 8 Jeeps, 62 crew
           1 Pioneer Platoon: 2 rifle/SMG/engineer secs, 2 LMG
           1 Test AA Platoon: 4 × .50" AAHMG on poor quality tripods (1942 only)
           1 MG Platoon: 4 × Vickers MMG, 34 crew
        1 Recce Platoon: 4 × Vickers MMG on 4 Jeeps (1943 onwards)

Notes
1. Radios were at Coy HQ and above.
2. Infantry had Type 74 or Type 75 anti-tank grenades.
3. In May 1943 the divisional artillery replaced the 3.7" howitzers with American 75mm pack howitzers.
4. First use of Horsa gliders was in November 1942 in Norway.
5. The AA Platoons in the Air Landing Battalions were discontinued, as the AA mounts were unreliable, continually breaking or toppling over.

1.14 BRITISH ANTI-AIRCRAFT DIVISIONS, 1939–OCTOBER 1942, BRITAIN

In 1939, there were 7 AA Divisions in the UK, two with 4 Brigades, five with 5 Brigades. In 1939–40 AA Brigades could consist of 2–5 Heavy AA Regiments with 3–5 S/L Regiments; 1–3 Heavy AA Regiments with 1–3 S/L Regiments, or 4–5 Light AA Regiments. Usually only one Brigade per Division contained Light AA Regiments. Of the 122 Regiments, 50 were Heavy AA, 23 Light AA, 49 Searchlight.

By 1941, the AA defence of the UK was reorganised into 3 AA Corps sharing 12 AA Divisions, each Division containing 3–5 Brigades. AA Brigades could consist of 5 Heavy AA Regiments; 1–4 Heavy AA and 1–4 Light AA Regiments; 1–3 Heavy AA, 1–3 Light AA and 1–3 S/L Regiments; 2–4 S/L Regiments; 3 Heavy AA with 1 S/L Regiments, or 1–2 Light AA with 2–4 S/L Regiments. Of the 165 Regiments, 55 were Heavy AA, 49 Light AA, 61 Searchlight. In October 1942, the AA defences were reorganised into 7 AA Groups.

Troops are rated at average training and average morale.

MAIN COMBAT ELEMENTS

Heavy AA Regiment
    RHQ (4 rifle secs, 2 LMG, radio vans or bunkers)
        3 Batteries, each: Battery HQ (2 rifle secs, 2 lorries or bunkers) 2 Troops, each: 4 × 3.7" or 4.5" AA, lorries or static in gunpits

Light AA Regiment
    RHQ (4 rifle secs, 2 LMG, 4 lorries)
        4 Batteries, each: Battery HQ (2 rifle secs, 2 lorries)
           3 Troops, each: 4 × 40mmL60 Bofors, 6 trucks, 2 LMG

Searchlight Regiment
    RHQ (2 rifle secs, 4 lorries)
        3 Batteries, each:
           4 Troops, each: 6 × 90cm or 150cm searchlights, AALMG, 8 trucks and lorries, 1 Boys A/T Rifle

Notes
1. Radios were not available, all being telephone linked.

1.15 BEF CORPS AND ARMY SUPPORT UNITS, OCTOBER 1939–JUNE 1940, FRANCE

Units are rated at average training and average morale.

SUPPORT UNITS

Corps Support Units
    3 MG Battalions, each:
        4 MG Companies, each: Coy HQ (1 rifle sec, 1 truck, 4 LMG)
           3 Platoons, each: 4 × MMG, 2 trucks
    4 Field Artillery Batteries, each: Battery HQ (4 rifle secs, 3 lorries)
        3 Troops, each: 4 × 25pdr Mk.1 or 18pdr, 4 trucks or Lt. Dragon, radio truck
    2 Medium Artillery Regiments, each: RHQ (6 rifle secs, 4 lorries)
        4 Batteries, each: 4 × 6" 26cwt, 4 lorries, radio van
    4 AA Companies, each: Coy HQ (1 rifle sec, 1 truck)
        3 Platoons, each: 4 × 40mm Bofors, 4 trucks

Army Support Units
    4 Royal Horse Artillery Batteries, each: Battery HQ (4 rifle secs, 4 trucks, 2 × Light Dragon IIC)
        2 Troops, each: 4 × 25pdr Mk.1, 4 × Light Dragon IIC/D, radio truck
    12 Field Artillery Batteries, each: Battery HQ (4 rifle secs, 3 lorries, 2 LMG)
        2 Troops, each: 4 × 4.5"L15 Mk.2 QF or 25pdr Mk.1 or 18pdr, 4 trucks, radio truck)
    5 Medium Artillery Regiments, each: RHQ (6 rifle secs, 4 lorries, 1 Boys, 2 LMG)
        4 Batteries, each: 4 × 6" 26cwt, 4 lorries or Medium Dragon III/IV, radio van, 2 Boys, 2 LMG
    1 Medium Artillery Regiment: RHQ (6 rifle secs, 4 lorry, 1 Boys, 2 LMG)
        4 Batteries, each: 4 × 60pdr, 4 lorries, radio van, 2 LMG, 2 Boys

British and Commonwealth Armies, 1939–43

  2 Medium Artillery Regiments, each: RHQ (6 rifle secs, 4 lorries, 1 Boys, 2 LMG)
    4 Batteries, each: 4 × 4.5"L43 Mk.1, 4 lorries, radio van, 2 Boys, 2 LMG
  1 Heavy Artillery Regiment: RHQ (8 rifle secs, 6 lorries, 2 LMG, 1 Boys)
    3 Batteries, each: 4 × 6" Mk.19, 4 lorries, radio van, 2 LMG, 4 Boys
    1 Battery: 4 × 9.2" BL Siege Mk.2, 2 LMG, 4 Boys (Static, pre-planned fire)
  1 Heavy Artillery Regiment: RHQ (8 rifle secs, 6 lorries, 2 LMG, 1 Boys)
    3 Batteries, each: 4 × 8" Mk.8 guns, 4 lorries, radio van, 2 LMG, 4 Boys
    1 Battery: 4 × 9.2" BL Siege Mk.2, 2 LMG, 4 Boys (Static, pre-planned fire)
  1 Heavy Artillery Regiment: RHQ (8 rifle secs, 6 lorries, 2 LMG, 1 Boys)
    4 Batteries, each: 4 × 9.2" BL Siege Mk.2, 4 Boys, 2 LMG (Static, pre-planned fire)
  2 Super-Heavy Artillery Batteries, each: 2 × 12" Siege MK.4 (Static, pre-planned fire)
  1 Super Heavy Rail Battery: 2 × 9.2" Mk.13 rail guns (Pre-planned fire only)
  6 AA Batteries, each: Battery HQ (1 rifle sec, 1 lorry)
    2 Troops, each: 4 × 3" 20cwt AA, 4 lorries
  7 AA Batteries, each: Battery HQ (1 rifle sec, 1 lorry)
    2 Troops, each: 4 × 3.7" AA, 4 lorries
  3 Light AA Batteries, each: Battery HQ (1 rifle sec, 1 lorry)
    3 Platoons, each: 4 × 40mm Bofors, 4 trucks
    (1 Battery Army HQ defence, 2 airfield defence)
  7 AA Batteries, each: Battery HQ (2 rifle secs, 4 lorries)
    2 Troops, each: 4 × 3.7" AA (Static rear area and airfield defence)
  8 AA Batteries, each: Battery HQ (2 rifle secs, 4 lorries)
    2 Troops, each: 4 × 3" 20cwt AA (Static rear area and airfield defence)
  2 AA Batteries, each: Battery HQ (2 rifle secs, 4 lorries)
    3 Troops, each: 6 × Lewis AAMG (Static airfield defence)
  3 AA Batteries, each: Battery HQ (2 rifle secs, 4 lorries)
    3 Troops, each: 4 × 2pdr pom-pom 40mm AA (Static airfield defence)
  9 Searchlight Batteries, each: 4 Troops, each: 6 × 90cm or 150cm searchlights, AALMG, 8 trucks and lorries,
    1 Boys A/T Rifle
  5 Engineer Companies, each: Coy HQ (2 rifle secs, 1 lorry)
    3 Platoons, each: 4 (12 man) rifle/engineer secs, 2 lorries, 1 LMG, 1 Boys A/T rifle
  3 Chemical Warfare Companies, each: Coy HQ (2 rifle/engineer secs, 2 trucks, 1 car)
    3 Platoons, each: 80 × gas projectors (7.5" mortar, 35lb gas shell, range 1700m), several trucks
  38 Pioneer Companies, each: Coy HQ (2 rifle secs) (poor training, average morale)
    4 Platoons, each: 3–4 rifle/pioneer secs, 1 LMG
  4 MG Battalions, each:
    4 MG Companies, each: Coy HQ (1 rifle sec, 1 truck, 4 LMG)
      3 Platoons, each: 4 MMG, 2 lorries
  1 Royal Marine Detachment: company strength from ships' detachments

Notes
1 Radios were in all AFVs and other Coy HQs.
2 Infantry had No.68 rifle A/T grenades or No.73 or 74 or 75 A/T grenades.
3 All artillery is rated as Assigned FC unless stated otherwise.
4 In practice the rail battery had no ammunition with it in France.

1.16 BRITISH CORPS AND ARMY SUPPORT UNITS, HOME DEFENCE, 1939–40, BRITAIN

Troops are rated as average or poor training and average morale.

SUPPORT UNITS

Corps Support Units

  1 Recce Regiment:
    RHQ: 4 × Armoured Cars or cars or trucks w/LMG
      3 Squadrons, each: Sqdn HQ (3 × A/C or cars or trucks w/LMG)
        5 Troops, each: 3 × A/C or trucks w/LMG
  6 Machine Gun Battalions, each:
    3 Companies, each: Coy HQ (1 rifle sec)
      3 Platoons, each: 3–4 MMG teams
  2 Field Artillery Regiments, each:
    2 Batteries, each: 2 Troops, each: 4 × 18pdr or 25pdr Mk.1, 6 trucks, 2 AALMG
  1 Medium Artillery Regiment:
    2 Batteries, each: 2 Troops, each: 4 × 6" 26cwt or 60pdr howitzers, horses or trucks
  1 Heavy Artillery Regiment:
    2 Batteries, each: 2 Troops, each: 4 × 6" Mk19 guns, 6 lorries
  2 Reserve A/T Regiments, each:
    3 Batteries, each: Battery HQ (1 rifle sec)
      3 Troops, each: 4 (4 man) rifle crew secs, 4 Boys, poss. 1 × 2pdr for training, 1 truck
  2 Cavalry Regiments each: RHQ (10 rifle secs, 8 lorries)
    3 Squadrons, each: Sqdn HQ (2 rifle secs, horses, sabres)
      3 Troops, each: 4 (8 man) rifle secs, horses, sabres
        1(9 man) rifle PHQ sec, 1 Lewis LMG, 1 Boys
    1 MG Troop: 4 × Vickers MMG, pack horses

1 A/T Troop: 4 × Boys A/T rifles, horses
1 Scout Troop: 9 × Austin 7 cars, 1 radio

Army Support Units
10 Medium Artillery Regiments, each: RHQ (6 rifle secs, 4 lorries)
    4 Batteries, each: 4 × 4.5"L43 Mk.1 or 6" 26cwt or 60pdr, 5 lorries
3 AA Batteries, each: 6 × lorry with 3pdr 47mm cannon (poor training)
3 Coastal Defence Mobile Batteries, each: 4 × 4" Naval Guns on lorries (poor training)
3 Machine Gun Companies, each: Coy HQ (1 rifle sec)
    3 Platoons, each: 3 MMG
1–2 AA Brigades
1 Pioneer Battalion: 4 Companies (poor training and morale)
3–9 Coastal Artillery Batteries

MISCELLANEOUS UNITS

Iceland Garrison, 1940
Garrison, 10–21 May (815 men):
    "Sturgesforce"
        2nd Royal Marine Battalion
        Y Battery, MNBD01: 2 × 4" naval guns semi-mobile mounts
        1st Anti-MTB Battery, MNBD01: 4 × 2pdr pom-pom
        1 Naval battery: 2 × 3.7" pack howitzers
British 147th Infantry Brigade reinforcements 19 May, including:
    Lord Lovat Cavalry Scout Regiment
    Y Battery, MNBD01: 2 × 4" naval guns semi-mobile mounts
    1st Anti-MTB Battery, MNBD01: 4 × 2pdr pom-pom
    1 Naval battery: 2 × 3.7" pack howitzers
July–October 1940:
    Royal Marine Fortress Unit 1: 201 men, digging gunpits for 18 × 3"–6" coastal defence guns, building huts for army units, survey work
September 1940 onwards:
    Z-Brigade: 2 Canadian Infantry Btns from 2nd Canadian Infantry Division,
    1 Canadian MG Battalion
    Y Battery, MNBD01: 2 × 4" naval guns (until 1941)

Northern Ireland Garrison, 1939–40
North Irish Horse Armoured Car Regiment
3rd AA Brigade: 2 Heavy AA Regiments, 1 S/L Regiment
1 Militia Cavalry Regiment
4 Regular Infantry Battalions (1939 only)
53rd Welsh Infantry Division (April 1940–41):
    3 Brigades, each of 3 Infantry Btns,[8] 1 Brigade A/T Coy
    3 Field Artillery Regts (old organisation)
    3 Engineer Companies, 1 Field Park Company
    1 A/T Regt (October 1940–41)

Notes
1   Radios were in all Coy HQs only. Artillery is rated as Assigned FC.
2   Infantry had no A/T weapons.
3   Armoured cars are Rolls-Royce or trucks with LMG.

---

8   158th Infantry Brigade – 4th, 6th and 7th Btns Royal Welch Fusiliers ; 159th Infantry Brigade – 3rd Btn Monmouthshire Regiment, 4th Btn King's Own Shropshire Light Infantry, 1st Btn Herefordshire Regiment ; 160th Infantry Brigade – 2nd Btn Monmouthshire Regiment, 4th and 1/5th Btns Welch Regiment.

PART 2
NORTH AFRICAN THEATRE 1938-43

2.1 BRITISH 7TH ARMOURED DIVISION, MARCH–SEPTEMBER 1940, NORTH AFRICA

The Division's main combat elements were:
- 4th Armoured Brigade (7th Hussars and 1st RTR)
- 7th Armoured Brigade (8th Hussars and 6th RTR)
- Divisional Recce Regiment (11th Hussars)
- 2 Divisional Motor Battalions (1st Btn King's Royal Rifle Corps, 2nd Btn Rifle Brigade)

The Division is rated at average training and good morale.

SUPPORT UNITS

Divisional Support
Included:
- 3rd Horse Artillery Regiment:
  - 4 A/T Batteries,: Battery HQ (1 rifle sec, 1 truck)
    - 3 Troops, each: 4 × 37mm Bofors on truck portées, 2 LMG
- 4th Royal Horse Artillery Regiment:
  - 2 Batteries, each: Battery HQ (4 rifle secs, 3 lorries, AALMG, radio van)
    - 2 Troops, each: 4 × 25pdr Mk.1, 4 trucks, radio truck, AALMG
- 2nd Field Engineer Squadron: Sqdn HQ (2 rifle secs, 1 lorry)
  - 4 Troops, each: 4 (12 man) rifle/engineer secs, 2 lorries
- 1 Engineer Park Company: (175 men)
  - 1 Workshop Section
  - 1 Bridging and Stores Section

Brigade Support
- 4th Armoured Brigade HQ (4 × A–9 Cruisers, 2 radio trucks)
- 7th Armoured Brigade HQ (4 × Vickers VIC, 4 × Rolls-Royce armoured cars)

MAIN COMBAT ELEMENTS

7th Hussars Armoured Regiment
- RHQ (2 × Vickers VIC)
- 2 Squadrons, each: Sqdn HQ (3 × Vickers Mk.VIB)
  - 3 Troops, each: 3 × Vickers VIB
- 1 Squadron: Sqdn HQ (1 × A–9)
  - 2 Troops, each: 3 × A–9 or A–10
- 1 Troop: 4 × 37mm Bofors A/T guns on truck portées

8th Hussars Armoured Regiment
- RHQ (4 × Vickers VIC)
- 3 Squadrons, each: Sqdn HQ (3 × Vickers VIB)
  - 5 Troops, each: 3 × Vickers VIB
- 1 Troop: 4 × 37mm Bofors A/T guns on truck portées

1st Royal Tank Regiment
- RHQ (2 × Vickers VIC, 2 × A–9)
- 2 Squadrons, each: Sqdn HQ (3 × Vickers Mk.VIB)
  - 3 Troops, each: 3 × Vickers VIB
  - 1 Troop: 3 × A–9
- 1 Squadron: Sqdn HQ (2 × A–9, 1 × A–10CS)
  - 4 Troops, each: 3 × A–9 or A–10

6th Royal Tank Regiment
- RHQ (2 × A–9 or A–10, 2 × A–9 without guns)
- 1 Squadron: Sqdn HQ (3 × Vickers VIB)
  - 3 Troops, each: 3 × Vickers VIB
- 2 Squadrons, each: Sqdn HQ (2 × A–9, 1 × A–10CS)
  - 1 Troop, each: 3 × A–9 or A–10
  - 1 Troop: 3 × A–9 or A–10 without guns

11th Hussars Divisional Recce Regiment ("The Cherry Pickers")
(rated at good training and good morale)
- RHQ (4 × Morris CS9 armoured cars)
- 3 Squadrons, each: Sqdn HQ (1 × Morris CS9, 2 × Rolls-Royce M1924)
  - 5 Troops, each: 2 × Rolls-Royce, 1 × Morris CS9

Divisional Motor Battalion

    Btn HQ (2 rifle secs, 2 trucks, 1 radio van)
        4 Companies, each: Coy HQ (1 rifle sec, 2 × MMG, 2 trucks)
            3 Platoons, each: 4 rifle secs, 3 LMG, 4 trucks, 4 Boys, 1 × 2" mortar
            1 Platoon: Pl HQ (1 × Bren Carrier, 1 staff car)
                3 Sections, each: 3 × Bren Carriers, 3 LMG
        1 A/T Troop: 4 × 37mm Bofors on truck portées, 2 LMG

Notes
1   Radios were in all AFVs and other Coy HQs. Artillery is rated as Assigned FC.
2   Infantry had No.68 rifle A/T grenades or No.73 or No.74 A/T grenades.

2.2 BRITISH 7TH ARMOURED DIVISION, OCTOBER 1940–FEBRUARY 1941, NORTH AFRICA

The Division's main combat elements were:
    4th Armoured Brigade (7th Hussars, 2nd and 6th RTR)
    7th Armoured Brigade (3rd and 8th Hussars, 1st RTR)
    Divisional Recce Regiment (11th Hussars)
    2 Divisional Motor Battalions (1st Btn King's Royal Rifle Corps, 2nd Btn Rifle Brigade)
The Division is rated at average training and good morale.

SUPPORT UNITS

Divisional Support

Included:
    2 Horse Artillery Batteries, each: Battery HQ (4 rifle secs, 3 lorries, radio van, 1 AALMG)
        2 Troops, each: 4 × 25pdr Mk.1, 5 trucks, radio truck, 1 AALMG, 1 Boys
    2 A/T Batteries, 3rd Royal Horse Artillery, each: Battery HQ (1 rifle sec, 1 truck)
        3 Troops, each: 4 × 2pdr portées, 2 LMG
    1 Engineer Squadron: Sqdn HQ (2 rifle secs, 1 lorry, 1 motorcycle)
        4 Troops, each: 4 (12 man) rifle/engineer secs, 3 LMG, 2 lorries
    1 Engineer Park Company: (175 men)
        1 Workshop Section
        1 Bridging and Stores Section
    1 attached RAF Armoured Car Squadron (average morale and average training)
        Sqdn HQ: 3 × Fordson or Rolls-Royce
            4 Troops, each: 3 × Fordson or Rolls-Royce
    106th Royal Horse Artillery Regiment (average morale and training)
        2 AA Batteries, each: Battery HQ (1 rifle sec, 1 truck)
            3 Troops, each: 4 × 20mm Breda AA, 4 trucks
        2 A/T Batteries, each: Battery HQ (1 rifle sec, 1 truck)
            3 Troops, each: 4 × 37mm Bofors A/T guns, 4 trucks, 2 LMG

Brigade Support

    Armoured Brigade HQ (4 × A–9 and 6 × Vickers VIB, 1 × ACV, 3 × Daimler S/C) with:
        1 attached A/T Battery, 3rd Royal Horse Artillery: Battery HQ (1 rifle sec, 1 truck)
            3 Troops, each: 4 × 2pdr portées, 1 LMG

MAIN COMBAT ELEMENTS

7th Hussars Armoured Regiment, 8th Hussars Regiment, 1st Royal Tank Regiment, 6th Royal Tank Regiment

Each:
    RHQ (4 × Vickers VIB, 3 × Scammel Wreckers)
        2 Squadrons, each: Sqdn HQ (4 × Vickers VIC)
            4 Troops, each: 3 × Vickers VIB
        1 Squadron: Sqdn HQ (2 × Vickers VIC, 1 × A–10)
            2 Troops, each: 3 × A–9 or A–10
            2 Troops, each: 3 × Vickers VIB

2nd Royal Tank Regiment

    RHQ (4 × Vickers VIB, 3 × Scammel Wreckers)
        2 Squadrons, each: Sqdn HQ (2 × A–13 Mk.2, 2 × A–10 CS)
            4 Troops, each: 3 × A–13 Mk.1 or Mk.2
        1 Squadron: Sqdn HQ (4 × Vickers VIC)
            4 Troops, each: 3 × Vickers VIB

3rd Hussars Armoured Regiment

    RHQ (4 × Vickers VIB, 3 × Scammel Wreckers)
        2 Squadrons, each: Sqdn HQ (4 × Vickers VIC)
            4 Troops, each: 3 × Vickers VIB
        1 Squadron: Sqdn HQ (2 × A–13 Mk.2, 2 × A–13 CS)
            4 Troops, each: 3 × A–13 Mk.1 or Mk.2

11th Hussars Divisional Recce Regiment
    RHQ (4 × Morris CS9 or Rolls-Royce)
        4 Sections, each: 3 × Daimler Scout Cars
        2 Squadrons, each: Sqdn HQ (4 × Morris CS9 or Rolls-Royce)
          5 Troops, each: 3 × A/C
        1 Squadron: Sqdn HQ (4 × Morris CS9 or Rolls-Royce)
          4 Troops, each: 3 × A/C
          1 Troop: 3 × Guy Mk.1 armoured cars (test troop)

Divisional Motor Battalion
    Btn HQ (2 trucks, 1 lorry, 2 rifle secs)
        3 Companies, each: Coy HQ (1 rifle sec, 1 × 2", 1 Boys, 2 trucks)
          3 Platoons, each: 4 rifle secs, 4 Boys, 1 × 2", 3 LMG, 4 trucks
          1 Platoon: 2 × 3" mortars, 2 MMG, 4 trucks
        1 Platoon: Pl HQ (1 × Carrier, 1 × Daimler S/C, 1 LMG)
          3 Sections, each: 3 × Carrier, 3 LMG, 1 Boys, 1 × 2", 1 rifle sec

Notes
1. Radios were in all AFVs and other Coy HQs. Artillery is rated as Assigned FC.
2. Infantry sections had No.68 rifle A/T grenades or No.73 or No.74 A/T grenades.
3. 2pdr fired AP only, 25pdr had no AP rounds.
4. Carrier is Bren or Scout Carrier. By 1941 could be Universal type.
5. For wargames purposes, armoured cars can be used in any mix, but usually have Morris as Sqdn HQ and Pl HQ vehicles. Up to one Armoured Troop can be equipped with Covenanters as a trials unit.

2.3 BRITISH 2ND ARMOURED DIVISION, MARCH–APRIL 1941, NORTH AFRICA

The Division's main combat elements were:
    3rd Armoured Brigade (3rd Hussars, 5th and 6th RTR)
    Divisional Recce Regiment (King's Dragoon Guards)
    Divisional Motor Battalion (1st Tower Hamlets Rifles)
The Division was all but destroyed in April 1941. Troops are rated at average training and average morale, with Brigade HQs as poor training and average morale.

SUPPORT UNITS

Divisional Support
Included:
    2 Horse Artillery Regiments, each:
        RHQ (4 rifle secs, 3 lorries, radio van, 4 AALMG, 1 Boys)
          2 Batteries, each Battery HQ (2 rifle secs, 4 trucks, 2 AALMG, 2 × Vickers VIA OP)
            2 Troops, each: 4 × 25pdr, 4 trucks, radio truck
    1 A/T Battery: Battery HQ (1 rifle sec, 1 truck)
        3 Troops, each 4 × 2pdr on portées, 2 LMG
    4th Field Engineer Squadron: Sqdn HQ (2 rifle secs, 1 lorry, 1 motorcycle)
        4 Troops, each: 4 (12 man) rifle/engineer secs, 3 LMG, 2 lorries
    143rd Engineer Park Company:
        1 Workshop Section
        1 Bridging and Stores Section
    1 Light AA Battery: Battery HQ (1 rifle sec, 1 truck)
        3 Troops, each: 4 × 40mm Bofors, 4 trucks
    1 Attached MG Company: Coy HQ (1 rifle sec, 1 truck)
        3 Platoons, each: 4 Vickers MMG, 2 trucks

Brigade Support
    Armoured Brigade HQ (3 × Vickers VIC, 1 × ACV, 3 × Daimler S/C)

MAIN COMBAT ELEMENTS

3rd Hussars Armoured Regiment
    RHQ (4 × Vickers VIB, 3 × Scammel Wreckers)
        B Squadron: Sqdn HQ (3 × M13/40)
          3 Troops, each: 3 × M13/40
        A, C Squadrons, each: Sqdn HQ (2 × Vickers VIC or VIB)
          3 Troops, each: 3 × Vickers VIB

5th Royal Tank Regiment
    RHQ (2 × A–9, 3 × Scammel Wreckers)
        2 Squadrons, each: Sqdn HQ (2 × A–9CS, 2 × A–13 Mk.II)
          2 Troops, each: 3 × A–13 Mk.1
          2 Troops, each: 3 × A–13 Mk.II

6th Royal Tank Regiment
    RHQ (4 × M–13/40, 3 × recovery lorries)

A, C Squadrons, each: Sqdn HQ (4 × M–13/40)
    4 Troops, each: 3 × M–13/40
B Squadron: Sqdn HQ (3 × Vickers VIC or VIB)
    3 Troops, each: 3 × Vickers VIB

King's Dragoon Guards Divisional Recce Regiment
RHQ (4 × Morris CS9 or Rolls-Royce)
    4 Sections, each: 3 × Daimler S/C
    3 Squadrons, each: Sqdn HQ (4 × A/C as in RHQ)
        4 Troops, each: 3 × A/C

Divisional Motor Battalion
Btn HQ (2 trucks, 1 lorry, 2 rifle secs)
    3 Companies, each: Coy HQ (1 rifle sec, 1 × 2", 1 Boys, 2 trucks)
        3 Platoons, each: 4 rifle secs, 4 Boys, 1 × 2", 3 LMG, 4 trucks
        1 Platoon: Pl HQ (1 × Universal Carrier, 1 × Daimler S/C, 1 LMG)
            3 Sections, each: 3 × Carrier, 3 LMG, 1 Boys, 1 × 2", 1 rifle sec
    0–1 Battery: 2 × 3" mortars, 2 trucks

Notes
1. Radios were in all AFVs and other Pl HQs, when working. Artillery is rated as Assigned FC.
2. Infantry sections had No.73 or No.74 or No.75 A/T grenades.
3. 2pdr fired AP only, 25pdr had no AP rounds.
4. Carrier was Bren or Scout Carrier or Universal Carrier.
5. For wargames purposes, armoured cars can be used in any variation. Up to one Armoured Troop can be equipped with Covenanters as a trials unit. Divisional AA batteries must be deployed around the artillery.
6. The M13/40s had sandbags on the hull front counting as an extra 1cm of improvised armour.
7. The 5th RTR had 6 × A–10Cs and 46 × A–13 tanks on strength, but many were inoperative.

2.4 BRITISH 7TH ARMOURED DIVISION, APRIL–MAY 1941, NORTH AFRICA

The Division's main combat elements were:
    7th Armoured Brigade (2nd RTR, converged Indian Cavalry Regiment, attached 6th Australian Divisional Cavalry Regiment)
    Divisional Recce Regiment (11th Hussars)
    2 Divisional Motor Battalions (1st Btn King's Royal Rifle Corps, 2nd Btn Rifle Brigade)
Majority of troops are rated average training and good morale, with the Indian troops rated at average training and poor morale.

SUPPORT UNITS

Divisional Support
Included:
    3 Artillery Batteries, each: Battery HQ (4 rifle secs, 3 lorries, radio van, 1 AALMG)
        2 Troops, each: 4 × 25pdr, 5 trucks, radio truck, 1 AALMG, 1 Boys
    1 A/T Battery: Battery HQ (1 rifle sec, 1 truck)
        3 Troops, each: 4 × 2pdr on portées, 2 LMG
    2 Australian A/T Batteries, each: Battery HQ (1 rifle sec, 1 truck)
        3 Troops, each: 4 × 2pdr A/T guns, 4 trucks, 2 LMG
    2 AA Batteries, each: Battery HQ (1 rifle sec, 1 truck)
        3 Platoons, each: 4 × 40mmL60 Bofors, 6 trucks
    1st Royal Tank Regiment (in Tobruk): RHQ (2 × A–13 Cruiser)
        3 Squadrons, each: 3 × A–13 Cruisers

Brigade Support
Armoured Brigade HQ: 3 × tanks, 1 × ACV, 3 × Daimler S/C

MAIN COMBAT ELEMENTS

2nd Royal Tank Regiment
RHQ (4 × A–13 Mk.2 Cruisers)
    1 Squadron: Sqdn HQ (2 × A–9, 2 × A–9 CS)
        4 Troops, each: 3 × A–10
    1 Squadron: Sqdn HQ (2 × A–13 Mk.2, 2 × A–13 CS)
        1 Troop: 3 × A–9
        3 Troops, each: 3 × A–10
    1 Recce Platoon: 2–3 Sections, each: 3 × Daimler S/C

Converged Indian Cavalry Regiment
(remnants of 3rd Indian Motorised Brigade)
    RHQ (2 rifle secs, 2 field cars, 2 trucks)
    3 Squadrons, each: Sqdn HQ (1 rifle sec, 1 truck)
        3 Troops, each: 3 rifle secs, 2 LMG, 0–1 × Boys A/T Rifle, 3 trucks
    1 A/T Battery: Battery HQ (1 rifle sec, 1 truck)
        3 Troops, each: 4 × 2pdr portées, 1 LMG

Attached Australian 6th Divisional Recce Regiment

RHQ (4 × Vickers VIB, 1 radio van, 4 × Scout Carriers)
   3 Squadrons, each: Sqdn HQ (2 × Vickers VIB, 2 × Scout Carriers)
     2 Troops, each: 3 × Vickers VIB or IIB light tanks
     4 Troops, each: 3 × Scout Carriers, 1 rifle sec, 3 Boys, 3 LMG

11th Hussars Divisional Recce Regiment

RHQ (4 × Marmon-Herrington I or II)
   4 Sections, each: 3 × Daimler S/C
   4 Squadrons, each: Sqdn HQ (2 × Marmon-Herrington I or II)
     4 Troops, each: 3 × Marmon-Herrington I or II

Divisional Motor Battalion

Btn HQ (2 trucks, 1 lorry, 2 rifle secs)
   3 Companies, each: Coy HQ (1 rifle sec, 1 × 2", 1 Boys, 2 trucks)
     3 Platoons, each: 4 rifle secs, 4 Boys, 1 × 2", 3 LMG, 4 trucks
     1 Platoon: 0–2 × 3" mortars, 2 MMG, 4 trucks
     1 Platoon: Pl HQ (1 × Carrier, 1 × Daimler S/C, 1 LMG)
       3 Sections, each: 3 × Carrier, 3 LMG, 1 Boys, 1 × 2", 1 rifle sec

Notes
1   Radios were in all AFVs and other Pl HQs. Artillery is rated as Assigned FC.
2   Infantry sections had No.73 or No.74 or No.75 A/T grenades.
3   2pdr fired AP only, 25pdr had no AP rounds, 37mm fired AP only.
4   Carrier is Universal type.

2.5 BRITISH 7TH ARMOURED DIVISION, JUNE–AUGUST 1941, NORTH AFRICA

The Division's main combat elements were:
   7th Armoured Brigade (2nd and 6th RTR)
   Divisional Recce Regiment (11th Hussars)
   2 Divisional Motor Battalions (1st Btn King's Royal Rifle Corps, 2nd Btn Rifle Brigade)
During this period an Army Tank Brigade with two regiments of Matilda II was also attached (see list 2.16), containing 4th and 7th RTR. The Division is rated at average training and good morale.

SUPPORT UNITS

Divisional Support

Included:
   3 Artillery Batteries, each: Battery HQ (4 rifle secs, 3 lorries, radio van, 1 AALMG)
     2 Troops, each: 4 × 25pdr, 5 trucks, radio truck, 1 AALMG, 1 Boys
   4th Royal Horse Artillery Regiment:
     2 Batteries, each: Battery HQ (4 rifle secs, 3 lorries, radio van, 1 AALMG)
       2 Troops, each: 4 × 25pdr, 5 trucks, radio truck, 1 AALMG, 1 Boys
   1 A/T Battery: Battery HQ (1 rifle sec, 1 truck)
     3 Troops, each: 4 × 2pdr on portées, 2 LMG
   1 Engineer Squadron: Sqdn HQ (2 rifle secs, 1 lorry)
     4 Troops, each: 4 (12 man) rifle/engineer secs, 3 LMG, 2 lorries
   3 AA Batteries, each: Battery HQ (1 rifle sec, 1 truck)
     3 Troops, each: 4 × 40mm Bofors, 6 trucks
   1 Squadron, 3rd Hussars: Sqdn HQ (3 × Vickers VIC)
     4 Troops, each: 3 × Vickers VIB light tanks
   7th Hussars Armoured Regiment (in Egypt, re-equipping): 18 × A–13 Cruisers
   3rd Hussars Armoured Regiment (in Egypt, re-equipping): some Vickers VIB

Brigade Support

Armoured Brigade HQ (4 × A–10, 1 × ACV, 3 × Daimler S/C)

MAIN COMBAT ELEMENTS

2nd Royal Tank Regiment

RHQ (4 × A–13 Mk.2 Cruisers, 3 × Scammel Wreckers)
   1 Squadron: Sqdn HQ (1 × A–9, 1 × A–13 Mk.2)
     3 Troops, each: 3 × A–9
   1 Squadron: Sqdn HQ (1 × A–10, 1 × A–10 CS, 1 × A–13 Mk.2)
     3 Troops, each: 3 × A–10
   1 Squadron: Sqdn HQ (1 × A–13 Mk2, 2 × A–13 CS)
     4 Troops, each: 3 × A–13
   1 Recce Troop: 2–3 sections, each: 3 × Daimler S/C

6th Royal Tank Regiment

RHQ (4 × Crusader I, 3 × Scammel Wreckers)
   3 Squadrons, each: Sqdn HQ (4 × Crusader I)
     4 Troops, each: 3 × Crusader I
   1 Recce Troop: 2–3 Sections, each: 3 × Daimler Scout Cars

11th Hussars Divisional Recce Regiment
    RHQ (4 × Marmon-Herrington II)
        4 Sections, each: 3 × Daimler S/C
        3 Squadrons, each: Sqdn HQ (4 × Marmon-Herrington II)
            4–5 Troops, each: 3 × Marmon-Herrington II

Divisional Motor Battalion
    Btn HQ (2 trucks, 1 lorry, 2 rifle secs)
        3 Companies, each: Coy HQ (1 rifle sec, 1 × 2", 1 Boys, 2 trucks)
            3 Platoons, each: 4 rifle secs, 4 Boys, 1 × 2", 3 LMG, 4 trucks
            1 Platoon: 2 × 3" mortars, 2 MMG, 4 trucks
            1 Platoon: Pl HQ (1 × Carrier, 1 × Daimler S/C, 1 LMG)
                3 Sections, each: 3 × Carrier, 3 LMG, 1 Boys, 1 × 2", 1 rifle sec

Notes
1. Radios were in all AFVs and other Pl HQs. Artillery is rated as Assigned FC.
2. Infantry sections had No.73 or No.74 or No.75 A/T grenades.
3. 2pdr fired AP only, 25pdr had no AP rounds.
4. Carrier is Universal type.
5. For wargames purposes, up to one Armoured Troop can replace Stuart with M2A4 from July 1941. Divisional AA batteries must be deployed around the artillery. Marmon-Herrington II armament could be (10% chance of each): 3.7cm PAK35; 20mm Breda AA; 47/32 A/T gun; Quad LMGAA; 25mmL72 A/T gun; turret Boys and co-axial MG; 2.8cm PzB41 A/T rifle; Twin LMGAA.

2.6 BRITISH 7TH ARMOURED DIVISION, SEPTEMBER–DECEMBER 1941, NORTH AFRICA
The Division's main combat elements were:
    4th Armoured Brigade (8th Hussars, 3rd and 5th RTR, 2nd Btn Scots Guards Motor Battalion)
    7th Armoured Brigade (7th Hussars, 2nd and 6th RTR)
    Attached 22nd Armoured Brigade[1] (3rd and 4th County of London Yeomanry)
    Attached 22nd Guards Motorised Brigade (3rd Btn Coldstream Guards and 9th Btn Rifle Brigade Motor Battalions)
    11th Hussars Divisional Recce Regiment
    Attached 4th South African Armoured Car Regiment
    2 Divisional Motor Battalions (1st Btn King's Royal Rifle Corps, 2nd Btn Rifle Brigade)

This reinforced Division was decimated in the Operation Crusader actions and withdrawn to reserve during December 1941 and January 1942. The Division is rated at average training and good morale.

SUPPORT UNITS

Divisional Support
Included:
    4 Artillery Batteries, each: Battery HQ (4 rifle secs, 3 lorries, radio van, 1 AALMG)
        2 Troops, each: 4 × 25pdr, 5 trucks, radio truck, 1 AALMG, 1 Boys
    3 A/T Batteries, each: Battery HQ (1 rifle sec, 1 truck)
        3 Troops, each: 4 × 2pdr on portées, 2 LMG
    1 Reinforced Light AA Battery: Battery HQ (1 rifle sec, 1 truck)
        4 Troops, each: 4 × 40mmL60 Bofors, 4 trucks
    1 Engineer Squadron: Sqdn HQ (2 rifle secs, 1 lorry)
        4 Troops, each: 4 (12 man) rifle/engineer secs, 3 LMG, 2 lorries
    1 Engineer Park Company:
        1 Workshop Section
        1 Bridging and Stores Section
    3 Armoured Car Squadrons, each: Sqdn HQ (4 × Marmon-Herrington II)
        4 Troops, each: 3 × Marmon-Herrington II

Brigade Support
    4th Armoured Brigade HQ (10 × M3A1 Stuart I, 1 × ACV, 3 × Daimler S/C) with:
        1 Royal Horse Artillery Regiment:
            2 Batteries, each: Battery HQ (4 rifle secs, 3 lorries, radio van, 1 AALMG)
                2 Troops, each: 4 × 25pdr, 5 trucks, radio truck, 1 AALMG, 1 Boys
        3 A/T Batteries, each: Battery HQ (1 rifle sec, 1 truck)
            3 Troops, each: 4 × 2pdr on portées, 2 LMG
        1 Light AA Battery: Battery HQ (1 rifle sec, 1 truck)
            2 Troops, each: 4 × 40mmL60 Bofors, 4 trucks
    7th Armoured Brigade HQ (5 × A–9CS, 5 × A–10, 1 × ACV, 3 × Daimler S/C) with:
        4th Royal Horse Artillery Regiment:
            2 Batteries, each: Battery HQ (4 rifle secs, 3 lorries, radio van, 1 AALMG)
                2 Troops, each: 4 × 25pdr, 5 trucks, radio truck, 1 AALMG, 1 Boys
        1 A/T Troop: 4 × 2pdr on portées, 2 LMG
        1 AA Troop: 4 × 40mmL60 Bofors, 4 trucks
        1 Motor Company: Coy HQ (1 rifle sec, 1 × 2", 1 Boys, 2 trucks)

---

1. This unit was detached from 1st Armoured Division.

3 Platoons, each: 4 rifle secs, 4 Boys, 1 × 2", 3 LMG, 4 trucks
1 Platoon: Pl HQ (1 × Carrier, 1 × Daimler S/C, 1 LMG)
3 Sections, each: 3 × Carrier, 3 LMG, 1 Boys, 1 × 2", 1 rifle sec
22nd Armoured Brigade HQ (8 × Crusader I/II, 1 × ACV, 3 × Daimler S/C) with:
1 Royal Horse Artillery Battery: Battery HQ (4 rifle secs, 3 lorries, radio van, 1 AALMG)
2 Troops, each: 4 × 25pdr, 5 trucks, radio truck, 1 AALMG, 1 Boys
1 A/T Troop: 4 × 2pdr on portées, 2 LMG
1 AA Troop: 4 × 40mmL60 Bofors, 4 trucks
1 Motor Company: Coy HQ (1 rifle sec, 1 × 2", 1 Boys, 2 trucks)
3 Platoons, each: 4 rifle secs, 4 Boys, 1 × 2", 3 LMG, 4 trucks
1 Platoon: Pl HQ (1 × Carrier, 1 × Daimler S/C, 1 LMG)
3 Sections, each: 3 × Carrier, 3 LMG, 1 Boys, 1 × 2", 1 rifle sec
22nd Guards Motorised Brigade HQ (4 rifle secs, 4 LMG, 6 trucks) with:
1 Field Artillery Battery: Battery HQ (4 rifle secs, 3 lorries, radio van, 1 AALMG)
3 Troops, each: 4 × 25pdr, 5 trucks, radio truck, 1 AALMG, 1 Boys
3 A/T Batteries, each: Battery HQ (1 rifle sec, 1 truck)
3 Troops, each: 4 × 2pdr on portées, 2 LMG
1 Light AA Battery: Battery HQ (1 rifle sec, 1 truck)
2 Troops, each: 4 × 40mmL60 Bofors, 4 trucks

MAIN COMBAT ELEMENTS

Armoured Regiment (4th Armoured Brigade)
RHQ (4 × M3A1 Stuart I)
3 Squadrons, each: Sqdn HQ (4 × Stuart I)
4 Troops, each: 3 × Stuart I
1 Recce Troop: 2–3 Sections, each: 3 × Daimler Scout Cars

7th Hussars Armoured Regiment (7th Armoured Brigade)
RHQ (4 × Crusader I, 2 × A–10)
1 Squadron: Sqdn HQ (4 × Crusader I)
4 Troops, each: 3 × Crusader I
1 Squadron: Sqdn HQ (2 × A–13 Mk.2, 2 × A–13 CS)
4 Troops, each: 3 × A–13 Mk.2
1 Squadron: Sqdn HQ (4 × A–10)
5 Troops, each: 3 × A–10
1 Recce Troop: 2–3 Sections, each: 3 × Daimler Scout Cars

2nd Royal Tank Regiment (7th Armoured Brigade)
RHQ (4 × A–13)
3 Squadrons, each: Sqdn HQ (2 × A–13, 2 × A–13 CS)
4 Troops, each: 3 × A–13
1 Recce Troop: 2–3 Sections, each: 3 × Daimler Scout Cars

6th Royal Tank Regiment (7th Armoured Brigade)
RHQ (4 × Crusader I/II)
3 Squadrons, each: Sqdn HQ (3 × Crusader I/II)
4 Troops, each: 3 × Crusader I/II
1 Recce Troop: 2–3 Sections, each: 3 × Daimler Scout Cars

Armoured Regiment (22nd Armoured Brigade)
RHQ (4 × Crusader II, 1 × Crusader ICS)
3 Squadrons, each: Sqdn HQ (1 × Crusader ICS, 2 × Crusader II)
4 Troops, each: 3 × Crusader I
1 Recce Troop: 3 Sections, each: 3 × Daimler Scout Cars

11th Hussars Divisional Recce Regiment /Armoured Car Regiment
RHQ (4 × Marmon-Herrington I or II OR Humber III)[2]
4 Sections, each: 3 × Daimler S/C
3 Squadrons, each: Sqdn HQ (4 × Marmon-Herrington I or II OR Humber III)
4–5 Troops, each: 3 × Marmon-Herrington I or II OR Humber III

Divisional Motor Battalion
Btn HQ (2 trucks, 1 lorry, 2 rifle secs)
3 Companies, each: Coy HQ (1 rifle sec, 1 × 2", 1 Boys, 2 trucks)
3 Platoons, each: 4 rifle secs, 4 Boys, 1 × 2", 3 LMG, 4 trucks
1 Platoon: 2 × 3" mortars, 2 MMG, 4 trucks
1 Platoon: Pl HQ (1 × Carrier, 1 × Daimler S/C, 1 LMG)
3 Sections, each: 3 × Carrier, 3 LMG, 1 Boys, 1 × 2", 1 rifle sec

---

[2] 11th Hussars Divisional Recce Regiment used Humber IIIs, and the attached 4th South African Armoured Car Regiment Marmon-Herringtons.

Other Motor Battalions
  Btn HQ (3 rifle secs, 2 × trucks, 1 lorry, 1 LMG)
    4 Companies, each: Coy HQ (2 rifle secs, 1 lorry)
      3 Platoons, each: 4 rifle secs, 3 LMG, 1 × 2", 1 Boys, 2 lorries
    1 Support Company: Coy HQ (1 rifle sec , 1 truck)
      1 Platoon: 4 × 3" mortars, 4 trucks, 1 radio truck, 2 Boys
      1 Platoon: 2 (8 man) rifle/engineer secs, 1 lorry
      0–1 Platoon: 4 MMG in 4 rifle secs, 1 Boys, 1 × 2", 2 lorries
      0–1 Platoon: 4 × 2pdr on portées, 4 LMG
      1 Platoon: Pl HQ (1 × Carrier, 1 × Daimler S/C, 1 LMG)
        4 Sections, each: 3 × Carrier, 3 LMG, 1 Boys, 1 × 2", 1 rifle sec

Notes
1 Radios were in all AFVs and other Pl HQs. Artillery is rated as Assigned FC.
2 Infantry sections had No.73 or No.74 or No.75 A/T grenades.
3 2pdr fired AP only, 25pdr had no AP rounds.
4 Carrier is Universal type.

2.7 BRITISH 1ST ARMOURED DIVISION, DECEMBER 1941–FEBRUARY 1942, NORTH AFRICA
  The Division's main combat elements were:
    2 Armoured Brigades (2nd – Queen's Bays, 9th Hussars, 10th Hussars Armoured Regiments and 9th Btn
      Rifle Brigade Motor Battalion; 22nd – 2nd Royal Gloucestershire Hussars, 3rd and 4th County of London
      Yeomanry Armoured Regiments)
    200th Guards (Motor) Infantry Brigade (3rd Btn Coldstream Guards, 2nd Btn Scots Guards)
    Divisional Recce Regiment (12th Lancers)
    2 Divisional Motor Battalions (2nd Btn King's Royal Rifle Corps, 1st Btn Rifle Brigade)

SUPPORT UNITS
Divisional Support
Included:
  1 Royal Horse Artillery Regiment:
    2 Batteries, each: Battery HQ (4 rifle secs, 3 lorries, radio van, 1 AALMG)
      2 Troops, each: 4 × 25pdr, 5 trucks, radio truck, 1 AALMG, 1 Boys
  1 A/T Regiment:
    3 A/T Batteries, each: Battery HQ (1 rifle sec, 1 truck)
      3 Troops, each: 4 × 2pdr on portées, 2 LMG
  1 Light AA Regiment:
    3 Light AA Batteries, each: Battery HQ (1 rifle sec, 1 truck)
      3 Troops, each: 4 × 40mmL60 Bofors, 4 trucks
  2 Engineer Squadrons, each: Sqdn HQ (2 rifle secs, 1 lorry)
    4 Troops, each: 4 (12 man) rifle/engineer secs, 3 LMG, 2 lorries

Brigade Support
  Armoured Brigade HQ (8 × Crusader II, 1 × ACV, 3 × Daimler S/C)
  200th then 201st Guards Infantry Brigade HQ (4 rifle secs, 6 trucks, 4 LMG)

MAIN COMBAT ELEMENTS
Armoured Regiment
  RHQ (4 × Crusader II and Stuart I)
    2 Squadrons, each: Sqdn HQ (2 × Crusader II)
      3 Troops, each: 3 × Crusader II
    1 Squadron: Sqdn HQ (2 × Stuart I)
      3 Troops, each: 3 × Stuart I

Motor Battalion
  Btn HQ (2 trucks, 1 lorry, 2 rifle secs)
    3 Companies, each: Coy HQ (1 rifle sec, 1 × 2", 1 Boys, 2 trucks)
      3 Platoons, each: 4 rifle secs, 4 Boys, 1 × 2", 3 LMG, 4 trucks
      1 Platoon: 2 × 3" mortars, 2 MMG, 4 trucks
      1 Platoon: Pl HQ (1 × Carrier, 1 × Daimler S/C, 1 LMG)
        3 Sections, each: 3 × Carrier, 3 LMG, 1 Boys, 1 × 2", 1 rifle sec

Guards Motorised Infantry Battalion
  Btn HQ (3 rifle secs, 2 trucks, 1 lorry, 1 LMG)
    4 Companies, each: Coy HQ (2 rifle secs, 1 lorry)
      3 Platoons, each: 4 rifle secs, 3 LMG, 1 × 2", 1 Boys, 2 lorries
    1 Support Company: Coy HQ (1 rifle sec , 1 truck)
      1 Platoon: 4 × 3" mortars, 4 trucks, 1 radio truck, 2 Boys
      1 Platoon: 2 (8 man) rifle/engineer secs, 1 lorry
      0–1 Platoon: 4 MMG in 4 rifle secs, 1 Boys, 1 × 2", 2 lorries
      0–1 Platoon: 4 × 2pdr on portées, 4 LMG

1 Platoon: Pl HQ (1 × Carrier, 1 × Daimler S/C, 1 LMG)
    4 Sections, each: 3 × Carrier, 3 LMG, 1 Boys, 1 × 2″, 1 rifle sec

12th Lancers Divisional Recce Regiment
RHQ (4 × Humber III)
    3 Sections, each: 3 × Daimler S/C
    3 Squadrons, each: Sqdn HQ (4 × Humber III)
        4 Troops, each: 3 × Humber III

Notes
1. Radios were in all AFVs and other Pl HQs. Artillery is rated as Assigned FC.
2. Infantry sections had No.73 or No.74 or No.75 A/T grenades.
3. 2pdr fired AP only. The 25pdr had no AP rounds.
4. Carrier is Universal type.
5. During January–February 1942 there were a variety of anti-tank and artillery units attached at different times from other divisions, for example, during late January, there were 12 Field Batteries, 1 Medium Battery and 8 Anti-Tank Batteries attached.

2.8 BRITISH ARMOURED DIVISIONS, MARCH–JULY 1942, NORTH AFRICA
The Division's main combat elements were loosely:
    1 Armoured Brigade (of 3 Armoured Regiments and 1 Motor Battalion)
    1 Motorised Brigade (3 Motorised Battalions)
    1 Divisional Recce Regiment
Specific examples:
    1st Armoured Division contained:
        2nd and 22nd Armoured Brigades[3] (2nd – Queen's Bays, 9th Lancers and 10th Hussars Armoured Regiments, 1st Btn Rifle Brigade Motor Battalion; 22nd – 2nd Royal Gloucestershire Hussars, 3rd and 4th County of London Yeomanry Armoured Regiments)
        201st Guards Motor Infantry Brigade (3rd Btn Coldstream Guards, 2nd Btn Scots Guards, 9th Btn Rifle Brigade)
        Divisional Recce Regiment (12th Lancers)[4]
    7th Armoured Division contained:
        4th Armoured Brigade[5] (8th Hussars, 3rd and 5th RTR, 1st Btn King's Royal Rifle Corps)
        1st Armoured Brigade[6] (4th Hussars, 1st and 6th RTR, 1st Btn Sherwood Foresters)
        7th Motor Infantry Brigade (2nd and 9th Btns, King's Royal Rifle Corps, 2nd Btn Rifle Brigade)
        Divisional Recce Regiment (King's Dragoon Guards)[7]
        3rd Indian Motorised Brigade attached – see list 2.21.
A typical strength is shown for the February–April 1942 period. Troops are rated at average training and good morale.

SUPPORT UNITS
Divisional Support
Included:[8]
    1 DHQ Escort Squadron: (June–July 1942)
        Sqdn HQ: 2 × Daimler II armoured cars, 1 × Grant I
        2 Platoons, each: 4 × Daimler II armoured cars
        2 AA Platoons, each: 4 × 40mmL60 Bofors, 4 trucks
        1 A/T Platoon: 1 × 2pdr portée, 1 LMG
    1 Engineer Park Company: (175 men)
        1 Workshop Section
        1 Bridging and Stores Section
    0–1 AA Battery: Battery HQ (1 rifle sec, 1 truck)
        3 Platoons, each: 4 × 40mm Bofors, 6 trucks

Brigade Support
    Armoured Brigade HQ (10 × Crusader II or Grant 1, 1 × ACV, 3 × Daimler S/C)
    Infantry Brigade HQ (4 rifle secs, 4 LMG, 6 trucks)
        Each Brigade HQ with up to:
            3 Artillery Batteries, each: Battery HQ (2 rifle secs, 2 trucks, radio van, 4 AALMG, 2 Boys)
                2 Troops, each: 4 × 25pdr, 4 trucks, radio truck, 2 AALMG, Assigned FC
            1 AA Battery: Battery HQ (1 rifle sec, 1 truck)
                3 Platoons, each: 4 × 40mm Bofors, 6 trucks
            1 Engineer Squadron: Sqdn HQ (2 rifle secs, 1 lorry, 1 motorcycle)
                4 Troops, each: 4 (12 man) rifle/engineer secs, 3 LMG, 2 lorries
            1 A/T Battery: Battery HQ (1 rifle sec, 1 truck)
                4 Platoons, each: 4 × 2pdr portées, 2 LMG

---

3. Each Armoured Regiment contained 1 Grant and 2 Crusader squadrons. By June, half of the Crusaders in 22nd Armoured Brigade had been replaced by Stuarts.
4. Equipped with Humber A/C.
5. Each Armoured Regiment contained 2 Grant and 1 Stuart squadrons, with Stuart RHQs.
6. The 1st Armoured Brigade was only available from May 1942 and in the event was used to fill losses in the 7th Armoured Brigade. It had been in Egypt since June 1941, slowly rebuilding.
7. Equipped with Marmon Herrington A/C.
8. Most divisional support units were allocated to Brigade HQs.

MAIN COMBAT ELEMENTS

Armoured Regiment
RHQ (4 × mix of Stuart I, Crusader II, Crusader IICS)
  1 Squadron: Sqdn HQ (1–3 × Grant 1 OR 3 × Stuart I)
    3 Troops, each: 3 × Grant 1 OR 4 Troops, each: 3 × Stuart I
  2 Squadrons, each: Sqdn HQ (3 × Stuart I OR 4 × Crusader II)
    4 Troops, each: 3 × Stuart I OR 4 Troops, each: 3 × Crusader II
  1 AA Troop: 0–2 Platoons, each: 4 × Vickers VI AA
  1 Recce Troop: 3 Sections, each: 3 × Daimler Scout Car

Armoured Regiment, 1st Armoured Brigade, February–April 1942, Egypt
RHQ (2 trucks, 2 × Stuarts, 3 × Daimler Scout Car)
  2 Squadrons, each: Sqdn HQ (1 × Stuart)
    3 Troops, each: 3 × Stuart
  1 Squadron: Sqdn HQ: 1 × Grant
    3 Troops, each: 3 × Grant

Motor Battalion, 201st Guards And 7th Motor Infantry Brigades
Btn HQ (2 rifle secs, 2 trucks, 1 LMG)
  4 Companies, each: Coy HQ (1 rifle sec, 1 lorry)
    3 Platoons, each: 4 rifle secs, 3 LMG, 0–1 Boys, 1 × 2" mortar, 2 lorries
  1 Support Company: Coy HQ (1 rifle sec, 1 truck)
    1 Platoon: 4 × 2pdr portées, 4 LMG
    1 Platoon: 2 (8 man) rifle/engineer secs, 1 (5 man) Pl HQ sec, 3 trucks
    1 Battery: 6 × 3" mortars, 6 trucks, radio truck (Assigned FC)
    1 Platoon: Pl HQ (1 × Universal Carrier, 1 LMG, 1 × Daimler S/C)
      4 Sections, each: 3 × Carriers, 3 LMG, 1 rifle sec, 1 × 2", 1 × Boys

Motor Battalion, All Other Units
Btn HQ (2 rifle secs, 2 trucks)
  3 Companies, each: Coy HQ (1 rifle sec, 0–1 × 2" mortar, 2 trucks)
    1 Battery (Assigned to Coy HQ): 2 × 3" mortars, 2 × Carriers
    2 Platoons, each: 4 rifle secs, 3 LMG, 1 × 2", 4 Boys, 4 trucks
    1 Platoon: 4 MMG, 4 × Carriers
    1 Platoon: Pl HQ (1 × Universal Carrier, 1 LMG, 1 × Daimler S/C)
      3 Sections, each: 3 × Carriers, 3 LMG, 1 rifle sec, 1 × 2", 1 × Boys
  1 A/Tank Company: Coy HQ (1 rifle sec, 1 truck)
    4 Platoons, each: 4 × 2pdr or 6pdr portées, 2 LMG

Divisional Recce Regiment
RHQ (4 × Humber III or Marmon-Herrington II armoured cars)
  0–4 Sections, each: 3 × Daimler Scout Cars
  3 Squadrons, each: Sqdn HQ (2 × Humber III or Marmon-Herrington II)
    4 Troops, each: 3 × Humber III or Marmon-Herrington II

Notes
1. Radios were in all tanks and armoured cars, and other Pl HQs.
2. Infantry sections had Hawkins 75 A/T grenades. 2pdr and 37mm had APC, 25pdr had AP.
3. For wargames purposes, Motorised and Motor Battalions can replace 2pdr with 6pdr 30% of the time.

2.9 BRITISH 1ST ARMOURED DIVISION, AUGUST 1942–MAY 1943, NORTH AFRICA

The Division's main combat elements were:
  2nd Armoured Brigade (The Bays, 9th Lancers, and 10th Hussars Armoured Regiments, Yorkshire Dragoons Motor Battalion)
  7th Motor Brigade (2nd Btn King's Royal Rifle Corps, 2nd Btn Rifle Brigade, 7th Btn Rifle Brigade, all Motor Battalions)
  Divisional Recce Regiment (12th Lancers)
Troops are rated at average training and good morale.

SUPPORT UNITS

Divisional Support
Included:
  2 Engineer Squadrons, each: Sqdn HQ (2 rifle secs, 1 lorry)
    4 Troops, each: 4 (12 man) rifle/engineer secs, 3 LMG, 2 lorries
  1 Engineer Park Company: (175 men)
    1 Workshop Section
    1 Bridging and Stores Section
  3 Artillery Batteries, each: Battery HQ (1 × ACV, 3 lorries, 4 rifle secs, 4 AALMG, 2 OP Teams)
    2 Troops, each: 4 × Bishop or M7 Priest, radio van, 2 AALMG
  6 Artillery Batteries, each: Battery HQ (4 rifle secs, 4 lorries, 4 AALMG, 3 OP Teams)
    2 Troops, each: 4 × 25pdr, 4 trucks, radio truck, 2 AALMG
  1–2 A/T Batteries, each: Battery HQ (2 × Carriers, 1 rifle sec)

2–3 Troops, each: 4 × Deacon, 1 × Deacon cargo
2 A/T Batteries, each: Battery HQ (1 rifle sec, 1 truck)
  3 Troops, each: 4 × 6pdr, 2 LMG, 4 trucks
  1 Troop: 4 × 6pdr or 17pdr, 2 LMG, 4 trucks
3 AA Batteries, each: Battery HQ (1 rifle sec, 1 truck)
  3 Troops, each: 6 × 40mm Bofors, 6 trucks

Brigade Support
Armoured Brigade HQ (3 × Sherman III or Grant 1, 2 × ACV, 1 × Vickers I AA)
Motorised Brigade HQ (4 rifle secs, 2 LMG, 2 trucks, 2 lorries) with:
  1 MG Company: Coy HQ (1 rifle sec, 1 truck)
    4 Platoons, each: 4 MMG in 4 rifle crew secs, 4 trucks

MAIN COMBAT ELEMENTS

Armoured Regiment, 2nd Armoured Brigade, 1942
RHQ (4 × Crusader II)
  2 Squadrons, each: Sqdn HQ (4 × Sherman II)
    4 Troops, each: 3 × Sherman II
  1 Squadron: Sqdn HQ (2 × Crusader II, 2 × Crusader IICS)
    2 Troops, each: 3 × Crusader II
    2 Troops, each: 3 × Crusader III
  1 AA Troop: 0–2 Platoons, each: 4 × Vickers VI AA
  1 Recce Troop: Troop HQ (1 × Daimler S/C)
    3 Sections, each: 3 × Daimler Scout Car

Armoured Regiment, 2nd Armoured Brigade, 1943
RHQ (4 × Sherman III)
  1 Squadron: Sqdn HQ (1 × Crusader II)
    2 Troops, each: 3 × Grant 1
    1 Troop: 3 × Crusader II
  1 Squadron: Sqdn HQ (4 × Sherman II)
    4 Troops, each: 3 × Sherman II
  1 Squadron: Sqdn HQ (2 × Crusader II, 2 × Crusader IICS)
    2 Troops, each: 3 × Crusader II
    2 Troops, each: 3 × Crusader III
  1 AA Troop: 0–2 Platoons, each: 4 × Vickers VI AA
  1 Recce Troop: Troop HQ (1 × Daimler S/C)
    3 Sections, each: 3 × Daimler Scout Car

Yorkshire Dragoons Motor Battalion
Btn HQ (2 rifle secs, 2 trucks)
  3 Companies, each: Coy HQ (1 rifle sec, 1 × 2" mortar, 2 trucks)
    1 Battery: 2 × 3" mortars, 3 × Carriers
    2 Platoons, each: 4 rifle secs, 3 LMG, 1 × 2", 0–4 Boys, 4 trucks
    1 Platoon: 4 MMG, 5 × Carriers
    1 Platoon: Pl HQ (1 × Universal Carrier, 1 LMG, 1 × Daimler S/C)
      3 Sections, each: 3 × Carriers, 3 LMG, 1 rifle sec, 1 × 2", 1 × Boys
  1 A/T Company: Coy HQ (1 rifle sec, 1 truck)
    4 Platoons, each: 4 × 2pdr or 6pdr, portéed or truck tows, 2 LMG

Motor Battalion, 7th Motor Brigade
Btn HQ (2 rifle secs, 2 trucks)
  4 Companies, each: Coy HQ (1 rifle sec, 1 lorry)
    3 Platoons, each: 4 rifle secs, 3 LMG, 0–1 Boys, 1 × 2" mortar, 2 lorries
  1 Support Company: Coy HQ (1 rifle sec, 1 truck)
    1 Platoon: 2 (8 man) rifle/engineer secs, 1 (5 man) Pl HQ sec, 3 trucks
    1 Battery: 6 × 3" mortars, 7 × Carriers or 6 trucks, radio truck
    2 Platoons, each: 4 × 2pdr or 6pdrs, 2 LMG, 4 trucks or Carriers
    1 Platoon: Pl HQ (1 × Universal Carrier, 1 LMG, 1 × Daimler S/C)
      4 Sections, each: 3 × Carriers, 3 LMG, 1 rifle sec, 1 × 2", 0–1 Boys

12th Lancers Divisional Recce Regiment
RHQ (4–2 × Humber III, 2 × Daimler Scout Cars)
  0–1 AA Troop: 4 × Humber AA
  3 Squadrons, each: Sqdn HQ (4 × Humber III)
    4 Troops, each: 3 × Humber III

British and Commonwealth Armies, 1939–43

Notes
1. Radios were in all tanks and armoured cars, Carrier Pl HQs, and other Coy HQs.
2. Infantry sections had No.74 or Hawkins 75 A/T grenades. Most units had dispensed with the Boys A/T rifle by this time.
3. 2pdr and 37mm had APCBC, 6pdr, 75mm and 25pdr had AP, the 6pdr had one load of APCBC. 17pdr had APC.
4. Artillery OP could be in truck, Carrier, Daimler S/C, Auster AOP, turretless Marmon-Herrington, or Stuart III tank.
5. 17pdr was not available until 1943.
6. By 1943 the three Armoured Regiments had one Sherman Squadron, one Crusader Squadron, one Squadron of 6 Grants and 3–4 Crusader II, and RHQ with Shermans.

2.10 BRITISH 7TH ARMOURED DIVISION, AUGUST 1942–MAY 1943, NORTH AFRICA

The Division's main combat elements were:
    22nd Armoured Brigade (1st and 5th RTR, 4th County of London Yeomanry Armoured Regiments, 1st Btn Rifle Brigade Motor Battalion)
    131st Queen's Lorried Infantry Brigade (1/5th, 1/6th and 1/7th Btns Queen's, Motor Battalions)
    Divisional Recce Regiment (11th Hussars)

During December 1942–January 1943 the 22nd Brigade was temporarily replaced by the 8th Armoured Brigade. 4th (Light) Armoured Brigade was also temporarily attached to the Division during part of this period.[9] Troops are rated at average training and good morale.

SUPPORT UNITS

Divisional Support
Included:
    2 Engineer Squadrons, each: Sqdn HQ (2 rifle secs, 1 lorry)
        4 Troops, each: 4 (12 man) rifle/engineer secs, 3 LMG, 2 lorries
    1 Engineer Park Company: (175 men)
        1 Workshop Section
        1 Bridging and Stores Section
    1 Field Artillery Regiment:
        3 Artillery Batteries, each: Battery HQ (4 rifle secs, 4 lorries, 4 AALMG, 3 OP Teams)
            2 Troops, each: 4 × 25pdr, 4 trucks, radio truck, 2 AALMG
    2 Field Artillery Regiments, each:
        2 Artillery Batteries, each: Battery HQ (4 rifle secs, 4 lorries, 4 AALMG, 3 OP Teams)
            2 Troops, each: 4 × 25pdr Bishop, 1 radio truck, 2 AALMG
    1 A/T Battery: Battery HQ (2 × Carriers, 1 rifle sec)
        3 Troops, each: 4 × Deacon, 1 × Deacon cargo
    3 A/T Batteries, each: Battery HQ (1 rifle sec, 1 truck)
        3 Troops, each: 4 × 6pdr, 2 LMG, 4 trucks
        1 Troop: 4 × 6pdr or 17pdr, 2 LMG, 4 trucks
    4 AA Batteries, each: Battery HQ (1 rifle sec, 1 truck)
        3 Troops, each: 4 × 40mm Bofors, 6 trucks

Brigade Support
    Armoured Brigade HQ (4 × Crusader II, 2 × ACV, 1 × Vickers I AA)
    Motorised Brigade HQ (4 rifle secs, 2 LMG, 2 trucks, 2 lorries) with:
        1 MG Company: Coy HQ (1 rifle sec, 1 truck)
            4 Platoons, each: 4 MMG in 4 rifle crew secs, 4 trucks

MAIN COMBAT ELEMENTS

1st Royal Tank Regiment, 22nd Armoured Brigade 1942
    RHQ (4 × Stuart I)
        2 Squadrons, each: Sqdn HQ (3 × Grant I)
            3 Troops, each: 3 × Grant I
        1 Squadron: Sqdn HQ (4 × Stuart I)
            3 Troops, each: 3 × Stuart I
        1 Recce Troop: Troop HQ (1 × Daimler S/C)
            2–3 Sections, each: 3 × Daimler S/C

5th Royal Tank Regiment, 22nd Armoured Brigade 1942
    RHQ (4 × Crusader II)
        2 Squadrons, each: Sqdn HQ (3 × Grant I)
            3 Troops, each: 3 × Grant I
        1 Squadron: Sqdn HQ (2 × Crusader II, 2 × Crusader III)
            2 Troops, each: 3 × Crusader II
            1 Troop: 3 × Crusader III
        1 Recce Troop: Troop HQ (1 × Daimler S/C)
            2–3 Sections, each: 3 × Daimler S/C

---

9. The Brigade contained Royal Scots Greys (2 squadrons of Stuarts and 2 of Grants), a Converged Hussars Regiment (Stuarts), 2nd Derbyshire Yeomanry (Humber A/C), and 1st Btn King's Royal Rifle Corps.

4th County Of London Yeomanry Armoured Regiment, 22nd Armoured Brigade 1942
RHQ (4 × Crusader II)
    2 Squadrons, each: Sqdn HQ (2 × Crusader II, 1 × Crusader III)
        2 Troops, each: 3 × Crusader II
        1 Troop: 3 × Crusader III
    1 Squadron: Sqdn HQ (3 × Grant I)
        2 Troops, each: 3 × Grant I
    1 Recce Troop: Troop HQ (1 × Daimler S/C)
        2–3 Sections, each: 3 × Daimler S/C

Armoured Regiment, 22nd Armoured Brigade 1943
RHQ (4 × Crusader III)
    1 Squadron: Sqdn HQ (3 × Grant I)
        5 Troops, each: 3 × Grant I
    1 Squadron: Sqdn HQ (4 × M4A2 Sherman III)
        4 Troops, each: 3 × Sherman III
    1 Squadron: Sqdn HQ (4 × Crusader III)
        4 Troops, each: 3 × Crusader III
    1 AA Troop: 0–2 Platoons, each: 4 × Vickers VI AA
    1 Recce Troop: Troop HQ (1 × Daimler S/C)
        3 Sections, each: 3 × Daimler S/C

1st Btn Rifle Brigade Motor Battalion, 22nd Armoured Brigade
Btn HQ (2 rifle secs, 2 trucks)
    3 Companies, each: Coy HQ (1 rifle sec, 1 × 2" mortar, 2 trucks)
        1 Battery: 2 × 3" mortars, 3 × Carriers
        2 Platoons, each: 4 rifle secs, 3 LMG, 1 × 2", 0–4 Boys, 4 trucks
        1 Platoon: 4 MMG, 5 × Carriers
        1 Platoon: Pl HQ (1 × Universal Carrier, 1 LMG, 1 × Daimler S/C)
            3 Sections, each: 3 × Carriers, 3 LMG, 1 rifle sec, 1 × 2", 1 × Boys
    1 A/T Company: Coy HQ (1 rifle sec, 1 truck)
        4 Platoons, each: 4 × 2pdr or 6pdr, portéed or truck tows, 2 LMG

Motor Battalion, 131st Queen's Lorried Infantry Brigade
Btn HQ (2 rifle secs, 2 trucks)
    4 Companies, each: Coy HQ (1 rifle sec, 1 lorry)
        3 Platoons, each: 4 rifle secs, 3 LMG, 0–1 Boys, 1 × 2" mortar, 2 lorries
    1 Support Company: Coy HQ (1 rifle sec, 1 truck)
        1 Platoon: 2 (8 man) rifle/engineer secs, 1 (5 man) Pl HQ sec, 3 trucks
        1 Battery: 6 × 3" mortars, 7 × Carriers or 6 trucks, radio truck
        2 Platoons, each: 4 × 2pdr, 2 LMG, 4 trucks or Carriers
        1 Platoon: Pl HQ (1 × Universal Carrier, 1 LMG, 1 × Daimler S/C)
            4 Sections, each: 3 × Carriers, 3 LMG, 1 rifle sec, 1 × 2", 0–1 Boys

11th Hussars Divisional Recce Regiment
RHQ (4 × Humber III, 2 × Daimler Scout Cars)
    0–1 AA Troop: 4 × Humber AA
    3 Squadrons, each: Sqdn HQ (4 × Humber III)
        5 Troops, each: 3 × Humber III

Notes
1   Radios were in all tanks and armoured cars, Carrier Pl HQs, and other Coy HQs.
2   Infantry sections had No. 74 or Hawkins 75 A/T grenades. Most units had dispensed with the Boys A/T rifle by this time.
3   2pdr and 37mm had APCBC, 6pdr, 75mm and 25pdr had AP, the 6pdr had one load of APCBC. 17pdr had APC.
4   Artillery OP could be in truck, Carrier, Daimler S/C, Auster AOP, turretless Marmon-Herrington, or Stuart III tank.
5   17pdr was not available until 1943.

2.11 BRITISH 10TH ARMOURED DIVISION, SEPTEMBER–NOVEMBER 1942, NORTH AFRICA
The Division's main combat elements were:
    2 Armoured Brigades (8th–3rd RTR, Nottinghamshire Yeomanry and Staffordshire Yeomanry Armoured Regiments, 1st Btn Buffs Motor Battalion; 24th–41st, 45th and 47th RTR, 11th Btn King's Royal Rifle Corps Motor Battalion)
    133rd Lorried Infantry Brigade (2nd, 4th and 5th Btns, Royal Sussex Regiment, Motor Battalions)
    Divisional Armoured Car Regiment (Royals)
Troops are rated at average training and good morale.

SUPPORT UNITS

Divisional Support
Included:
    3 Artillery Regiments, each:
        3 Batteries, each: Battery HQ (4 rifle secs, 4 lorries, 4 AALMG, 3 OP Teams)
            2 Troops, each: 4 × 25pdr, 6 trucks, 2 AALMG

14th A/T Regiment:
    4 Batteries, each: Battery HQ (1 rifle sec, 1 truck)
        4 Troops, each: 4 × 6pdr, 4 trucks or Carriers, 2 LMG
53rd Light AA Regiment:
    2 AA Batteries, each: Battery HQ: 1 rifle sec, 1 truck
        3 Troops, each: 6 × 40mmL60 Bofors, 6 trucks
    1 AA Battery: Battery HQ (1 rifle sec, 1 truck)
        2 Troops, each: 4 × 40mmL60 Bofors, 4 trucks
2 Engineer Squadrons, each: Sqdn HQ (2 rifle secs, 1 lorry)
    4 Troops, each: 4 (12 man) rifle/engineer secs, 2 LMG, 2 lorries
1 Field Park Squadron:
    1 Bridge Section
    1 Workshop Section

Brigade Support
8th Armoured Brigade HQ (2 × Crusader II, 1 × ACV, 3 × Daimler S/C)
24th Armoured Brigade HQ (2 × Grant I, 1 × ACV, 3 × Daimler S/C)
133rd Lorried Infantry Brigade HQ (6 rifle secs, 2 LMG, 6 trucks) with:
    1 MG Company: Coy HQ (1 rifle sec, 1 truck)
        4 Platoons, each: 4 Vickers MMG, 2 trucks

MAIN COMBAT ELEMENTS

Armoured Regiment, 8th Armoured Brigade
RHQ (4 × Grant I)
    1 Squadron: Sqdn HQ (2 × Crusader II, 1 × Crusader CS)
        3 Troops, each: 3 × Crusader II
        1 Troop: 3 × Crusader III
    1 Squadron: Sqdn HQ (3 × Grant I)
        4 Troops, each: 3 × Grant I
    1 Squadron: Sqdn HQ (1 × M4A1 Sherman II)
        3 Troops, each: 3 × Sherman II

Armoured Regiment, 24th Armoured Brigade
RHQ (3 × Sherman II)
    1 Squadron: Sqdn HQ (2 × Crusader II, 1 × Crusader CS)
        3 Troops, each: 3 × Crusader II
        1 Troop: 3 × Crusader III
    2 Squadrons, each: Sqdn HQ (2 × M4A1 Sherman II)
        4 Troops, each: 3 × Sherman II

11th Battalion King's Royal Rifle Corps Motor Battalion
Btn HQ (2 rifle secs, 2 trucks)
    3 Companies, each: Coy HQ (1 rifle sec, 1 truck, 1 × 2" mortar)
        2 Platoons, each: 4 (8 man) rifle secs, 4 trucks, 3 LMG, 4 trucks
        1 Platoon: 4 Vickers MMG, 5 × Universal Carrier
        1 Platoon: 2 × 3" mortars, 2 trucks
        1 Platoon: Pl HQ (1 × Universal Carrier, 1 LMG, 1 × Scout Car)
            3 Sections, each: 3 × Carrier, 3 LMG, 1 rifle sec, 1 Boys, 1 × 2" mortar
    1 A/T Company: Coy HQ (1 rifle sec, 1 truck)
        4 Troops, each: 4 × 6pdr portées, 2 LMG

Motor Battalion, 133rd Lorried Infantry Brigade
Btn HQ (2 rifle secs, 2 trucks)
    4 Companies, each: Coy HQ (1 rifle sec, 1 lorry)
        3 Platoons, each: 4 rifle secs, 3 LMG, 1 × 2" mortar, 1 Boys, 2 lorries
    1 Support Company: Coy HQ (1 rifle sec, 1 truck)
        1 Platoon: 2 (8 man) rifle/engineer secs, 1 (5 man) Pl HQ sec, 1 lorry, 2 LMG
        1 Battery: 6 × 3" mortars, 6 trucks
        2 Platoons, each: 4 × 2pdr A/T guns, 4 trucks, 2 LMG
        1 Platoon: Pl HQ (1 × Universal Carrier, 1 LMG, 1 × Scout Car)
            4 Sections, each: 3 × Carrier, 3 LMG, 1 rifle sec, 1 Boys, 1 × 2" mortar

Royals Divisional Armoured Car Regiment
RHQ (4 × Humber III)
    3 Squadrons, each: Sqdn HQ (2 × Humber III)
        4 Troops, each: 3 × Humber III
        0–1 AA Troop: 4 × Humber AA
        0–1 Communications Troop: 3 Sections, each: 3 × Daimler S/C

Notes
1   Radios were in all AFVs, Carrier Pl HQs and other Pl HQs.
2   Infantry had No.74 or No.75 Hawkins anti-tank grenades.
3   2pdr had APCBC. 6pdr, 25pdr and 75mm had AP. 6pdr had one load of APCBC.
4   Artillery OP could be in truck, scout car, Carrier or turretless Marmon-Herrington.

2.12 BRITISH 6TH ARMOURED DIVISION, NOVEMBER 1942–MAY 1943, TUNISIA

The Division's main combat elements were:
- 26th Armoured Brigade (16th/5th Lancers, 17th/21st Lancers, 2nd Lothian and Border Horse Mixed Armoured Regiments, 10th Btn Rifle Brigade Motor Battalion)
- 38th Lorried Infantry Brigade (6th Btn Royal Inniskilling Fusiliers, 2nd Btn London Irish Rifles, 1st Btn Royal Irish Fusiliers, Motor Battalions)
- Divisional Armoured Car Regiment (1st Derbyshire Yeomanry)

Troops are rated at average training and average morale.

SUPPORT UNITS

Divisional Support
Included:
- 2 Engineer Squadrons, each: Sqdn HQ (2 rifle secs, 1 lorry)
  - 4 Troops, each: 4 (12 man) rifle/engineer secs, 3 LMG, 2 lorries
- 1 Engineer Park Company: (175 men)
  - 1 Workshop Section
  - 1 Bridging and Stores Section
- 2 Artillery Regiments, each:
  - 3 Artillery Batteries, each: Battery HQ (4 rifle secs, 4 lorries, 4 AALMG, 3 OP Teams)
    - 2 Troops, each: 4 × 25pdr, 4 trucks, radio truck, 2 AALMG
- 72nd A/T Regiment:
  - 3 A/T Batteries, each: Battery HQ (1 rifle sec, 1 truck)
    - 3 Troops, each: 4 × 6pdr, 2 LMG, 4 trucks
- 1 A/T Battery: Battery HQ (2 × Carriers, 1 rifle sec)
  - 3 Platoons, each: 4 × Deacon, 1 × Deacon cargo
- 51st Light AA Regiment:
  - 2 AA Batteries, each: Battery HQ (1 rifle sec, 1 truck)
    - 3 Troops, each: 6 × 40mm Bofors, 6 trucks

Brigade Support
- Armoured Brigade HQ (3 × Sherman III or Grant I, 2 × ACV, 1 × Vickers I AA)
- Motorised Brigade HQ (4 rifle secs, 2 LMG, 2 trucks, 2 lorries)

MAIN COMBAT ELEMENTS

Armoured Regiment, March 1943 Onwards
- RHQ (4 × Sherman II)
  - 3 Squadrons, each: Sqdn HQ (4 × Sherman II)
    - 3 Troops, each: 3 × Sherman II
    - 2 Troops, each: 3 × Sherman II or III
    - 1 AA Troop: 4 × Vickers VI AA
    - 1 Recce Troop: Troop HQ (1 × Daimler S/C)
      - 3 Sections, each: 3 × Daimler S/C

Armoured Regiment (Mixed)
- RHQ (4 × Valentine III and Crusader II)
  - 3 Squadrons, each: Sqdn HQ (2 × Valentine III or V, 2 × Crusader IICS)
    - 2 Troops, each: 3 × Crusader III, 1 × Crusader II Troop HQ
    - 2 Troops, each: 3 × Valentine III or V, 1 × Valentine VIII (6pdr)
    - 1 AA Troop: 1–2 × Vickers VI AA
    - 1 Recce Troop: Troop HQ (1 × Daimler S/C)
      - 3 Sections, each: 3 × Daimler S/C

10th Battalion Rifle Brigade Motor Battalion
- Btn HQ (2 rifle secs, 2 trucks)
  - 1 Battery: 4 × 3" mortars, 5 × Carriers
  - 3 Companies, each: Coy HQ (1 rifle sec, 1 × 2" mortar, 2 trucks)
    - 2 Platoons, each: 4 rifle secs, 3 LMG, 1 × 2", 4 Boys, 4 trucks
    - 1 Platoon: 4 MMG, 4 trucks
    - 1 Platoon: Pl HQ (2 × Universal Carrier, 1 LMG, 1 × Daimler S/C)
      - 3 Sections, each: 3 × Carriers, 3 LMG, 1 rifle sec, 1 × 2", 1 Boys
  - 1 A/T Company: Coy HQ (1 rifle sec, 1 truck)
    - 3 Platoons, each: 4 × 2pdr, portéed or truck tows, 2 LMG

Motor Battalion, 38th Lorried Infantry Brigade
- Btn HQ (2 rifle secs, 2 trucks)
  - 4 Companies, each: Coy HQ (1 rifle sec, 1 lorry)
    - 3 Platoons, each: 4 rifle secs, 3 LMG, 1 Boys, 1 × 2" mortar, 2 lorries
  - 1 Support Company: Coy HQ (1 rifle sec, 1 truck)
    - 1 Platoon: 4 × 2pdr, 2 LMG, 4 trucks
    - 1 Platoon: 2 (8 man) rifle/engineer secs, 1 (5 man) Pl HQ sec, 1 lorry
    - 1 Battery: 6 × 3" mortars, 7 × Universal Carriers

1 Platoon: Pl HQ (1 × Universal Carrier, 1 LMG, 1 × Daimler S/C)
    4 Sections, each: 3 × Carriers, 3 LMG, 1 rifle sec, 1 × 2", 0–1 Boys

1st Derbyshire Yeomanry Divisional Armoured Car Regiment

RHQ (4 × Humber III, 2 × Daimler S/C)
  0–1 AA Troop: 4 × Humber AA
  3 Squadrons, each: Sqdn HQ (2 × Daimler II, 2 × Humber III)
    5 Troops, each: 2 × Humber III, 1 × Daimler II

Notes
1. Radios were in all tanks and armoured cars, Carrier Pl HQs, and other Coy HQs.
2. Infantry sections had No.74 or Hawkins 75 A/T grenades.
3. 2pdr and 37mm had APCBC, 6pdr, 75mm and 25pdr had AP, the 6pdr had one load of APCBC.
4. Artillery OP could be in truck, Daimler Scout car or Auster AOP.
5. The Division was fully equipped with Shermans by March 1943.
6. For wargames purposes, from January 1943 one A/T Troop could replace 6pdr with 17pdrs.

2.13 BRITISH BLADE FORCE, 6TH ARMOURED DIVISION, NOVEMBER 1942, TUNISIA

The Brigade's main combat element was:
17th/21st Lancers Armoured Regiment
The force represented the initial elements of 6th Armoured Division that landed in Tunisia. The troops are rated at average training and average morale.

SUPPORT UNITS

Brigade Support

Brigade HQ (2 × Crusader II, 1 × Crusader III, 1 × Vickers VI AA, 2 × ACV) with:
  B Recce Squadron: Sqdn HQ (2 × Daimler II, 2 × Humber III, 2 × Daimler S/C)
    5 Troops, each: 2 × Humber III, 1 × Daimler II
  1 Field Artillery Battery: Battery HQ (4 rifle secs, 6 trucks, 2 AALMG, 3 OP Teams)
    2 Troops, each: 4 × 25pdr, 4 trucks, radio truck, 2 AALMG
  1 A/T Troop: 4 × 6pdr guns, 2 LMG, 4 trucks
  1 AA Troop: 6 × 40mm Bofors, 6 trucks
  1 Motor Company: Coy HQ: 1 rifle sec, 1 × 2" mortar, 2 trucks
    2 Platoons, each: 4 rifle secs, 1 × 2", 3 LMG, 4 Boys, 4 trucks
      1 Section: 2 × 3" mortars, 2 × Carriers
    1 Platoon: 4 MMG, 4 trucks
    1 Platoon: Pl HQ (2 × Carrier, 1 × Daimler S/C, 1 LMG)
      3 Sections, each: 3 × Carrier, 1 rifle sec, 1 × 2", 1 Boys, 3 LMG
  1 Engineer Troop: 4 (12 man) rifle/engineer secs, 2 lorries, 2 LMG

MAIN COMBAT ELEMENTS

17th/21st Lancers Armoured Regiment

RHQ (4 × Valentine III and Crusader II)
  3 Squadrons, each: Sqdn HQ (2 × Valentine III or V, 2 × Crusader IICS)
    2 Troops, each: 3 × Crusader III, 1 × Crusader II Troop HQ
    2 Troops, each: 3 × Valentine III or V, 1 × Valentine VIII (6pdr)
  1 AA Troop: 1–2 × Vickers VI AA
  1 Recce Troop: Troop HQ (1 × Daimler S/C)
    3 Sections, each: 3 × Daimler S/C

Notes
1. Radios were in all AFVs and Coy HQs, except for Carriers, in which case they were in Pl HQs only.
2. Infantry sections had No.74 or Hawkins 75 A/T grenades.
3. The 2pdr fired APCBC, 6pdr had AP with one load of APCBC.
4. Artillery OP was in Daimler S/C or truck.

2.14 BRITISH 4TH LIGHT ARMOURED BRIGADE, MID–1942–MAY 1943, NORTH AFRICA

The Brigade's main combat elements were:
  2 Armoured Regiments (Royal Scots Greys, Converged Hussars Regiment)
  1 Armoured Car Regiment (2nd Derbyshire Yeomanry)
  1 Motor Battalion (1st Btn King's Royal Rifle Corps)
Troops are rated at average training and average morale.

SUPPORT UNITS

Brigade Support

Brigade HQ (9 × A/C, 1 × ACV, 3 × Daimler S/C) with:
  3 Artillery Batteries, each: Battery HQ (4 rifle secs, 5 lorries, 4 AALMG, 2 Boys, 3 OP Teams)
    2 Troops, each: 4 × 25pdr, 4 trucks, radio truck, 2 AALMG, 1 Boys

MAIN COMBAT ELEMENTS

Royal Scots Greys Armoured Regiment
RHQ (3 × Stuart I, 2 × Grant I)
    1 Squadron: Sqdn HQ (4 × Stuart I)
        3 Troops, each: 4 × Stuart I
    1 Squadron: Sqdn HQ (3 × Grant I) (September 1942 onwards only)
        3 Troops, each: 3 × Grant I
    1 Recce Troop: 2 Sections, each: 3 × Daimler S/C

Converged Hussars Armoured Regiment
RHQ (3 × Stuart I)
    3 Squadrons, each: Sqdn HQ (3 × Stuart I)
        3 Troops, each: 4 × Stuart I
    1 Recce Troop: 2–3 Sections, each: 3 × Daimler S/C

1st Battalion King's Royal Rifle Corps Motor Battalion
Btn HQ (2 rifle secs, 2 trucks)
    3 Companies, each: Coy HQ (1 rifle sec, 1 × 2" mortar, 2 trucks)
        1 Battery: 2 × 3" mortars, 3 × Carriers (Assigned FC)
        2 Platoons, each: 4 rifle secs, 3 LMG, 1 × 2", 0–4 Boys, 4 trucks
        1 Platoon: 4 MMG, 5 × Carriers
        1 Platoon: Pl HQ (1 × Universal Carrier, 1 LMG, 1 × Daimler S/C)
            3 Sections, each: 3 × Carriers, 3 LMG, 1 rifle sec, 1 × 2", 1 Boys
    1 A/T Company: Coy HQ (1 rifle sec, 1 truck)
        4 Platoons, each: 4 × 6pdr portées

2nd Derbyshire Yeomanry Armoured Car Regiment
RHQ (4 × Humber III)
    0–4 Sections, each: 3 × Daimler S/C
    3 Squadrons, each: Sqdn HQ (2 × Humber III)
        4 Troops, each: 3 × Humber III

Notes
1. Radios were in all AFVs, Carrier Pl HQs, and other Coy HQs.
2. Infantry sections had No.74 or Hawkins 75 A/T grenades.
3. 2pdr and 37mm had APC, with APCBC from September 1942. 6pdr, 75mm and 25pdr had AP, the 6pdr having one load of APCBC.
4. Artillery OPs are in trucks, Daimler S/C or Stuart I

2.15 BRITISH ARMY TANK BRIGADE, OCTOBER 1940–FEBRUARY 1942, NORTH AFRICA

The 1st Brigade had one regiment until early 1941, when a second regiment arrived. By late 1941 the Brigade had three regiments – 8th, 42nd and 44th RTR. From October 1941 two (1st, 32nd) Brigades existed, each containing two Matilda regiments and a third regiment (Cruisers in 32nd Brigade, Valentine I in 1st Brigade). Troops are rated at average training and good morale.

SUPPORT UNITS

Brigade Support
Tank Brigade HQ (4 × Matilda II, 2 × ACV, 6 × Scout Cars)

MAIN COMBAT ELEMENTS

Armoured Regiment
Btn HQ (2 × Matilda IICS, 2 × Matilda II, 4 × Vickers VIB)
    3 Companies, each: Coy HQ (1 × Matilda II, 2 × Matilda IICS or II)
        3 Platoons, each: 3 × Matilda II

Armoured Regiment, 32nd Tank Brigade, October 1941 Onwards
Btn HQ (1–3 × A–10 or A–13 Mk2, 3 × Vickers VIB)
    1 Company, each: Coy HQ (1 × A–13 Mk2, 2 × A–9 CS)
        3 Platoons, each: 3 × A–13 Mk2 Cruiser
    1 Company: Coy HQ (1 × A–10, 2 × A–9 CS, 1 × Vickers VIB)
        1 Platoon: 3 × A–13 Mk2
        2 Platoons, each: 3 × Vickers VIB
    1 Company: Coy HQ (1 × A–10, 2 × A–9 CS, 1 × Vickers VIB)
        2 Platoons, each: 3 × A–10
        1 Platoon: 3 × Vickers VIB or A–10

Notes
1. Radios were in all AFVs.
2. If equipped with Valentines, then the CS-tanks were Matilda IICS.
3. The organisation of the Cruiser Regiment in 32nd Brigade is provisional – it had 29–39 Cruisers and 10–19 Vickers VIB depending on the source quoted. The Brigade formed part of the Tobruk garrison. Following the relief of Tobruk the 32nd Brigade deployed to Palestine, during January–April 1942.

2.16 BRITISH ARMY TANK BRIGADE, MARCH–JULY 1942, NORTH AFRICA

The 1st Brigade contained three regiments of Valentines, the 32nd Brigade had two regiments of Matildas. In July 1942 a third brigade (23rd Armoured) arrived with three regiments of Valentines. This was from 8th Armoured Division and was completely untrained in the infantry support role. After being decimated in July 1942, the 23rd Brigade was rebuilt using the 24th Armoured Brigade of the 8th Armoured Division. Troops are rated at average training and good morale.

SUPPORT UNITS

Brigade Support
Tank Brigade HQ (4 × Matilda II or Valentine III, 2 × ACV, 6 × S/C, 2 × Vickers VI AA)

MAIN COMBAT ELEMENTS

Armoured Regiment
RHQ (2 × Matilda IICS, 2 × Matilda II OR 4 × Valentine III)
   3 Squadrons, each: Sqdn HQ (2 × Matilda II or 2 × Valentine III, 2 × Matilda IICS)
      4 Troops, each: 3 × Matilda II OR 3 Troops, each: 3 × Valentine III
   1 Recce Platoon: Pl HQ (1 × Daimler S/C)
      3 Sections, each: 3 × Daimler S/C
   1 AA Platoon: 4 × Vickers VI AA tanks

Notes
1   Radios were in all AFVs.
2   2pdr had APC.

2.17 BRITISH 23RD ARMOURED BRIGADE, AUGUST 1942–JANUARY 1943, NORTH AFRICA

The Brigade's main combat element was:
   3 Armoured Regiments (40th, 46th and 50th RTR)
   1 Motor Battalion (11th Btn King's Royal Rifle Corps)
From December 1942, the Brigade's tank assets were reduced to a single effective regiment. The troops are rated at average training and good morale.

SUPPORT UNITS

Brigade Support
Tank Brigade HQ (4 × Valentine III, 2 × ACV, 6 × Scout Cars, 2 × Vickers VI AA)

MAIN COMBAT ELEMENTS

Armoured Regiment
RHQ (2 × Matilda IICS, 2 × Valentine II or III)
   3 Squadrons, each: Sqdn HQ (2 × Valentine II, III, V, or VII)
      4 Troops, each: 3 × Valentine II, III, or V
   1 Recce Platoon: Pl HQ (1 × Daimler S/C)
      3 Sections, each: 3 × Daimler S/C
   1 AA Troop: 2 Platoons, each: 4 × Vickers VI AA tanks

Motor Battalion
Btn HQ (2 rifle secs, 2 trucks)
   3 Companies, each: Coy HQ (1 rifle sec, 1 × 2" mortar, 2 trucks)
      1 Battery: 2 × 3" mortars, 3 × Carriers
      2 Platoons, each: 4 rifle secs, 3 LMG, 1 × 2", 0–4 Boys, 4 trucks
      1 Platoon: 4 MMG, 5 × Carriers
      1 Platoon: Pl HQ (1 × Universal Carrier, 1 LMG, 1 × Daimler S/C)
         3 Sections, each: 3 × Carriers, 3 LMG, 1 rifle sec, 1 × 2", 1 × Boys
   1 A/T Company: Coy HQ (1 rifle sec, 1 truck)
      4 Platoons, each: 4 × 2pdr or 6pdr, portéed or truck tows, 2 LMG

Notes
1   Radios were in all AFVs.
2   2pdr had APCBC.
3   One Regiment was issued with 12 AMRA mine roller sets in October 1942, of which 5 were used.

2.18 BRITISH ARMY TANK BRIGADE, JANUARY–MAY 1943, TUNISIA

The two brigades, the 21st and 25th, each contained three Infantry Tank Regiments – 21st: 12th RTR, 48th RTR, 8th Duke of Wellington's; 25th – 11th RTR, 51st RTR, 7th Suffolks. Troops are rated at average training and good morale.

SUPPORT UNITS

Brigade Support
Tank Brigade HQ (4 × Sherman II, 2 × ACV, 6 × S/C, 2 × Vickers VI AA)

MAIN COMBAT ELEMENTS

Infantry Tank Regiment
    RHQ (2 × Churchill III, 2 × Churchill V or 1 CS, 1 × Stuart III OP)
        3 Squadrons, each: Sqdn HQ (2 × Churchill III, 2 × Churchill V, 1 × Daimler Scout Car)
            4–5 Troops, each: 3 × Churchill III
        1 Squadron: Sqdn HQ (3 × Stuart III or 1 × Daimler S/C)
            3 Troops, each: 3 × Stuart III or 3 × Daimler S/C

Notes
1   Radios were in all AFVs.
2   2pdr and 37mm had APCBC. 6pdr had AP with one load of APCBC.

2.19 INDEPENDENT ARMOURED UNITS, 1940–MAY 1943, NORTH AFRICA

Units are rated at average training and good morale, except Searchlight Regiments, which are average training and morale, and Tank Training units, which are poor training and average morale.

ARMY-LEVEL SUPPORT UNITS
Included:
    2nd New Zealand Divisional Cavalry Regiment (March 1940–February 1941)
        RHQ (2 radio trucks, 4 cars, 2 rifle secs)
            3 Recce Squadrons, each: Sqdn HQ (2 × Vickers VIB, 2 × Scout Carrier)
                1 Troop: 3 × Vickers VIB light tanks
                4 Troops, each: 2 × Bren Carriers
    1 Recce Regiment (October 1940–Feb 1942)
        RHQ (4 × Vickers VIB, 2 × radio vans)
            3 Recce Squadrons, each: Sqdn HQ (2 × Vickers VIB, 2 × Scout Carrier)
                2 Troops, each: 3 × Vickers VIB
                4 Troops, each: 3 × Scout Carriers, 1 rifle sec, 1 radio
    1 Recce Regiment (August 1942 onwards)
        RHQ (4 × Marmon-Herrington II or Humber II)
            3 Recce Squadrons, each: Sqdn HQ (2 × Marmon-Herrington II or Humber II)
                3 Platoons, each: 4 × Marmon-Herrington II or Humber II
    2 Tank Training Squadrons (October 1940–April 1941), each:
        Sqdn HQ (2 × Vickers Medium II, 2 × Vickers Medium IICS)
            4 Troops, each: 3 × Vickers Medium II
    1 Army Tank Test Troop (Kingforce): 6 × Churchill III (November 1942 only)
    8th Army HQ Protection Squadron (August 1942 onwards): Sqdn HQ (3 × Grant I)
        1 Troop: 6 × 40mm Bofors, 6 trucks
        1 Troop: 4 × Grant I
        1 Troop: 4 × Marmon-Herrington II A/C
    1 Tank Squadron (August 1942 onwards): Sqdn HQ (2 × Matilda II, 2 × Matilda IICS)
        4 Troops, each: 3 × Matilda II Scorpion flails
    1 Tank Squadron (January 1943 onwards): Sqdn HQ (3 × Grant I)
        4 Troops, each: 3 × Grant I Scorpion
    3 Searchlight Regiments (August 1942 onwards), each:
        RHQ (2 × Matilda IICS, 2 × Matilda II, 2 Scout Cars)
            2–3 Squadrons, each: Sqdn HQ (2 × Matilda II, 2 × Matilda IICS)
                5 Troops, each: 3 × Matilda II CDL

Notes
1   Radios were in all AFVs and other Pl HQs.
2   The Searchlight Regiments were never used in action.

2.20 INDIAN 3RD MOTORISED BRIGADE, FEBRUARY–APRIL 1941, NORTH AFRICA

The Brigade's main combat element was a single Cavalry Regiment. The remnants of the Brigade joined the 7th Armoured Division in May 1941. Troops are rated at average training and morale, except for the Australians, with average training and good morale.

SUPPORT UNITS

Brigade Support
    Motorised Brigade HQ (4 rifle secs, 6 trucks, 2 field cars, 2 AA LMG) with:
        1 Engineer Squadron: Sqdn HQ (1 rifle sec, 1 truck)
            3 Platoons, each: 2–3 rifle/engineer secs, 3 trucks, 1 LMG, 0–1 Boys
        1 Attached Australian A/T Battery: Battery HQ (1 rifle sec, 1 truck)
            3 Troops, each: 4 × 2pdr A/T guns, 4 trucks, 1 LMG

MAIN COMBAT ELEMENT

Cavalry Regiment
    RHQ (4 rifle secs, 2 field cars, 4 trucks)
        3 Squadrons, each: Sqdn HQ (1 rifle sec, 1 truck)
            3 Troops, each: 4 rifle secs, 3 LMG, 0–1 Boys A/T Rifle, 4 trucks
            0–1 Troop: 2 MMG, 2 × 3" mortars, 4 trucks

Notes
1. Radios were in all Coy HQs
2. Infantry had no anti-tank grenades. In practice few LMG or Boys were available. The heavy weapons troop in each squadron was never raised, as the unit was overrun in April 1941, at Mechili, near Tobruk.

2.21 INDIAN 3RD MOTORISED BRIGADE, JANUARY–MAY 1942, NORTH AFRICA

The Brigade's main combat elements were:
    3 Cavalry Carrier Regiments (2nd Royal Lancers, 11th Prince Albert Victor's Own Cavalry, 18th King Edward VII's Own Cavalry)

Attached to the 7th Armoured Division, the Brigade was overrun and virtually destroyed during the Gazala line fighting in May 1942, the remnants retired to Syria and were converted to a Lorried Infantry Brigade in the 31st Indian Armoured Division. Troops are rated at average training and average morale.

SUPPORT UNITS

Brigade Support

Motorised Brigade HQ (4 rifle secs, 6 trucks, 2 staff cars or scout cars) with:
  2nd Indian Field Artillery Regiment:
    3 Batteries, each: Battery HQ (1 radio van, 4 trucks, 4 rifle secs, 2 AALMG
      2 Troops, each: 4 × 25pdr, 4 trucks, radio van, 1 LMG
  1 Engineer Squadron: Sqdn HQ (1 rifle sec, 1 truck)
    4 Troops, each: 4 (12 man) rifle/engineer secs, 1 Boys, 1 AALMG, 2 lorries
  1 A/T Battery: Battery HQ (1 rifle sec, 1 truck)
    4 Troops, each: 4 × 2pdr A/T guns, 4 × Universal Carriers

MAIN COMBAT ELEMENTS

Cavalry (Carrier) Regiment

RHQ (4 rifle secs, 4 trucks, 1 car, 1 Boys, 2 LMG)
  2 Recce Squadrons, each: Sqdn HQ (3 × Universal Carriers, 1 (12 man) rifle crew sec
    4 Troops, each: 3 × Universal Carrier, 1 (12 man) rifle crew sec, 3 LMG, 1 × Boys
  1 A/T Squadron: Sqdn HQ (3 × Universal Carriers, 1 rifle crew HQ sec)
    4 Troops, each: 4 × 2pdr A/T guns, 4 × Universal Carriers, 4 LMG

Notes
1. Radios were in all Pl HQs and above.
2. Infantry had no anti-tank grenades.
3. When overrun, the Brigade was caught at only half-strength in A/T guns.

2.22 BRITISH AND COMMONWEALTH INFANTRY DIVISIONS, JUNE 1941–43, NORTH AFRICA

The Division's main combat elements were:
    3 Infantry Brigades (each of 3 Infantry Battalions)
    1 Divisional Recce Regiment

This list can be used for independent brigades and Commonwealth infantry units in North Africa up to July 1942, including South African Divisions, and Canadian troops in Sicily during 1943. Troops are rated at average training and good morale.

SUPPORT UNITS

Divisional Support

Included:
  9 Artillery Batteries, each: Battery HQ (1 radio van, 4 trucks, 4 rifle secs, 1 Boys, 2 AALMG
    2 Troops, each: 4 × 25pdr Mk.1, 4 trucks, radio van, 1 LMG
  3 A/T Batteries, each: Battery HQ (1 rifle sec, 1 truck)
    3 Troops, each: 4 × 2pdr or 6pdr, 4 truck portées, 2 LMG
  3 Engineer Companies, each: Coy HQ (1 rifle sec, 2 × Scout Cars)[10]
    3 Platoons, each: 4 (12 man) rifle/engineer secs, 1 Boys, 1 AALMG
  1 MG Battalion:[11]
    3 MG Companies, each: Coy HQ (1 rifle sec, 1 truck)
      4 Platoons, each: 4 MMG, 1 Boys, 2 trucks
  3 AA Batteries, each: Battery HQ (1 rifle sec, 1 truck)
    3 Troops, each: 6 × 40mm Bofors, 6 trucks

Brigade Support

Infantry Brigade HQ (10 rifle secs, 3 LMG, 1 × 2", 1 × Boys) with:
  1 Support Company:[12] Coy HQ (1 rifle sec, 1 truck)
    3 Platoons, each: 4 Vickers MMG, 4 trucks, 4 rifle crew secs
    2 Platoons, each: 4 × 4.2" mortars, 4 trucks, radio truck

---

10. 1943 onwards.
11. Only in 5th, 44th, 50th, 4th British Infantry Divisions from 1943, and in all Commonwealth Divisions, 1941–43.
12. Only if 1943 onwards, and if there was no Divisional MG Battalion.

MAIN COMBAT ELEMENTS

Infantry Battalion
Btn HQ (5 rifle secs, 1 LMG)
    4 Companies, each: Coy HQ (1 rifle sec)
        3 Platoons, each: 4 rifle secs, 3 LMG, 1 × 2", 1 Boys
    1 Support Company: Coy HQ: 1 rifle sec
        1 Platoon: 4 or 6 × 3" mortars, 3 Boys, 6 Carriers
        1 Platoon: 2 rifle/engineer secs, 1 lorry
        1 Platoon: Pl HQ (1 × Carrier, 1 × Daimler S/C, 1 LMG)
            4 Sections, each: 3 × Carrier, 3 LMG, 1 Boys, 1 × 2", 1 rifle sec
        2 Platoons, each: 4 × 2pdr, 4 × Carriers (1942 onwards)
        1 Platoon:[13] 4 × Vickers MMG, 4 trucks

Infantry Battalion, North Africa/Sicily, November 1942 Onwards
Btn HQ (5 rifle secs, 1 LMG)
    4 Companies, each: Coy HQ (1 rifle sec)
        3 Platoons, each: 4 rifle secs, 3 LMG, 1 × 2", 1 Boys
    1 Support Company: Coy HQ (1 rifle sec)
        1 Platoon: 4 or 6 × 3" mortars, 3 Boys, 6 × Carriers
        1 Platoon: 2 rifle/engineer secs, 1 lorry
        1 Scout Platoon: Pl HQ (1 × Carrier, 1 × Daimler S/C, 1 LMG)
            1 Section: 3 × Carrier, 3 LMG, 1 Boys, 1 × 2", 1 rifle sec
        2 Platoons, each: 4 × 2pdr, 4 × Carriers
        1 MG Platoon: 4 × Vickers MMG, 8 × Universal Carriers

Divisional Recce Regiment
RHQ (4 × Marmon-Herrington I or II, 0–12 × Daimler S/C)
    3 Squadrons, each: Sqdn HQ (3 × Marmon-Herrington I or II)
        4 Troops, each: 3 × Marmon-Herrington I or II

Divisional Recce Regiment, Libya/Tunisia/Sicily, July 1942–Late 1943
RHQ (3 rifle secs, 3 LMG, 3 × Light Recce Car)
    3 Squadrons, each: Sqdn HQ (3 rifle secs, 1 LMG, 3 trucks, 1 Light Recce Car, 1 Jeep)
        3 Troops, each: Troop HQ (1 × Carrier, 1 LMG, 1 Boys, 1 × 2" mortar)
            1 Section: 3 × Humber Light Recce IIIA, 2 × Humber III or Marmon-Herrington II+47mmL32
            2 Sections, each: 3 × Carrier, 1 Boys, 3 LMG, 1 × 2", 1 rifle sec
        1 Troop: 4 rifle secs, 5 trucks, 4 LMG, 1 Jeep
    1 Mortar Battery: 6 × 3" mortars, 7 × Universal Carriers, 1 Jeep
    1 A/T Platoon: Pl HQ (1 Jeep, 4 × Lloyd Carriers)[14]
        3 Troops (1942), each: 4 × 2pdr A/T guns, 4 × Lloyd Carriers
        OR 2 Troops (1943), each: 4 × 2pdr or 6pdr A/T guns, 4 × Lloyd Carriers
    1 AA Platoon: 2 × twin AALMG on trucks

Divisional 2nd Cavalry Regiment, New Zealand 2nd Infantry Division, Egypt, August 1941–March 1942
RHQ (2 × Vickers VIB, 2 × Universal Carrier)
    3 Squadrons, each: Sqdn HQ (2 × Vickers VIB, 2 × Universal Carrier)
        2 Troops, each: 3 × Vickers VIB light tanks
        4 Troops, each: 3 × Universal Carriers, 3 LMG, 1 Boys, 1 × 2" mortar, 1 rifle sec

Notes
1. Radios were in all Coy HQs and AFVs. All artillery is rated as Assigned FC up to July 1942. After that it is rated as Flexible FC, with one OP team per battery in truck, Daimler S/C or turretless Marmon-Herrington.
2. Infantry sections had No.74 or No.75 Hawkins A/T grenades. By August 1942 the Boys was dispensed with.
3. Divisional A/T batteries did not have 6pdr until July 1942.
4. For wargames purposes, from 1942 the Divisional Recce Regiment could have Humber IIIs mixed in, and could replace the Daimler S/C with Humber Light Recce Mk II or III. From August 1942, each Recce Squadron could add one troop of 6 jeeps (unarmed).
5. In 1942 25pdr had AP. From May 1942 the 2pdr had APC, with APCBC from August 1942.
6. 2pdr A/T guns could be towed by Lloyd Carriers.

2.23 AUSTRALIAN INFANTRY DIVISION, 1940–41, NORTH AFRICA

The Division's main combat elements were:
2–3 Infantry Brigades (each of 3–4 Infantry Battalions)
Troops are rated at average training and good morale.

---

13   South African battalions only.
14   For extra ammunition.

SUPPORT UNITS

Divisional Support
Included:
 6 Artillery Batteries, each: Battery HQ (1 radio van, 4 trucks, 4 rifle secs, 2 AALMG)
  3 Troops, each: 4 × 25pdr, 4 trucks, radio van, 1 AALMG
 4 A/T Companies, each: Coy HQ (1 rifle sec, 1 truck)
  3 Troops, each: 4 × 2pdr, 4 trucks
 3 Engineer Companies, each: Coy HQ (1 rifle sec)
  3 Platoons, each: 4 (12 man) rifle/engineer secs, 2 lorries
 4 MG Companies, each: Coy HQ (1 rifle sec, 1 truck)
  3 Platoons, each: 4 × MMG, 2 trucks

Brigade Support
Infantry Brigade HQ (6 rifle secs, 4 lorries, 1 Boys, 3 LMG)

MAIN COMBAT ELEMENTS

Infantry Battalion
Btn HQ (2 rifle secs)
 4 Companies, each: Coy HQ (1 rifle sec)
  3 Platoons, each: 4 rifle secs, 3 LMG, 1 × 2", 0–1 Boys
 1 Support Company: Coy HQ (1 rifle sec)
  1 Platoon: 2 × 3" mortars (Assigned FC)
  1 Platoon: 2 rifle/engineer secs
  1 Platoon: 4 × Twin AALMG
  1 Platoon: Pl HQ (1 × Bren Carrier, 1 LMG)
   3 Sections, each: 3 × Bren Carrier, 3 LMG, 1 (6 man) rifle sec

Divisional Recce Regiment[15]
RHQ (4 × Vickers VIB, 1 radio van, 4 × Scout Carriers)
 3 Squadrons, each: Sqdn HQ (2 × Vickers VIB, 2 × Scout Carriers)
  2 Troops, each: 3 × Vickers VIB or IIB light tank
  4 Troops, each: 3 × Scout Carriers, 1 rifle sec, 3 Boys, 3 LMG

Notes
1 Radios were in all AFVs and other Coy HQs. Artillery is rated as Assigned FC.
2 Infantry sections had no A/T grenades.
3 For wargames purposes, in 1941 could replace Bren Carriers with Universal type, adding 4 riflemen, 1 Boys, 1 × 2" mortar to each Carrier section.
4 This list can also be used for Australian and New Zealand divisions operating in Greece in 1941.

2.24 AUSTRALIAN INFANTRY DIVISION, MID 1942–43, NORTH AFRICA

The Division's main combat elements were:
 3 Infantry Brigades (each of 3 Infantry Battalions)
Troops are rated at average training and good morale.

SUPPORT UNITS

Divisional Support
 9 Artillery Batteries, each: Battery HQ (6 trucks, 4 rifle secs, 2 AALMG, 2 OP Teams)
  2 Troops, each: 4 × 25pdr, 4 trucks, radio van, 1 LMG
 3 A/T Companies, each: Coy HQ (1 rifle sec, 1 truck)
  3 Platoons, each: 4 × 6pdr, 4 truck portées, 2 LMG
 3 AA Companies, each: Coy HQ (1 rifle sec, 1 truck)
  3 AA Platoons, each: 6 × 40mm Bofors, 6 trucks
 1 Pioneer Battalion:
  3 Pioneer Companies, each: Coy HQ (1 rifle sec, 1 truck)
   3 Platoons, each: 4 (12 man) rifle/pioneer secs, 2 LMG, 2 lorries
  1 MMG Platoon: 4 × Vickers MMG, 2 trucks
 1 MG Battalion:
  4 MG Companies, each: Coy HQ (1 rifle sec, 1 truck)
   4 Platoons, each: 4 × MMG, 2 trucks
 1 Pioneer Company: Coy HQ (1 rifle sec, 1 truck) (average morale, poor training)
  3 Platoons, each: 4 rifle/pioneer secs, 2 lorries

Brigade Support
Infantry Brigade HQ (10 rifle secs, 10 trucks/lorries, 3 LMG, 1 × 2" mortar)

---

15 In 1941 the Divisional Recce Regiment had 5 × M11/39 and 5 × M13/40 tanks (captured at Tobruk), distributed amongst the Squadrons.

MAIN COMBAT ELEMENTS
Infantry Battalion
Btn HQ (5 rifle secs, 1 LMG)
    4 Companies, each: Coy HQ (1 rifle sec)
        3 Platoons, each: 4 rifle secs, 3 LMG, 1 × 2" mortar
    1 Support Company: Coy HQ (1 rifle sec)
        1 Platoon: 6 × 3" mortars, 7 × Carriers
        1 Platoon: 4 × 2pdr or 6pdr A/T guns, 4 × Carriers
        1 Platoon: 2 rifle/engineer secs, 1 stores truck
        1 Platoon: 4 × Vickers MMG, 4 trucks
        1 Platoon: Pl HQ (1 × Carrier, 1 × Daimler S/C, 1 LMG)
            4 Sections, each: 3 × Carrier, 3 LMG, 1 × 2", 1 rifle sec

Divisional Cavalry Regiment[16]
RHQ (1 × Stuart I, 1 radio van, 4 × Carriers or Daimler Scout Cars)
    3 Squadrons, each: Sqdn HQ (1 × Stuart I, 2 × Carriers)
        2 Troops, each: 3 × Crusader II
        3 Troops, each: 3 × Carriers, 1 rifle sec, 3 Boys, 3 LMG
    2 MG Troops, each: 4 × Vickers MMG, 4 × Carriers

Notes
1   Radios were in all tanks, all Carrier Pl HQ and other Coy HQs.
2   Infantry sections had No.74 or No.75 Hawkins A/T grenades.
3   Artillery OPs were in trucks or Daimler Scout Car.
4   25pdr had AP, 6pdr had AP, APC and one load of APCBC, 37mm and 2pdr had APCBC.

2.25 NEW ZEALAND 2ND DIVISION, MID 1942–43, NORTH AFRICA

In early 1943, the Division's main combat elements were:
    6th Infantry Brigade (24th, 25th and 26th Infantry Battalions)
    4th Armoured Brigade (18th, 19th and 20th Armoured Regiments, 22nd Motor Battalion)
    2nd Divisional Cavalry Regiment
Troops are rated at average training and good morale, except for the Maori Battalion, which is rated as average training and excellent morale.

SUPPORT UNITS
Divisional Support
Included:
    DHQ Escort Troop (1 × Stuart III-HQ (dummy gun, extra radio), 3 × Stuart I)
    9 Artillery Batteries, each: Battery HQ (4 lorries, 4 rifle secs, 4 AALMG, 2 OP Teams)
        2 Troops, each: 4 × 25pdr, 4 trucks, radio van, 2 AALMG
    3 A/T Companies, each: Coy HQ (1 rifle sec, 1 truck)
        3 Platoons, each: 4 × 6pdr, 4 truck portées, 2 LMG
    3 AA Companies, each: Coy HQ (1 rifle sec, 1 truck)
        3 AA Platoons, each: 6 × 40mm Bofors, 6 trucks
    3 Engineer Companies, each: Coy HQ (1 rifle sec, 1 truck)
        3 Platoons, each: 4 (12 man) rifle/engineer secs, 2 LMG, 2 lorries
    1 MG Battalion:
        3 MG Companies, each: Coy HQ (1 rifle sec, 1 truck)
            3 Platoons, each: 4 × MMG, 2 trucks

Brigade Support
    Infantry Brigade HQ (6 rifle secs, 8 trucks/lorries, 2 LMG)
    Armoured Brigade HQ (2 × Grant I, 1 × Vickers VI AA, 2 × ACV)

MAIN COMBAT ELEMENTS
Infantry Battalion
Btn HQ (5 rifle secs, 1 LMG)
    4 Companies, each: Coy HQ (1 rifle sec)
        3 Platoons, each: 4 rifle secs, 3 LMG, 1 × 2"
    1 Support Company: Coy HQ (1 rifle sec)
        1 Platoon: 6 × 3" mortars, 7 × Carriers
        2 Platoons, each: 4 × 2pdr or 6pdr, 4 × Carrier
        1 Platoon: 2 rifle/engineer secs
        1 Platoon: Pl HQ (1 × Carrier, 1 × Daimler S/C, 1 LMG)
            4 Sections, each: 3 × Carrier, 3 LMG, 1 × 2" mortar, 1 rifle sec

---

16   Provisional.

Armoured Regiment Variant 1
    Btn HQ (3 × Sherman II)
        3 Squadrons, each: Sqdn HQ (2 × Sherman II)
            3 Troops, each: 3 × Sherman II
        1 Recce Platoon: Pl HQ (1 × Daimler Scout Car)
            3 Sections, each: 3 × Daimler Scout Car

Armoured Regiment Variant 2
    Btn HQ (1 × Crusader II, 2 × Grant I)
        2 Squadrons, each: Sqdn HQ (2 × Crusader II, 2 × Crusader IICS)
            2 Troops, each: 3 × Crusader II
            2 Troops, each: 3 × Crusader III
        1 Squadron: Sqdn HQ (1 × Grant I)
            3 Troops, each: 3 × Grant I
        1 Recce Platoon: Pl HQ (1 × Daimler Scout Car)
            3 Sections, each: 3 × Daimler Scout Car

Armoured Regiment Variant 3
    Btn HQ (3 × Grant I)
        2 Squadrons, each: Sqdn HQ (1 × Grant I)
            3 Troops, each: 3 × Grant I
        1 Squadron: Sqdn HQ (2 × Crusader II, 2 × Crusader IICS)
            4 Troops, each: 3 × Crusader II
        1 Recce Platoon: Pl HQ (1 × Daimler Scout Car)
            3 Sections, each: 3 × Daimler Scout Car

Divisional 2nd Cavalry Regiment, June 1942
    RHQ (3 trucks, 4 × field cars, 2 rifle secs)
        3 Squadrons, each: Sqdn HQ (2 × Vickers VIB light tanks, 2 × Universal Carrier)
            2 Troops, each: 3 × Universal Carrier, 1 (12 man) rifle sec, 3 LMG, 1 × 2" mortar

Divisional 2nd Cavalry Regiment, July–August 1942
    RHQ (4 × Vickers VIB, 4 × Daimler Scout Car)
        3 Squadrons, each: Sqdn HQ (2 × Stuart I, 2 × Universal Carrier)
            2 Troops, each: 3 × Universal Carrier, 1 (12 man) rifle sec, 3 LMG, 1 × 2" mortar
            1 Troop: 3 × Stuart I

Divisional 2nd Cavalry Regiment, September 1942–May 1943
    RHQ (2 × Stuart I, 4 × Daimler Scout Car, 2 trucks)
        3 Squadrons, each: Sqdn HQ (2 × Stuart I, 2 × Universal Carrier)
            2 Troops, each: 3 × Stuart I
            3 Troops, each: 3 × Universal Carrier, 1 (12 man) rifle sec, 3 LMG, 1 × 2" mortar

Divisional 2nd Cavalry Regiment, August 1943 Onwards
    RHQ (4 × Humber Scout Cars)
        3 Squadrons, each: Sqdn HQ (4 × Staghound 1, 1 × Daimler Scout Car, 1 × LAD truck)
            3–5 Troops, each: 2 × Staghound 1, 1 × Staghound 2 (3" CS)
            1 Troop: 4 (8 man) rifle secs, 4 trucks, 3 LMG, 1 × 2" mortar, 1 PIAT
            0–1 Battery: 6 × 3" mortars, 7 × Universal Carrier, LP
            0–1 Platoon: 4 × 6pdr A/T guns, 5 × Universal Carrier, 2 LMG

22nd Motor Battalion
    Btn HQ (2 rifle secs, 2 trucks)
        3 Companies, each: Coy HQ (2 trucks, 1 rifle sec, 1 × 2" mortar)
            2 Platoons, each: 4 rifle secs, 3 LMG, 1 × 2", 4 trucks
            1 Platoon: Pl HQ (1 × Carrier, 1 × Daimler S/C, 1 LMG)
                4 Sections, each: 3 × Carrier, 3 LMG, 1 × 2", 1 rifle sec
            1 Platoon: 2 × 3" mortars, 2 × Carrier
            1 Platoon: 4 MMG, 5 × Carrier
        1 A/T Company: Coy HQ (1 rifle sec, 1 truck)
            4 Platoons, each: 4 × 2pdr or 6pdr, 4 trucks portées

Notes
1   Radios were in all tanks, Carrier Pl HQs, and other Coy HQs.
2   Infantry sections had No.74 or No.75 Hawkins A/T grenades.
3   Artillery OPs are in Stuart III, truck, Carrier or Daimler Scout Car.
4   75mm and 25pdr had AP, 6pdr had APC with one load of APCBC, 2pdr and 37mm had APCBC.

2.26 INDIAN INFANTRY DIVISION, 1940–41, NORTH AFRICA
The Division's main combat elements were:
    3 Infantry Brigades (each of 3–4 Infantry Battalions)
Troops are rated at average training and good to average morale.

SUPPORT UNITS
Divisional Support
Included:
    9 Field Artillery Batteries, each: Battery HQ (1 radio van, 4 trucks, 4 rifle secs, 2 AALMG)
        2 Troops, each: 4 × 25pdr, 4 trucks, radio van, 1 LMG
    3 Engineer Companies, each: Coy HQ (1 rifle sec, 1 truck)
        3 Platoons, each: 4 (12 man) rifle/engineer secs, 2 lorries
    1–3 A/T Companies, each: Coy HQ (1 rifle sec, 1 truck)
        3 Platoons, each: 4 × 2pdr, 4 trucks

Brigade Support
    Infantry Brigade HQ (6 rifle secs, 1 LMG, 6 trucks)

MAIN COMBAT ELEMENTS
Infantry Battalion
    Btn HQ (5 rifle secs, 1 LMG)
        4 Companies, each: Coy HQ (1 rifle sec)
            3 Platoons, each: 4 rifle secs, 3 LMG, 1 × 2", 1 Boys
        1 Support Company: Coy HQ (1 rifle sec)
            1 Platoon: 2 × 3" mortars
            1 Platoon: 2 rifle/engineer secs
            1 Platoon: 4 × Twin LMGAA in 2 rifle secs
            1 Platoon: Pl HQ (1 × Bren Carrier, 1 LMG)
                3 Sections, each: 3 × Bren Carriers, 3 LMG, 1 (6 man) rifle sec

Notes
1. Radios were in all armoured cars and other Coy HQs. Artillery is rated Assigned FC.
2. Infantry sections had no A/T grenades.
3. Infantry were usually motorised in 2 lorries per Platoon and 1 truck per Coy HQ.
4. This list primarily represents the 4th Indian Infantry Division in North Africa 1940.

2.27 INDIAN INFANTRY DIVISION, EARLY 1942–43, NORTH AFRICA
The Division's main combat elements were:
    3 Infantry Brigades (each of 3 Infantry Battalions. Of the 9 Battalions in the Division, two were Gurkha, one Scottish)
Independent Indian Infantry Brigades were similar, having three Infantry Battalions and one Artillery Regiment. The Infantry Battalions had only one A/T Platoon. Troops are rated at average training and good morale, except Gurkhas, rated at good training and excellent morale.

SUPPORT UNITS
Divisional Support
    9 Artillery Batteries, each: Battery HQ (4 lorries, 4 rifle secs, 2 AALMG, 2 OP Teams)
        2 Troops, each: 4 × 25pdr, 4 trucks, radio van, 1 LMG
    3 A/T Companies, each: Coy HQ (1 rifle sec, 1 truck)
        3 Platoons, each: 4 × 6pdr, 4 truck portées, 2 LMG
    3 AA Companies, each: Coy HQ (1 rifle sec, 1 truck)
        3 AA Platoons, each: 6 × 40mm Bofors, 6 trucks
    3 Indian Engineer Companies, each: Coy HQ (1 rifle sec, 1 truck)
        3 Platoons, each: 4 (12 man) rifle/engineer secs, 1 AALMG, 2 lorries
    Indian Machine Gun Battalion:
        3 MG Companies, each: Coy HQ (1 rifle sec, 1 truck)
            4 Platoons, each: 4 × MMG, 2 trucks
    1 Tank Battalion (deception unit with dummy tanks based on lorries)
    1 Bridging Section, Indian Engineers

Brigade Support
    Infantry Brigade HQ (10 rifle secs, 10 trucks/lorries, 3 LMG, 1 × 2" mortar)

MAIN COMBAT ELEMENTS
Infantry Battalion
    Btn HQ (5 rifle secs, 1 LMG)
        4 Companies, each: Coy HQ (1 rifle sec)
            3 Platoons, each: 4 rifle secs, 3 LMG, 1 × 2" mortar
        1 Support Company: Coy HQ (1 rifle sec)
            1 Platoon: 6 × 3" mortars, 7 × Carriers, 3 Boys
            2 Platoons, each: 4 × 2pdr A/T guns, 4 × Carrier
            1 Platoon: 2 rifle/engineer secs, 1 lorry
            1 Platoon: Pl HQ (1 × Carrier, 1 × Daimler S/C, 1 LMG)
                4 Sections, each: 3 × Carrier, 3 LMG, 1 × 2", 1 rifle sec, 1 Boys

Gurkha Battalion
    Btn HQ (5 rifle secs, 1 LMG, kukris)
        4 Companies, each: Coy HQ (1 rifle sec, kukris)
            3 Platoons, each: 4 rifle secs, 3 LMG, 1 × 2" mortar, kukris
        1 Support Company: Coy HQ (1 rifle sec)
            1 Platoon: 6 × 3" mortars, 7 × Carriers, 3 Boys
            1 Platoon: 4 × 2pdr A/T guns, 4 × Carrier
            1 Platoon: 2 rifle/engineer secs, 1 lorry

Notes
1. Radios were in all Carrier Pl HQ and other Coy HQs.
2. Infantry section had No.74 or No.75 Hawkins A/T grenades.
3. Artillery OPs were in trucks or Daimler Scout Car.
4. 25pdr had AP, 6pdr had AP, APC and one load of APCBC, 2pdr had APCBC.
5. For wargames purposes, could replace towed 2pdr with towed 6pdr guns in 1943.

2.28 BRITISH PARACHUTE BRIGADE, NOVEMBER 1942–MAY 1943, TUNISIA

The Brigade's main combat elements were:
    3 Parachute Battalions

In addition to the Brigade in Tunisia, 4th Parachute Brigade was training in Egypt, Palestine and Libya between December 1942 and September 1943. Paratroops are rated at good training and excellent morale.

SUPPORT UNITS

Brigade Support
    Airborne Brigade HQ (6 rifle/SMG secs) with:
        1 HQ Defence Platoon (4 rifle/SMG secs, 3 LMG, 1 × 2" mortar

MAIN COMBAT ELEMENTS

Parachute Battalion
    Btn HQ (2 rifle/SMG secs)
        3 Companies, each: Coy HQ (2 (8 man) rifle secs)
            3 Platoons, each: 1 (6 man) rifle/SMG Pl HQ sec, 3 rifle/SMG secs, 3 LMG, 1 × 2"
        1 Battery: 4 × 3" mortars (Assigned FC)
        1 MG Platoon: 4 × Vickers MMG, 1 Boys

Notes
1. Radios were at Coy HQ and above.
2. Infantry had Type 74 or Type 75 anti-tank grenades.

2.29 BRITISH CORPS SUPPORT, 1938–40, EGYPT

Units are rated at average training and average morale.

SUPPORT UNITS

Corps Support Units
    2 AA Troops, each: 4 × 3" 20cwt AA, 4 lorries
    1st Royal Marine AA Battery (Alexandria, August–December 1939):
        2 Sections, each: 4 × 3.7" AA
    4 Machine Gun Companies, each: Coy HQ (1 rifle sec, 2 trucks, 4 LMG)
        3 Platoons, each: 4 MMG, 2 trucks
    Cairo and Canal British Infantry Brigades, each:[17]
        2 Infantry Battalions
        1 British Field Artillery Regiment: 2 Batteries, each: 1 Troop w/18pdrs, 1 Troop w/ 4.5"L15
        1 British Field Engineer Company
    11th Indian Infantry Brigade:
        2nd Btn Queen's Own Cameron Highlanders
        1st Btn 6th Rajputana Rifles
        4th Btn 7th Rajput Regiment
        1 Artillery Regiment: 2 Batteries, each: 1 Troop w/ 4 × 18pdrs, 1 Troop w/4 × 4.5"L15
        1 Bombay Sapper Company
    7th Medium Artillery Regiment:
        1 Battery: 2 Troops, each: 4 × 60pdr guns
        1 Battery: 2 Troops, each: 4 × 6" 26cwt howitzers
    2nd RAF Armoured Car Company:[18] Coy HQ (4 × Rolls-Royce 1920 Pattern Mk I A/C)
        3 Flights, each: 4 × Rolls-Royce 1920 Pattern Mk I A/C (w/Vickers MMG and Lewis AAMG)
        1 Reserve Flight: 4 × spare Rolls-Royce 1920 Pattern Mk I A/C

---

17. Cairo (18th Brigade) – 1st Btn Royal Northumberland Fusiliers, 1st Btn Bedfordshire and Hertfordshire Regiment. Canal Brigade – 1st Btn Royal Sussex Regiment, 1st Btn Essex Regiment.
18. Available from January 1940.

Aviation Support At Corps Level
    6 Bomber Flights, each: 4 × Bombay bomber-transports
    18 Bomber Flights, each: 4 × Blenheim I
    15 Fighter Flights, each: 4 × Gladiator I
    6 Recce Flights, each: 4 × Lysander I
    2 Maritime Recce Flights, each: 5 × Short Sunderland I

Notes
1   Radios were in all Coy HQs. Artillery is rated as Assigned FC.

2.30 BRITISH CORPS AND ARMY SUPPORT, OCTOBER 1940–APRIL 1941, NORTH AFRICA

Units are rated at average training and good morale.

SUPPORT UNITS

Corps Support Units
    1 Medium Artillery Regiment: RHQ (6 rifle secs, 4 lorries, 2 AALMG)
        3 Batteries, each: 4 × 6" 26cwt or 60pdr, 4 lorries, radio van
        1 Battery: 4 × 6" Mk19 guns, 4 lorries, radio van
    1 Medium Artillery Regiment: RHQ (6 rifle secs, 4 lorries, 2 AALMG)
        4 Batteries, each: 4 × 4.5" Mk1 BL, 4 lorries, radio van
    9 Artillery Batteries, each: Battery HQ (4 rifle secs, 4 lorries, 1 AALMG)
        2 Troops, each: 4 × 25pdr Mk1, 5 trucks, radio truck, 1 AALMG
    4 Indian MG Companies, each: Coy HQ (1 rifle sec, 1 truck)
        3 Platoons, each: 4 MMG, 2 trucks

Army Support Units
    4 AA Batteries, each: 4 × 3.7" guns, 4 lorries, radio van
    9 AA Batteries, each: 6 × 40mm Bofors, 6 trucks
    5 Naval Batteries, each: 1 × 6" or 2 × 4.5" guns (Pre-planned fire only, coastal areas only)
    11 Naval Batteries, each: 2 × 15" guns (Pre-planned fire only, coastal areas only)
    15th Coastal Artillery Regiment (Suez):
        2 Squadrons, each: 2 Batteries, each: 4 × 6" naval guns, 120 crew, 4 AAMG
    Royal Marine AA Brigade, MNBDO 1 (Egypt, March 1941 only):
        1st, 2nd Royal Marine AA Regiments, each: RHQ:
            2 Batteries, each: Coy HQ (1 rifle sec)
                2 Troops, each: 4 × 3" 20cwt AA, 4 trucks, 1 Vickers MMG
            1 Light AA Battery: Coy HQ (2 (8 man) rifle squads)
                4 Troops, each: 4 × 40mmL60 Bofors, 52 crew
    2nd RAF Armoured Car Company: Coy HQ (4 × Fordson A/C)
        3 Flights: 4 × Fordson A/C (w/Vickers MMG, Lewis AAMG)
        1 Reserve Flight: 4 × spare Fordson A/C

Notes
1   Radios were in all AFVs and other Coy HQs. Artillery is rated as Assigned FC.

2.31 BRITISH CORPS AND ARMY SUPPORT UNITS, APRIL 1941–FEBRUARY 1942, NORTH AFRICA

Units are rated at average training and good morale, unless noted otherwise.

SUPPORT UNITS

Corps Support Units
    4 Artillery Regiments, each: RHQ (6 rifle secs, 4 lorries, 2 AALMG)
        4 Batteries, each: 4 × 6" 26cwt or 60pdr, 4 lorries, radio van
    1 MG Battalion:
        4 MG Companies, each: Coy HQ (1 rifle sec, 1 truck, 4 LMG)
            3 Platoons, each: 4 MMG, 2 trucks

Army Support Units
    4 AA Troops, each: 4 × 3.7" guns, 4 lorries, radio van
    9 AA Troops, each: 6 × 40mm Bofors, 6 trucks
    1 Artillery Troop: 4 × 6" Mk.19 guns or 155mm M1918, 4 lorries, radio van
    15th Coastal Artillery Regiment (Suez):
        2 Squadrons, each: 2 Batteries, each: 4 × 6" naval guns, 120 crew, 4 AAMG
    1st RM AA Regiment (June–December 1941, Egypt):
        A, C Batteries, each: 2 Troops, each: 4 × 3.7" AA, 8 × twin Lewis AAMG w/shield
        R Searchlight Battery: 24 searchlights
        22nd Light AA Battery: 2 Troops, each: 4 × 40mmL60 Bofors
    2nd RM AA Regiment (June–December 1941, Egypt):
        C, D Batteries, each: 1 Troop: 2–4 × 3" or 3.7" AA
        23rd Light AA Battery: 2 Troops, each: 2–3 × 40mmL60 Bofors

Tobruk Garrison, November 1941

70th (British) Infantry Division:
- 14th, 16th, 23rd Infantry Brigades, each: 3 Infantry Battalions
- 1 MG Btn: 4 Companies, each: 3 Platoons, each: 4 MMG
- 1 RHA Artillery Regiment: 2 Batteries, each: 2 Troops, each: 4 × 25pdr field guns
- 2 RHA Artillery Regiments, each: 2 Batteries, each: 3 Troops, each: 4 × 25pdr
- 1 Field Artillery Regiment: 2 Batteries, each:
    - 3 Troops, each: 4 × 25pdr
    - 1 Troop: 4 × 60pdr guns
- 3 A/T Batteries, each: 4 Troops, each: 4 × 2pdr
- 3 Engineer Companies, 1 Field Park Company

32nd Army Tank Brigade (see list 2.15)

King's Dragoon Guards Recce Regiment: 29 × Marmon-Herrington II in 1 Squadron

Polish Carpathian Brigade:
- 3 Infantry Battalions
- 1 Recce Battalion (no vehicles)
- 1 Artillery Regiment
- 1 MG Company
- 1 A/T Battery

11th Czech Infantry Battalion: 4 companies (poor training, average morale)

3 Heavy AA Batteries, each: 2 Troops, each: 4 × 3.7" AA

7 Light AA Batteries, each: 3 Troops, each: 4 × 40mm Bofors

2 Coastal batteries, each: 2 × 4" naval guns

1 Coastal battery: 2 × 6" guns

Notes

1 Radios were in all AFVs and other Pl HQs. Artillery is rated as Assigned FC.

2.32 BRITISH CORPS AND ARMY SUPPORT, FEBRUARY–JULY 1942, NORTH AFRICA

Troops are rated at average training and good morale.

SUPPORT UNITS

Corps Support Units

2 Artillery Regiments, each: RHQ (8 rifle secs, 6 lorries) (Assigned FC)
- 4 Batteries, each: 4 × 4.5" or 5.5" or 155mm M1918, 4 lorries, radio van, 2 AALMG

1 Machine Gun Battalion:
- 4 MG Companies, each: Coy HQ (1 rifle sec, 1 truck)
- 3 Platoons, each: 4 MMG, 2 trucks

Army Support Units

2 Heavy AA Regiments, each: RHQ (6 rifle secs, 8 lorries)
- 2 Batteries, each: Battery HQ (2 rifle secs, 2 lorries)
    - 2 Troops, each: 4 × 3.7" AA, 4 lorries, 1 radio van

9 AA Batteries, each: Battery HQ (2 rifle secs, 2 lorries)
- 3 Platoons, each: 6 × 40mm Bofors, 6 trucks

3 RAF Regiment Squadrons, each:[19]
- 2 Flights, each: Sqdn HQ (2 rifle secs, 2 lorries)
- 1 Flight: 4 × Humber Mk III Light Recce Cars
- 1 AA Flight: 6 Lewis AAMG OR 4 × 40mm Bofors, 6 trucks

2 A/T Regiments, each: (average morale and training)
- 3 Batteries, each: Battery HQ (1 rifle sec, 1 truck)
    - 3 Troops, each: 4 × 2pdr, 4 truck portées, 2 LMG

Notes

1 Radios were in all tanks and armoured cars, and other Pl HQs.
2 Infantry sections had Hawkins 75 A/T grenades.
3 2pdr and 37mm had APC, 25pdr had AP.

2.33 BRITISH CORPS AND ARMY SUPPORT, AUGUST 1942–MAY 1943, NORTH AFRICA

Troops are rated at average training and good morale.

SUPPORT UNITS

Corps Support Units

3 Medium Artillery Regiments, each: RHQ (8 rifle secs, 8 lorries, 4 AALMG)
- 4 Batteries, each: 4 × 5.5" or 4.5", 4 lorries, radio van, 2 AALMG

1 Heavy Artillery Regiment:[20] RHQ (8 rifle secs, 10 lorries, 4 AALMG)
- 3 Batteries, each: 6 × 7.2" Mk.5, 6 lorries, radio van

---

19 185 men per Squadron.
20 Tunisia only.

1 Chemical Smoke Company: Coy HQ (2 rifle secs, 4 lorries, 2 AALMG)
    3 Batteries, each: 4 × 4.2" mortars, 4 trucks, radio truck
3 Artillery Batteries, each:
    Battery HQ (2 rifle secs, 2 trucks, radio van, 3 OP Teams, 4 AALMG)
        2 Troops, each: 4 × Bishop, 1 radio truck, 2 AALMG
1 AA Battery: Battery HQ (2 rifle secs, 2 lorries)
    3 Platoons, each: 6 × 40mm Bofors, 6 trucks

Army Support Units

12 AA Batteries, each: Battery HQ (2 rifle secs, 2 lorries)
    3 Troops, each: 6 × 40mm Bofors, 6 trucks
2 Heavy AA Regiments, each: RHQ (6 rifle secs, 8 lorries)
    2 Batteries, each: Battery HQ (2 rifle secs, 2 lorries)
        2 Troops, each: 4 × 3.7" AA, 4 lorries, 1 radio van
2 Heavy AA Troops, each: 4 × 3.7" AA, 4 lorries, radio van
2 African Engineer Companies, each: Coy HQ (2 rifle secs)
    3 Platoons, each: 5 rifle/pioneer secs
1 Chemical Smoke Company:[21] Coy HQ (2 rifle secs, 4 lorries, 2 AALMG)
    3 Batteries, each: 4 × 4.2" mortars, 4 trucks, radio truck
3 Dummy Tank Regiments, each: approx 50 dummy Crusader tanks on truck bodies
RAF Servicing Commando:
    6 Parties, each: 2 Sections, each: 10–16 aircraft engineers, trucks, jeeps

Aviation Support At Army Level

6 Bomber Flights, each: 3 × Boston III
12 Bomber Flights, each: 3 × Baltimore III
12 US Bomber Flights, each: 3 × B–25C Mitchell
3 A/T Flights, each: 4 × Hurricane IID
36 Fighter-Bomber Flights, each: 4 × Hurricane IIC
18 Fighter-Bomber Flights, each: 4 × Kittyhawk IA, II, III
3 Fighter-Bomber Flights, each: 4 × Tomahawk
9 Fighter Flights, each: 4 × Spitfire Vc
3 Fighter Flights, each: 4 × Spitfire IX (March 1943 onwards)
12 US Fighter Flights, each: 4 × P–40F Warhawk

Notes
1   Radios were in all AFVs and other Pl HQs.
2   2pdr and 37mm had APCBC. 6pdr had AP with one load of APCBC. 75mm and 25pdr had AP.
3   Artillery OPs could be in Stuart III, truck, Carrier, Daimler S/C or turretless Marmon-Herringtons.
4   RAF Servicing Commandos were teams equipped to operate fighter-bombers from forward airstrips, in existence from November 1942. Five operated in North Africa and Tunisia.

---

21   Tunisia only.

PART 3
MIDDLE EAST, CENTRAL AND WEST AFRICAN THEATRES 1938–43

3.1 INDIAN 1ST/31ST ARMOURED DIVISION, APRIL–DECEMBER 1941, IRAQ/PERSIA

In June 1941, the Division's main combat elements were:
    1st Armoured Brigade (5th Probyn's Lancers, 9th Royal Deccan Horse Armoured Regiments, 2/4th Bombay Grenadiers Motor Battalion)
    2nd Armoured Brigade (4th Hodson's Lancers, 3rd (British) Carabiniers, 26th (British) Hussars Armoured Regiments, 1/4th Bombay Grenadiers Motor Battalion)
    19th Lancers Divisional Armoured Car Regiment

In April 1941, the Division moved from India into Iraq and Persia, deploying into existing garrison areas already used by agreement. It was renamed 31st Indian Armoured Division in June 1941. Troops are rated at average training and average morale.

SUPPORT UNITS

Brigade Support[1]

Armoured Brigade HQ (3 × Vickers VIB, 3 lorries, 3 rifle secs) with:
    1 Engineer Squadron: Sqdn HQ (2 rifle secs, 2 × Carrier IP Mk.1, 2 LMG, 2 lorries
    2 Troops, each: 4 (12 man) rifle/engineer secs, 5 lorries

MAIN COMBAT ELEMENTS

British Armoured Regiment

RHQ (4 × Vickers VIB light tanks, 1 truck)
    3 Squadrons, each: Sqdn HQ (2 × Vickers VIB, 2 × Universal Carriers, 2 LMG)
    2 Troops, each: 3 × Vickers VIB
    2 Troops, each: 3 × trucks w/LMG or 3 × Universal Carriers, 2 LMG, 1 Boys

Indian Cavalry Armoured Regiment

RHQ (2 × Vickers VIB light tanks, 1 truck OR (April 1941 onwards) 3 × Stuart I
    2 Squadrons, each: Sqdn HQ (3 × A/C, Chevrolet Indian Pattern)
    5 Troops, each: 3 × A/C, Chevrolet, Indian Pattern
    1 Squadron: Sqdn HQ (3 × Vickers VIB, 2 × Wheeled Carrier IP Mk.1)
    3 Troops, each: 3 × Vickers VIB

1/4th Bombay Grenadiers Motor Battalion

Btn HQ (2 rifle secs, 2 trucks, 2 LMG)
    3 Companies, each: Coy HQ (1 rifle sec, 1 truck)
    3 Platoons, each: 4 (8 man) rifle secs, 4 LMG, 1 Boys, 4 trucks
    1 Platoon: Pl HQ (2 × Bren Carrier, 1 LMG, 1 Boys)
        3 Sections, each: 3 × Bren Carrier, 2 LMG, 1 Boys

2/4th Bombay Grenadiers Motor Battalion

Btn HQ (2 rifle secs, 2 trucks, 1 Boys)
    4 Companies, each: Coy HQ (2 rifle secs, 2 trucks, 1 LMG, 1 × 2" mortar, 1 Boys)
    3 Platoons, each: 4 (12 man) rifle secs, 3 LMG, 4 trucks
    1 Battery: 4 × 3" mortars, 4 trucks, Assigned FC
    1 HQ Defence Platoon: 4 rifle secs, 3 LMG, 1 Boys, 4 trucks

19th Lancers Divisional Armoured Car Regiment

RHQ (4 × A/C)
    3 Squadrons, each: Sqdn HQ (1 × A/C)
        3 Troops, each: 5 × A/C

Notes
1   Radios were in all tanks and other Coy HQs.
2   Infantry sections had no anti-tank grenades.
3   Tanks and Armoured Cars were in short supply, so for wargames purposes, can replace any with trucks w/LMGs or possibly Wheeled Carrier, Indian Pattern, Mk.1.

---

1   There were no divisional-level support units.

3.2 INDIAN 2ND ARMOURED BRIGADE, AUGUST 1941, PERSIA

The Brigade's main combat elements were:
14th/20th (British) Hussars Armoured Regiment
2 Motorised Gurkha Battalions (2/7th and 1/5th Gurkha Rifles)
The Brigade saw brief action against Persian forces. Troops are rated at average training and good morale.

SUPPORT UNITS

Brigade Support

Brigade HQ (3 rifle secs, radio van, 2 lorries, 3 × Vickers VIB) with:
    1 Medium Artillery Battery: 4 × 6" 26cwt howitzers, 4 lorries, radio van
    3 Artillery Batteries, each: BHQ (4 rifle secs, 2 AALMG, 5 trucks, Assigned FC)
        2 Troops, each: 4 × 25pdr, 4 trucks, radio truck
    1 British Yeomanry Squadron: Sqdn HQ (1 rifle sec, 1 truck)
        3 Platoons, each: 4 (6 man) rifle secs, 1 Boys, 1 × 2" mortar, 3 LMG, 4 trucks

MAIN COMBAT ELEMENTS

14th/20th Hussars Armoured Regiment

RHQ (4 × Vickers VIB, 1 radio van)
    3 Squadrons, each: Sqdn HQ (2 × Vickers VIB, 2 × Universal Carriers, 2 LMG)
        2 Troops, each: 3 × Vickers VIB
        2 Troops, each: 3 × Universal Carrier, 2 LMG, 1 Boys

Motorised Gurkha Battalion

Btn HQ (3 rifle secs, 1 LMG, Kukris, 2 lorries)
    4 Companies, each: Coy HQ (2 rifle secs, Kukris, 1 lorry)
        3 Platoons, each: 4 rifle secs, 3 LMG, 1 × 2" mortar, 1 Boys, Kukris, 2 lorries
    1 Support Company: Coy HQ (1 rifle sec, 1 truck)
        1 Battery: 4 × 3" mortars, 2 lorries, Assigned FC
        1 Platoon: 4 MMG, 2 lorries

Notes
1   Radios were in all tanks and Carrier Pl HQs, and other Coy HQs.
2   Infantry had no anti-tank grenades.

3.3 SOUTH AFRICAN 7TH ARMOURED BRIGADE, SEPTEMBER–NOVEMBER 1942, MADAGASCAR

The Brigade's main combat elements were:
    3 Infantry Battalions (First City/Capetown Highlanders, Pretoria Regiment, 9th Cape Corps Motor Battalion,
        1 Battalion each)
The Brigade took part in the occupation of central and southern Madagascar. Troops are rated at average training and good morale. This list includes support units available at divisional-level.

SUPPORT UNITS

Divisional-Level Support Units

Included:
    31st South African Armoured Car Commando:
        Coy HQ: 3 × Marmon-Herrington Mk.III, 1 × Daimler S/C
        4 Platoons, each: 3 × Marmon-Herrington Mk.III
    British 9th Field Artillery Regiment:
        3 Artillery Batteries, each: Battery HQ (4 rifle secs, 2 Boys, 4 AALMG, 6 trucks)
            2 Troops, each: 4 × 25pdr Mk2, 2 LMG, 5 trucks, radio truck
    3 Engineer Companies,[2] each:
        Coy HQ: 1 rifle sec, 1 truck
        3 Platoons, each: 4(12 man) rifle/engineer secs, 2 lorries
    6 Naval Batteries, each: 3 × 6" guns from light cruisers
    6 Naval Batteries, each: 2 × 4" guns from various warships
    9 Naval Batteries, each: 2 × 4.7" guns from destroyers
    3 Naval Batteries, each: 2 × 5.9" guns from Dutch cruiser
    4 Naval Batteries, each: 2 × 15" guns from HMS Warspite
    3 Fleet Air Arm Flights, each: 3 × Swordfish I
    6 Fleet Air Arm Flights, each: 3 × F-4F4 Martlet IV fighters
    3 South African Air Force Flights, each: 4 × Kittyhawk IA fighter-bombers

Brigade Support

Infantry Brigade HQ (6 rifle secs, 4 lorries) with up to:
    1 Defence Platoon: 4 rifle secs, 3 LMG, 1 × 2" mortar

---

2   1 British, 1 East African, 1 South African.

MAIN COMBAT ELEMENTS

Infantry Battalion
Btn HQ (5 rifle secs, 1 LMG)
    3 Companies, each: Coy HQ (1 rifle sec)
        3 Platoons, each: 4 rifle secs, 3 LMG, 1 × 2" mortar
    1 Support Company: Coy HQ (1 rifle sec)
        1 Battery: 4–6 × 3" mortars, trucks or Carriers
        1 Platoon: 4 × AALMG in 2 rifle crew secs
        1 Platoon: 2 rifle/engineer secs
        0–1 Platoon: Pl HQ (1 × Universal Carrier, 1 LMG)
            4 Sections, each: 3 × Carrier, 1 rifle sec, 1 × 2" mortar, 3 LMG

Notes
1   Radios were in all A/C, Carrier Pl HQs, and other Coy HQs.
2   Infantry had no anti-tank grenades.
3   Naval fire support in coastal areas only. Guns of the same calibre could be grouped into larger batteries. Fire was pre-planned only.

3.4 AFRICAN INFANTRY DIVISION, JULY–NOVEMBER 1940, EAST AFRICA

There were two divisions, whose main combat elements were:
    1st African Division
        1st (East Africa) Infantry Brigade – 2/6th, 1/4th and 1/2nd King's African Rifles Battalions
        3rd (Nigeria) Infantry Brigade – 1st, 2nd and 3rd Battalions, Nigeria Regiment
    2nd African Division
        4th (Gold Coast) Infantry Brigade – 1st, 2nd and 3rd Battalions, Gold Coast Regiment
        2nd (East Africa) Infantry Brigade – 1st, 5th and 6th King's African Rifles Battalions

Troops are rated at poor training and good morale. Deployed in East Africa, the divisions were redesignated in November 1940.

SUPPORT UNITS

Divisional Support
Included:
    1 Light Battery (4 × 3.7" Mountain Guns, 4 trucks, radio truck)
    2 Engineer Companies, each: Coy HQ (1 rifle sec, 1 truck)
        3 Platoons, each: 4 rifle/engineer secs, 2 lorries

Brigade Support
Infantry Brigade HQ (4 rifle secs, 3 lorries)

MAIN COMBAT ELEMENTS

Infantry Battalion (Nigerian, Gold Coast Or King's African Rifles)
Btn HQ (2 rifle secs, 1 lorry)
    4 Companies, each: Coy HQ (1 (13 man) rifle sec)
        3 Platoons, each: 4 rifle secs, 3 LMG, 1 × 2" mortar
    1 Support Company: Coy HQ (1 rifle sec, 1 truck)
        1 Platoon: 4 × 3" mortars, pack horses
        1 Platoon: 4 × Twin AALMG or 2 × Lewis AAMG
        1 Platoon: 2 rifle/engineer secs, 1 truck

Notes
1   Radios were in all Btn HQ and above. All artillery is rated Assigned FC.
2   Infantry sections had no A/T grenades.
3   All troops were black Africans with white officers.

3.5 AFRICAN INFANTRY DIVISION, NOVEMBER 1940–NOVEMBER 1941, EAST AFRICA

In late 1940 there were two divisions, whose main combat elements were:
    11th African Division
        21st (East Africa) Infantry Brigade – 1/4th and 1/2nd King's African Rifles Battalions, 1st Northern Rhodesia Regiment
        23rd (Nigerian) Infantry Brigade – 1st, 2nd and 3rd Battalions, Nigeria Regiment
    12th African Division
        24th (Gold Coast) Infantry Brigade – 1st, 2nd and 3rd Battalions, Gold Coast Regiment
        1st South African Infantry Brigade – 1st Btn Natal Carabineers, Duke of Edinburgh's Own Rifles, 1st Btn Transvaal Scottish Regiment

The divisions fought in south and central Abyssinia and were pitted against Italian Colonial Infantry and Savoia Grenadier Divisions. No Corps support was available. Troops are rated at average training and good morale, some at excellent morale.

SUPPORT UNITS

Divisional Support
Included:
    1 Armoured Car Squadron: Sqdn HQ (1–3 × Rolls-Royce or Marmon-Herrington I)
        1–5 Troops, each: 3 × A/C as in Sqdn HQ
    1–3 Artillery Batteries, each: 4 × 25pdr Mk.1, 4 trucks, radio truck, 1 LMG
    1 South African or 3 British A/T Troops, each: 4 × 37mm Bofors, 4 trucks, 1 LMG
    0–1 AA Troop: 4 × 40mm Bofors, 4 trucks

Brigade Support
Infantry Brigade HQ (4 rifle secs, 3 lorries) with:
    1 South African Recce Squadron: Sqdn HQ (3 × Marmon-Herrington I)
        3–5 Troops, each: 3 × Marmon-Herrington I
    1 South African Artillery Brigade: Brigade HQ (4 trucks, radio van, 4 rifle secs, 2 AALMG)
        2 Batteries, each: 4 × 18pdr Mk.IV, 4 trucks, radio truck, 1 LMG
    1 Battery: 4 × 3.7" Mountain Guns or 4.5" QF howitzers, 4 trucks, radio truck
    OR 1 African Light Battery: 4 × 3.7" Mountain Guns, 4 trucks, radio truck
    1 Engineer Company: Coy HQ (1 rifle sec, 1 truck)
        3 Platoons, each: 4 rifle/engineer secs, 2 lorries

MAIN COMBAT ELEMENTS

Infantry Battalion
Btn HQ (2 rifle secs, 1 lorry)
    4 Companies, each: Coy HQ (1 (13 man) rifle sec, 1 lorry)
        3 Platoons, each: 4 rifle secs, 3 LMG, 1 × 2", 1 Boys, 2 lorries
    Support Company: Coy HQ (1 rifle sec, 1 truck)
        1 Platoon: 4 × 3" mortars, 2 trucks, radio truck
        1 Platoon: 4 × Twin AALMG, 4 Boys, 4 trucks
        1 Platoon: 2 rifle/engineer secs, 1 lorry

Notes
1. Radios were in all Coy HQs and AFVs. All artillery is rated as Assigned FC.
2. Infantry sections had no A/T grenades.
3. All troops were black Africans with white officers except for the South African units.
4. For wargames purposes, only the South African Brigade can use the South African brigade-level support units.

3.6 INDIAN INFANTRY DIVISION, OCTOBER 1940–NOVEMBER 1941, EAST AFRICA

The Division's main combat elements were:
    2–3 Infantry Brigades (each of 3–4 Infantry Battalions)
    1 Divisional Cavalry Regiment

This list also includes Indian corps-level support units. The divisions fought in north and central Abyssinia. Troops are rated at average training and good morale.

SUPPORT UNITS

Corps-Level Support Units
Included:
    1 A/T Troop: 4 × 2pdr, 4 trucks, 2 LMG
    B Squadron, 4th RTR: Sqdn HQ (3 × Vickers VIB OR 3 × Matilda II)
        1 Troop: 3 × Vickers VIB OR 3 × Matilda II
        2 Troops, each: 3 × A–13 Mk.1 OR 3 × Matilda II
    2 Medium Batteries, each: 4 × 60pdr, 4 lorries, 2 LMGAA, 1 radio van
    2 Batteries, each: 4 × 3.7" Mountain Guns, 4 trucks, radio truck
    1 AA Battery: 6 × 40mm Bofors, 6 trucks
    Gazelle Force
        HQ (2 rifle secs, 2 trucks)
            2 Sudanese MG Companies, each: Coy HQ (1 × A/C w/Boys, LMG)
                2 Platoons, each: 3 × A/C
                2 Platoons, each: 4 trucks w/AALMG
                2 Platoons, each: 3 rifle secs, 2 trucks
        1 Battery: 4 × 18pdr or 25pdr, 4 trucks, radio truck, 2 LMG
        1 Battery: 2 × 40mm Bofors AA, 2 trucks
    Commando Battalion (good training, good morale)
        Btn HQ (2 rifle secs, 1 LMG, radio)
            2 Companies, each: 5 Troops, each: 5 rifle/SMG secs, 5 LMG, 1 Boys, radio

Divisional Support
Included:
    3 Field Artillery Batteries, each: Battery HQ (1 radio van, 4 trucks, 4 rifle secs, 2 AALMG)
        2 Troops, each: 4 × 25pdr, 4 × trucks, radio van, 1 LMG

6 Field Artillery Batteries, each: Battery HQ (1 radio van, 4 trucks, 4 rifle secs, 2 AALMG)
2–3 Troops, each: 4 × 18pdr Mk.IV, 4 trucks, radio van, 1 LMG
3 Engineer Companies, each: Coy HQ (1 rifle sec)
3 Platoons, each: 4 (12 man) rifle/engineer secs, 3 LMG

Brigade Support
Infantry Brigade HQ (4 rifle secs, 2 staff cars, 2 lorries)

MAIN COMBAT ELEMENTS
Infantry Battalion
Btn HQ (3 rifle secs, 1 LMG)
4 Companies, each: Coy HQ (1 rifle sec, 1–3 Boys)
3 Platoons, each: 4 rifle secs, 3 LMG, 1 × 2"
1 Support Company: Coy HQ (1 rifle sec)
1 Platoon: 2 × 3" mortars
1 Platoon: 2 rifle/engineer secs
1 Platoon: 2 × Twin LMGAA
1 Platoon: Pl HQ (1 × Carrier, 1 LMG)
1–4 Sections, each: 3 × Carrier, 3 LMG, 1 Boys, 1 × 2", 1 rifle sec

Divisional Cavalry Regiment (Skinner's Horse Or Central Indian Horse)
RHQ (2 rifle secs, 2 trucks)
3 Companies, each: Coy HQ (1 rifle sec, 1 truck)
3 Troops, each: 4 rifle secs, 4 Boys, 3 LMG, 1 × 2", 4 trucks
1 Company:[3] Coy HQ: 1 rifle sec, 1 truck
1 Battery: 6 × 3" mortars, 3 trucks
3 Platoons, each: Pl HQ (1 Carrier, 1 LMG)
4 Sections, each: 3 × Carriers, 1 rifle sec, 3 LMG, 1 Boys, 1 × 2"

Notes
1   Radios were in all AFVs and Carrier Pl HQs, and other Coy HQs. Artillery is rated as Assigned FC.
2   Infantry sections had no A/T grenades.
3   The tank squadron used Vickers and A-13s until receiving Matilda IIs in January 1941.

3.7 INDIAN INFANTRY DIVISION, 1940–41, IRAQ/PERSIA
The Division's main combat elements were:
3 Infantry Brigades (each of 3–4 Infantry Battalions)
This list should be used for the 8th and 10th Indian Divisions, in Iraq and Iran from April 1941. Troops are rated average training and good morale.

SUPPORT UNITS
Divisional Support
Included:
3 Field Artillery Regiments, each:
3 Batteries, each: Battery HQ (1 radio van, 4 trucks, 4 rifle secs, 2 AALMG)
2 Troops, each: 4 × 25pdr, 4 × trucks, radio van, 1 LMG
3 Engineer Companies, each: Coy HQ (1 rifle sec, 1 truck)
3 Platoons, each: 4 (12 man) rifle/engineer secs, 2 lorries
1–3 A/T Batteries, each: Battery HQ (1 rifle sec, 1 truck)
3 Troops, each: 4 × 2pdr, 4 trucks
2 Lancer Squadrons, each: Sqdn HQ (2 × M1923 Indian Pattern Chevrolet A/C) (Persia only)
2 Troops, each: 3 × A/C as in Sqdn HQ
1 Cavalry Squadron: Sqdn HQ (1 rifle sec, 1 truck) (Persia only)
3 Platoons, each: 4 rifle secs, 1 Boys, 1 × 2", 3 LMG, 4 trucks

Brigade Support
Infantry Brigade HQ (6 rifle secs, 1 LMG, 6 trucks)

MAIN COMBAT ELEMENTS
Infantry Battalion
Btn HQ (5 rifle secs, 1 LMG)
4 Companies, each: Coy HQ (1 rifle sec)
3 Platoons, each: 4 rifle secs, 3 LMG, 1 × 2", 1 Boys
1 Support Company: Coy HQ (1 rifle sec)
1 Platoon: 2 × 3" mortars
1 Platoon: 2 rifle/engineer secs
1 Platoon: 4 × Twin LMGAA in 2 rifle secs

3   February 1941 onwards.

Notes
1 Radios were in all armoured cars and other Coy HQs. Artillery is rated Assigned FC.
2 Infantry sections had no A/T grenades.
3 Infantry were usually motorised in 2 lorries per platoon and 1 truck per Coy HQ.

3.8 SOUTH AFRICAN 1ST INFANTRY DIVISION, OCTOBER 1940–FEBRUARY 1941, EAST AFRICA

The Division's main combat elements were:
    2 South African Infantry Brigades (5th – 3rd Transvaal Scottish, 1st South African Irish, 2nd Regiment Botha,
        1 Battalion each; 2nd – 1st Natal Mounted Rifles, 1st and 2nd Field Force Battalions, 1 Battalion each)
    1 East African Infantry Brigade (21st (East Africa) Infantry Brigade – 1/4th and 1/2nd King's African Rifles
        Battalions, 1st Northern Rhodesia Regiment)

The Division fought in southern Abyssinia against Italian Colonial Divisions. Troops are rated as average training and good morale, except for the Somali Irregulars, who are rated as poor training with good morale. This list includes corps-level support units.

SUPPORT UNITS

Corps-Level Support Units
Included:
    2 Ethiopian Native Companies, each:
        150 men with obsolete rifles, 3 LMG
    1 South African Armoured Squadron:
        Sqdn HQ (1–3 × Vickers VIB, plus 1 × M11/39 in June 1941)
            3–4 Troops, each: 3 × Vickers Light VIB or IIB or III
    13 Abyssinian Patriot Companies,[4] each:
        150 men with obsolete rifles, 3 LMG, leader on horse
    1 British Medium Artillery Battery: 4 × 6" 26cwt, 4 lorries, 1 radio van, 1 LMG
    1 British Medium Artillery Battery: 4 × 60pdrs, 4 lorries, radio van, 1 LMG
    1 British AA Battery:[5] Battery HQ: 1 rifle sec, 1 truck
        2 Troops, each: 4 × 3" 20cwt AA, 4 trucks
    4 British MG Companies, each: Coy HQ (1 rifle sec, 1 truck)
        3 Platoons, each: 4 MMG, 2 trucks, 1 Boys
    1 East African Recce Squadron:
        Sqdn HQ: 3 × Rolls-Royce or Marmon-Herrington I or Light A/C
            3–5 Troops, each: 3 × A/C as in Sqdn HQ
    2 Somali Irregular Companies, each:
        250 men, rifles, swords, spears, camels

Divisional Support
Included:
    1 AA Troop: 3 × 20mm Breda AA, 6 × Lewis AAMG, 6 trucks
    1 A/T Troop: 4 × 37mm Bofors A/T guns, 1 LMG, 4 trucks
    1 Engineer Company: Coy HQ (1 rifle sec, 1 truck)
        3 Platoons, each: 4 rifle/engineer secs, 2 lorries
    2 Abyssinian Patriot Companies,[6] each:
        150 men with obsolete rifles, 3 LMG, leader on horse
    2 Motorcycle Recce Companies, each: Coy HQ (2 rifle secs, 3 trucks)
        3 Platoons, each: 11 M/C Combos, 3 trucks, 3 M/C, 3 rifle secs, 3 LMG
    1 Artillery Brigade:[7] Brigade HQ (4 trucks, radio van, 4 rifle secs, 2 AALMG)
        2 Batteries, each: 4 × 18pdr Mk.IV, 4 trucks, radio truck, 1 LMG
        1 Battery: 4 × 4.5"L13 QF Mk2 howitzers, 4 trucks, radio truck, 1 LMG

Brigade Support
Infantry Brigade HQ (4 rifle secs, 3 lorries) with up to:
    1 Engineer Company: Coy HQ (1 rifle sec, 1 truck)
        3 Platoons, each: 4 rifle/engineer secs, 2 lorries
    1 Armoured Car Squadron:[8] Sqdn HQ (4 × Marmon-Herrington I or South African Armoured Recce Car Mk.1)
        6 Troops, each: 3 × A/C as in Sqdn HQ
Following units were only in East African Infantry Brigade:
    1 Light Battery: 6 × 3.7" Mountain Guns, 6 lorries, 1 radio truck
    1 Somali Camel Corps Troop: 4 × Light A/C w/turret MG

4 May 1941 onwards. Rated at poor training and good morale.
5 1941 onwards.
6 Rated at poor training and good morale.
7 1941 onwards.
8 Only in South African infantry brigades.

MAIN COMBAT ELEMENTS

Infantry Battalion
Btn HQ (2 rifle secs, 1 staff car, 2 trucks)
  3 Companies, each: Coy HQ: 1(13 man) rifle sec, 1 lorry
    3 Platoons, each: 4 rifle secs, 3 LMG, 1 × 2", 1 Boys, 2 lorries
  1 Support Company: Coy HQ: 1 rifle sec, 1 truck
    1 Platoon: 4 × 3" mortars, 2 trucks, radio truck
    1 Platoon: 4 × Twin AALMG, 4 Boys, 4 trucks
    1 Platoon: 2 rifle/engineer secs, 1 lorry
    1 Platoon: Pl HQ (1 × Carrier, 1 × Daimler S/C, 1 LMG)
      1–3 Sections, each: 3 × Carriers, 3 LMG, 1 Boys, 1 rifle sec, 1 × 2"

Notes
1 Radios were in Coy HQs and all AFVs. Artillery is rated Assigned FC.
2 Infantry sections had No.68 rifle A/T grenades.
3 The Light Armoured Car was an unknown South African type, very similar in appearance to the Humber Light Recce Mk.III, but with only a turreted LMG as armament.
4 The obsolete rifles of the native companies were Martini-Henry 1890s type and other similar single-shot breech loading types.

3.9 AUSTRALIAN INFANTRY DIVISION, 1941, SYRIA

The Division's main combat elements were:
  2–3 Australian Infantry Brigades (each of 3–4 Infantry Battalions)
  1 Divisional Recce Regiment
  1 Tank Troop
  'The Kelly Gang'
Troops are rated average training and good morale. This list includes corps-level support units.

SUPPORT UNITS

Corps-Level Support Units
Included:
  1 British Medium Artillery Regiment: RHQ (6 rifle secs, 4 lorries, 2 AALMG)
    4 Batteries, each: 4 × 6" 26cwt, 4 lorries, 1 radio van
  1 Indian Armoured Car Squadron: Sqdn HQ (3 × Chevrolet Indian Pattern A/C)
    3 Troops, each: 3 × Chevrolet Indian Pattern A/C
  11th British Commando Battalion (good training and morale)
    Btn HQ (1 rifle/SMG sec, radio)
      5 Troops, each: 4 rifle/SMG secs, 1 Boys, 4–6 LMG, 1 × 2" mortar, 1 radio
  4 Naval Batteries, each: 2–3 × 6" guns (Pre-planned fire)
  1 Naval Battery: 4 × 4" guns (Pre-planned fire)
  12 Naval Batteries, each: 1–2 × 4.7" guns (Pre-planned fire)

Divisional Support
Included:
  6 Artillery Batteries, each: Battery HQ (1 radio van, 4 trucks, 4 rifle secs, 2 AALMG)
    3 Troops, each: 4 × 25pdr, 4 trucks, radio van, 1 AALMG
  4 A/T Companies, each: Coy HQ (1 rifle sec, 1 truck)
    3 Troops, each: 4 × 2pdr, 4 trucks
  3 Engineer Companies, each: Coy HQ (1 rifle sec)
    3 Platoons, each: 4 (12 man) rifle/engineer secs, 2 lorries
  1 MG Battalion:
    4 MG Companies, each: Coy HQ (1 rifle sec, 1 truck)
      3 Platoons, each: 4 × MMG, 2 trucks

Brigade Support
Infantry Brigade HQ (6 rifle secs, 4 lorries, 1 Boys, 3 LMG)

MAIN COMBAT ELEMENTS

Infantry Battalion
Btn HQ (2 rifle secs)
  4 Companies, each: Coy HQ (1 rifle sec)
    3 Platoons, each: 4 rifle secs, 3 LMG, 1 × 2", 0–1 Boys A/T Rifle
  1 Support Company: Coy HQ: 1 rifle sec
    1 Platoon: 2 × 3" mortars, Assigned FC
    1 Platoon: 2 rifle/engineer secs
    1 Platoon: 4 × Twin AALMG
    1 Platoon: Pl HQ (1 × Universal Carrier, 1 LMG)
      3 Sections, each: 3 × Universal Carrier, 3 LMG, 1 rifle sec, 1 × 2" mortar

Divisional Recce Regiment
Divisional Recce Regiment
   RHQ (4 × Vickers VIB, 1 radio van, 4 × Scout Carriers)
      3 Squadrons, each: Sqdn HQ (2 × Vickers VIB, 2 × Scout Carriers)
         2 Troops, each: 3 × Vickers VIB or IIB light tanks
         4 Troops, each: 3 × Scout Carriers, 1 rifle sec, 3 Boys, 3 LMG

Tank Troop
   4 × captured R-35

'The Kelly Gang'
   'The Kelly Gang': 3 rifle secs, horses (captured Arab horses)

Notes
1   Radios were in all AFVs and other Coy HQs. Artillery is rated Assigned FC.
2   Infantry sections had no A/T grenades.
3   For wargames purposes, naval batteries of the same calibre could be combined to form larger batteries. Naval batteries and the Commandos could only be used in coastal areas of Syria

3.10 EAST AFRICAN 22ND BRIGADE, SEPTEMBER-NOVEMBER 1942, MADAGASCAR

The Brigade's main combat elements were:
   3 Infantry Battalions (5th, 1/1st and 1/6th King's African Rifles Battalions)

The Brigade took part in the occupation of central and southern Madagascar. Troops are rated at average training and good morale.

SUPPORT UNITS

Brigade Support
Infantry Brigade HQ (6 rifle secs, 4 lorries) with:
   1 Defence Platoon: 4 rifle secs, 3 LMG, 1 × 2" mortar, 4 trucks

MAIN COMBAT ELEMENTS

Infantry Battalion
Btn HQ (5 rifle secs, 1 LMG, 4 lorries)
   4 Companies, each: Coy HQ (1 rifle sec, 1 lorry)
      3 Platoons, each: 4 rifle secs, 3 LMG, 1 × 2", 2 lorries
   1 Support Company: Coy HQ (1 rifle sec, 1 truck)
      1 Battery: 4 × 3" mortars, 2 lorries, radio truck
      1 Platoon: 4 × MMG or AALMG, 2 trucks
      1 Platoon: 2 rifle/engineer secs, 1 lorry

Notes
1   Radios were in all Coy HQs and above.
2   Infantry sections had no A/T grenades.
3   Can use divisional support units from South African 7th Infantry Brigade (list 3.9).

3.11 BRITISH CAVALRY DIVISION, JULY 1940-MARCH 1942, PALESTINE

The Division's main combat elements were:
   4th, 5th and 6th Cavalry Brigades (4th–1st Household Cavalry Regiment, Royal Wiltshire Yeomanry, Warwickshire Yeomanry; 5th – Cheshire Yeomanry, Yorkshire Dragoons, North Somerset Yeomanry; 6th – Royal Scots Greys, Yorkshire Hussars, Staffordshire Yeomanry)

In 1941 the 4th Brigade was detached to form Habforce (see list 3.17). The remaining two brigades served in Syria. In August 1941 the Division was converted to the 10th Armoured Division, leaving only the 5th Cavalry Brigade as a garrison in Syria and Palestine until disbanded in March 1942. Troops are rated at average training and average morale.

SUPPORT UNITS

Divisional Support
Included:
   3 attached Artillery Regiments, each: RHQ (4 rifle secs, 4 lorries)
      2 Batteries, each: Battery HQ (4 rifle secs, 2 AALMG, 2 trucks)
         2 Troops, each: 3–4 × 25pdr field guns, 2 AALMG, 6 trucks
   1 Engineer Squadron: Sqdn HQ (2 rifle secs, 1 lorry)
      4 Troops, each: 4 (12 man) rifle/engineer secs, 1 LMG, 2 lorries
   1 Field Park Squadron:
      1 Bridge Section: lorries
      1 Workshop Section

Brigade Support
Cavalry Brigade HQ (6 rifle secs, 6 trucks, 2 LMG, 1 Boys)

MAIN COMBAT ELEMENTS

Cavalry Regiment (1940)
    RHQ (8 rifle secs, 6 lorries)
        2 Squadrons, each: Sqdn HQ (2 rifle secs, horses, sabres)
            3 Troops, each: 4 (8 man) rifle secs, horses, sabres
                1 (9 man) rifle HQ sec, 1 Lewis LMG, 1 Boys
        1 Squadron: Sqdn HQ (1 rifle sec, 1 truck)
            3 Troops, each: 4 (8 man) rifle secs, 4 trucks
                1 (8 man) rifle sec, 1 LMG, 1 Boys
        1 MG Troop: 4 × Vickers MMG, pack horses
        1 A/T Troop: 4 × Boys A/T rifles, horses OR 4 × 2pdr A/T guns, 4 trucks
        1 Scout Troop: 9 × saloon cars, 1 radio

Cavalry Regiment (1941–42)
    RHQ: 6 rifle secs, 4 lorries
        2 Squadrons, each: Sqdn HQ (1 rifle sec, horses, sabres)
            3 Troops, each: 1 (5 man) Troop HQ rifle sec, 2 LMG, horse, sabres
                3 (6 man) rifle secs, horses, sabres
        1 Squadron: Sqdn HQ (1 rifle sec, 1 truck)
            3 Troops, each: 1 (5 man) rifle Troop HQ sec (2 LMG, 1 truck)
                3 (6 man) rifle secs, 3 trucks
        1 MG Troop: 4 × Vickers MMG, 4 Boys A/T rifles, pack horses
        1 A/T Troop: 4 × 2pdr A/T guns, 4 trucks, 4 Boys
        1 Scout Troop: 9 × saloon cars, 1 radio
        1 Mortar Troop: 4 × 3" mortars, pack horses (1942 only)

Notes
1   Radios were in all Sqdn HQ and artillery troops, and where noted.
2   Troops had no anti-tank grenades.

3.12 SUDANESE HOME DEFENCE FORCES, 1939–SEPTEMBER 1940, SUDAN

These forces defended Sudan from Italian incursions directed from West Abyssinia, and were also in place to repel attacks from Chad had it become controlled by Vichy France. Troops are rated at average training and good morale unless noted.

SUPPORT UNITS
    6 Sudanese Motor MG Companies, each: Coy HQ (1 × A/Car w/Boys, MG)
        2 Platoons, each: 3 × A/C
        2 Platoons, each: 4 × trucks w/AALMG
        2 Platoons, each: 3 rifle secs, 2 trucks
    6+ Sudanese Frontier Camel Corps Companies, each: Coy HQ (1 rifle sec, camels, horses)
        3 Platoons, each: 4 rifle secs, 1 LMG, camels, swords
    1 Sudanese Saluting Battery: 4 × 2.95" Mountain Guns M01, pack mules (Obsolete FC) (poor training, average morale)
    6 Equatorial Corps Companies, each: Coy HQ (1 rifle sec) (poor training, average morale)
        2–3 Platoons, each: 3–4 rifle secs

MAIN COMBAT ELEMENTS

1 Sudanese Frontier Battalion
    Btn HQ (2 rifle secs)
        4 Companies, each: Coy HQ (1 rifle sec, 1 Boys, 1 LMG)
            2 Platoons, each: 3 rifle secs, 1 LMG, machetes
        1 Support Company: Coy HQ (1 rifle sec)
            1 Platoon: 3 MMG
            1 Battery: 4 × 3" mortars, Assigned FC

2+ Frontier Police Units
(poor training, average morale)
    Coy HQ (1 rifle sec)
        2 Platoons, each: 3 rifle secs

2 British Infantry Battalions
(August 1940 onwards), each:
    Btn HQ (2 rifle secs, 1 staff car, 2 trucks)
        3 Companies, each: Coy HQ (1 (13 man) rifle sec)
            3 Platoons, each: 4 rifle secs, 3 LMG, 1 × 2", 1 Boys
        1 Support Company: Coy HQ (1 rifle sec)
            1 Platoon: 4 × 3" mortars
            1 Platoon: 4 × Twin AALMG, 1 Boys

Notes
1   Radios were in all Coy HQs.
2   Infantry sections had no A/T grenades.

3.13 BRITISH GARRISON FORCES, 1939–AUGUST 1940, BRITISH SOMALILAND

The garrison in British Somaliland consisted of a North Rhodesian Battalion, a King's African Rifles (Kenyan) Battalion, a Black Watch Infantry Battalion, and the Somaliland Camel Corps. All these forces fought together, delaying an overwhelming Italian attack long enough to allow evacuation from Berbera to Aden. Troops are rated average training and good morale.

SUPPORT UNITS

Brigade Support
Brigade HQ (4 rifle secs, 3 lorries) with:
    2 Punjabi Companies, each: Coy HQ (1 rifle sec)
        3 Platoons, each: 3–4 rifle secs, 3 LMG, 1 × 2"
    1 East African Light Battery: 4 × 3.7" Mountain Guns, pack mules (Obsolete FC)
    1 Naval Battery: 1 × 3pdr 47mm Saluting Gun on improvised mount loaned from the Royal Navy.

MAIN COMBAT ELEMENTS

British Infantry Battalion
Btn HQ (2 rifle secs)
    4 Companies, each: Coy HQ (1 (13 man) rifle sec, 1 Boys)
        3 Platoons, each: 4 rifle secs, 3 LMG, 1 × 2" mortar
    1 Support Company: Coy HQ (1 rifle sec)
        1 Platoon: 4 × 3" mortars, Assigned FC
        1 Platoon: 4 × Twin AALMG, 1 Boys

Somaliland Camel Corps
Btn HQ (4 rifle secs, camels, ponies or 4 trucks)
    2 Camel Companies, each: Coy HQ (2 rifle secs, camels)
        3 Platoons, each: 3 rifle secs, 1 Lewis LMG, camels
    1 Platoon: 3 rifle secs, 1 Lewis LMG, ponies
        1 Motorised Company: Coy HQ (4 (9 man) rifle secs, 2 trucks)
            4 Platoons, each: 3 rifle secs, 1 Lewis LMG, 3 trucks
            1 MG Platoon:[9] 4 × Vickers MMG, 4 trucks, 4 (6 man) crew secs

Notes
1   Radios were at Btn HQ and above.
2   Infantry sections had no A/T grenades.

3.14 KENYAN HOME DEFENCE FORCES, 1939–NOVEMBER 1940, KENYA, SOUTH ABYSSINIA

These forces had to defend the Kenyan-Abyssinian border from Italian incursions from July 1940. Troops are rated average training and good morale.

MAIN COMBAT ELEMENTS

1+ King's African Rifles Infantry Battalions,
each:
    Btn HQ (2 rifle secs, 1 staff car, 2 trucks)
        4 Companies, each: Coy HQ (1 rifle sec, 1 Boys)
            3 Platoons, each: 4 rifle secs, 3 LMG, 1 × 2" mortar
        1 Support Company: Coy HQ (1 rifle sec)
            1 Platoon: 4 × 3" mortars, Assigned FC
            1 Platoon: 4 × Twin AALMG, 1 Boys

1 East African Recce Squadron (white settlers)
Sqdn HQ (1 truck w/AALMG)
    2 Troops, each: 3 trucks, 2 rifle secs, 3 AALMG

2 Somali Irregular Companies,
each:
    25 rifle secs, obsolete rifles, swords, spears (poor training, good morale)

2nd Ethiopian Battalion
Btn HQ (1 rifle sec)
    2 Companies, each: Coy HQ (1 rifle sec, 1 Boys)
        3 Platoons, each: 3 rifle secs, 2 LMG
        1 Platoon: 2 MMG

2+ Abyssinian Patriot Companies,
each:
    Coy HQ (1 leader on horse, standard bearer)

---
9   1940 onwards.

3 Platoons, each: 50 men, spears, obsolete Martini-Henry rifles (poor training, good morale)

Notes
1 Radios were in all Btn HQs only.
2 Infantry sections had no A/T grenades.
3 Possibly up to 2 batteries, each 4 × 3.7" Mountain Guns with pack mules could be added to this list.

3.15 GIDEON FORCE, DECEMBER 1940–MAY 1941, WEST SUDAN, WEST ABYSSINIA

Gideon force escorted Emperor Haile Selassie from Sudan to Addis Ababa, the capital of Abyssinia, routing 4 Italian colonial brigades in the process. Troops are rated average training and good morale.

SUPPORT UNITS

Force Support
Mission 101 Force HQ (1 British rifle sec, long range radios)

MAIN COMBAT ELEMENTS

2nd Ethiopian Battalion
Btn HQ (1 rifle sec)
  2 Companies, each: Coy HQ (1 rifle sec, 1 Boys)
    3 Platoons, each: 3 rifle secs, 2 LMG
    1 Platoon: 2 MMG

1 Sudanese Frontier Battalion
Btn HQ (2 rifle secs)
  2 Bodyguard rifle/pistol secs with large standard (average training, excellent morale)
  4 Companies, each: Coy HQ (1 rifle sec, 1 Boys, 1 LMG)
    2 Platoons, each: 3 rifle secs, 1 LMG, machetes
  1 Support Company: Coy HQ (1 rifle sec)
    1 Platoon: 3 MMG
    1 Battery: 4 × 3" mortars, Obsolete FC

13 Ethiopian Patriot Companies,
each:
  Coy HQ (leader on horse, standard bearer)
    15 rifle secs, spears, 0–5 LMG (good morale, poor training)

Notes
1 Radios were in all Btn HQs.
2 Infantry sections had no A/T grenades.

3.16 BRITISH GARRISON FORCES, 1940–41, HABBINIYA AIRBASE, IRAQ

These forces were besieged by Iraqi forces at Habbaniya airfield in Iraq during April 1941, then later carried out offensive actions in the area in conjunction with Habforce.

MAIN COMBAT ELEMENTS

1 Assyrian Levy Battalion
(poor training, average morale)
Btn HQ (2 rifle secs)
  6 Companies, each: Coy HQ (2 rifle secs, 1 × 2" mortar)
    3 Platoons, each: 4 rifle secs, 3 LMG
  1 Support Company: Coy HQ (1 rifle sec)
    1 Platoon: 4 × 3.7" Mountain Guns, 4 trucks (May 1941 onwards only)
    1 Platoon: 4 × AALMG in 2 rifle crew secs
    1 Platoon: 2 rifle/engineer secs

2 RAF Armoured Car Squadrons,
each: (average training, average morale)
  Coy HQ (3 × Rolls-Royce M1920 Type A)
    2 Troops, each: 3 × Rolls-Royce Type A

1 Gate Guard Battery
(average training, average morale)
  2 × 4.5" QF Mk 1 howitzers, 2 trucks

1st Battalion, King's Own Royal Regiment (British Infantry Battalion)
flown in from Basra, April 1941 (average training, average morale)
Btn HQ (1 rifle sec)
  3 Companies, each: Coy HQ (1 rifle sec)
    3 Platoons, each: 4 rifle secs, 1 Boys, 3 LMG, 1 × 2" mortar

10 RAF Garrison Platoons,[10]
each: (poor training, average morale)
   3 rifle secs, 1 LMG

Notes
1. Number 4 Service Training School at Habbaniya in Iraq possessed the following aircraft:
   - 12 × Audax, each: 2 × 250lb bombs
   - 7 × Gordon, each: 2 × 250lb bombs
   - 3 × Gloster Gladiator fighters
   - 18 × Audax, each: 8 × 20lb bombs
   - 25 × Hawker Hart, each: 2 × 250lb bombs
   - 27 × Oxford, each: 8 × 20lb bombs
   - 3 × Valentia

   However there were only 39 pilots to fly this assortment. During the May 1941 siege reinforcements consisted of:
   - 6 × Blenheim IVL
   - 4 × Blenheim IVF
   - 9 × Gladiators
   - 2 × Hurricane IIC

   Support from Basra included a few DC-2s and 10 × Wellington 1c
2. Radios were in all Btn HQs and armoured cars.
3. Infantry sections had no A/T grenades.

3.17 BRITISH HABFORCE, MAY–JULY 1941, IRAQ/SYRIA

Habforce's main combat elements were:
   4th Cavalry Brigade (Household Cavalry Regiment, Royal Wiltshire Yeomanry, Warwickshire Yeomanry Motorised Cavalry Battalions, 1st Btn Essex Regiment Motor Infantry Battalion)
   1st Mechanised Regiment Transjordan Frontier Force
   Arab Legion Desert Mechanised Regiment

Habforce invaded Iraq from the west in May 1941, then Syria from the east the following month. Troops are rated at average training and good morale unless otherwise noted.

SUPPORT UNITS

Force Support
4th Cavalry Brigade HQ (4 rifle secs, 4 trucks) with up to:
  2 Artillery Batteries, each:
    Battery HQ (4 rifle secs, 3 lorries, radio van, 2 AALMG), Assigned FC
      1 Troop: 4 × 25pdr, 4 trucks, radio truck, 1 LMG
  2 A/T Troops, each: 2 × 2pdr, 4 trucks, 1 LMG
  1 Engineer Company: Coy HQ (1 rifle sec, 1 truck)
    3 Platoons, each: 4 rifle/engineer secs, 2 lorries
  1 RAF Recce Company: Coy HQ (3 × Fordson A/C)
    2 Platoons, each: 3 × Fordson A/C
  2 Yeomanry Squadrons, each:[11] Sqdn HQ (1 rifle sec, 1 truck)
    3 Platoons, each: 4 (6 man) rifle secs, 1 Boys, 2 LMG, 4 trucks

MAIN COMBAT ELEMENTS

Motorised Cavalry Regiment
Btn HQ (2 rifle secs, 2 trucks)
  3 Squadrons, each: Sqdn HQ (1 rifle sec, 1 × 2", 1 Boys, 1 truck)
    3 Troops, each: 3 rifle secs, 2 LMG, 4 trucks, 0–1 Boys, 0–1 × 2" mortar
  1 Troop: 2 MMG, 2 × 3" mortars, 4 trucks

1st Btn Essex Regiment Motor Infantry Battalion
Btn HQ (2 rifle secs, 1 staff car, 2 trucks)
  4 Companies, each: Coy HQ (1 rifle sec, 1 lorry)
    3 Platoons, each: 4 rifle secs, 3 LMG, 1 × 2", 1 Boys, 2 lorries
  1 Support Company: Coy HQ (1 rifle sec, 1 truck)
    1 Platoon: 4 × 3" mortars, 2 trucks, radio truck
    1 Platoon: 4 × Twin AALMG, 1 Boys, 3 trucks
    1 Platoon: 2 rifle/engineer secs, 1 lorry
    1 Platoon: Pl HQ (1 × Bren Carrier, 1 LMG)
      3 Sections, each: 3 × Bren Carrier, 3 LMG, 1 (6 man) rifle sec

1st Mechanised Regiment Transjordan Frontier Force
(average training, average morale)
  Force HQ (2 rifle secs, 2 trucks)
    3 Companies, each: Coy HQ (1 rifle sec, 1 × 2", 1 Boys, 1 truck)
      3 Platoons, each: 3 (8 man) rifle secs, 2 LMG, 3 trucks, 0–1 Boys
    1 Platoon: 2 MMG, 2 × 3" mortars, 4 trucks

---

10. Ground crew personnel, cooks, etc.
11. Syria only.

Arab Legion Desert Mechanised Regiment
(good training, good morale)
>Legion HQ (1 rifle sec, 2 trucks, 2 LMG)
>>2 Troops, each: 3 × Ford A/C 1939 pattern
>>2 Troops, each: 3 trucks w/Lewis AAMG, 3 rifle secs, 1 Boys

Notes
1. Radios were in all Coy HQs and Fordsons. All artillery is rated Assigned FC.
2. Infantry sections had no A/T grenades.

3.18 BRITISH FORCE 121, MAY–SEPTEMBER 1942, MADAGASCAR

Force 121's main combat elements were:
>29th Independent Infantry Brigade (1st Royal Scots Fusiliers, 2nd Royal Welsh Fusiliers, 2nd East Lancashire Regiment, 1 Battalion each, all trained for amphibious warfare)
>17th Infantry Brigade Group (2nd Royal Scots Fusiliers, 2nd Northamptonshire Regiment, 6th Seaforth Highlanders, 1 Battalion each)

Force 121 invaded Madagascar in May 1942; in September, 29th Brigade took part in the occupation of southern and central Madagascar. Troops are rated average training, average to good morale. Marines are rated good training and good morale. The 29th Brigade went on to serve in India in the 36th Indian Infantry Division.

SUPPORT UNITS

Force 121 Support Units
>8 Fleet Air Arm Flights, each: 3 × Swordfish I or Albacore
>6 Fleet Air Arm Flights, each: 4 × Sea Hurricane 1B or F–4F4 Martlet IV or Fulmar I
>4 Naval Batteries, each: 2 × 15" guns from HMS Ramillies
>4 Naval Batteries, each: 2 × 8" gun from heavy cruiser
>5 Naval Batteries, each: 2 × 5.25" guns from HMS Hermoine
>4 Naval Batteries, each: 2 × 4" guns (ships' secondary armaments)
>20 Naval Batteries, each: 2 × 4.7" guns from destroyers
>1 × Backaquero class LST (2 × LCM, 3 × 2pdr AA, 6 × 20mm AA, 2 × 4.2" smoke mortars, 2 AALMG w/cargo of 200 infantry, 22 × 25t AFV or lorries)
>Numerous LCM, LCVP landing craft
>50 Marines from HMS Ramillies (leaving 97 on board) used in landings.

29th Independent Brigade Support
>Infantry Brigade HQ (6 rifle secs, 6 trucks) with attached support:
>>B Special Service Tank Squadron (good training, good morale)
>>>Sqdn HQ (2 × Valentine II)
>>>>4 Troops, each: 1 × Valentine II, 2 × Tetrarch
>>455th Light Artillery Battery: Battery HQ (2 rifle secs, 4 trucks), Assigned FC
>>>1 Troop: 4 × 3.7" Mountain guns, 4 trucks, radio truck
>>>1 Troop: 2 × 25pdr field guns, 2 trucks, radio truck
>>>1 AA Troop: 4 × 40mmL60 Bofors, 4 trucks
>>5 Commando (good training, good morale):
>>>Btn HQ (1 rifle/SMG sec, radio)
>>>>5 Troops, each: 5 rifle/SMG secs, 1 Boys, 5 LMG, 1 × 2" mortar, radio

17th Infantry Brigade Group Support
>Brigade HQ (6 rifle secs, 4 lorries) with:
>>3 Artillery Batteries, each: BHQ (4 rifle secs, 4 AALMG, 6 trucks), Assigned FC
>>>2 Troops, each: 4 × 25pdr Mk2, 2 LMG, 5 trucks, radio truck
>>1 Engineer Company: Coy HQ (1 rifle sec)
>>>3 Platoons, each: 4 (12 man) rifle/engineer secs, 3 LMG

MAIN COMBAT ELEMENTS

Infantry Battalion
>Btn HQ (4 rifle secs, 1 LMG)
>>4 Companies, each: Coy HQ (1 rifle sec)
>>>3 Platoons, each: 4 rifle secs, 3 LMG, 1 × 2" mortar
>>1 Support Company: Coy HQ (1 rifle sec)
>>>1 Battery: 4 × 3" mortars, trucks or Carriers
>>>1 Platoon: 4 × AALMG in 2 rifle crew secs
>>>1 Platoon: 2 rifle/engineer secs
>>>1 Platoon: Pl HQ (1 × Universal Carrier, 1 LMG, 1 × Daimler S/C)
>>>>4 Sections, each: 3 × Carrier, 1 rifle sec, 1 × 2" mortar, 3 LMG

Notes
1. Radios were in all tanks and other Coy HQs, and in Carrier Pl HQs.
2. Infantry had no A/T grenades.
3. For wargames purposes, may add one Boys A/T rifle per company if desired.
4. Naval artillery was only available in coastal areas. Batteries of the same calibre could be grouped together. Fire was pre-planned only.

PART 4
MEDITERRANEAN THEATRE
1939–43

4.1 BRITISH 2ND ARMOURED BRIGADE, APRIL 1941, GREECE

The Brigade's main combat elements were:
   3rd Royal Tank Regiment
   4th Hussars Armoured Regiment
   1 Motor Battalion (1st Btn Rangers)
Troops are rated average training and good morale.

SUPPORT UNITS

Brigade Support

Brigade HQ (3 × Vickers VIB, 7 × A–10 or A–13 Mk.2 tanks, radio vans) with:
   1 A/T Regiment:
      3 A/T Batteries, each: Battery HQ (1 rifle sec, 1 truck)
         3 Troops, each: 4 × 2pdr A/T guns, 4 trucks or portées
   3rd Field Engineer Squadron: Sqdn HQ (2 rifle secs, 1 lorry)
      4 Troops, each: 4 (12 man) rifle/engineer secs, 2 lorries, 1 LMG
   142nd Field Engineer Park Squadron: stores, bridges, explosives, lorries
   1 Horse Artillery Regiment:
      2 Batteries, each: Battery HQ (4 rifle secs, 3 lorries, radio van, 1 AALMG)
         2 Troops, each: 4 × 25pdr field guns, 6 trucks, 1 AALMG

MAIN COMBAT ELEMENTS

3rd Royal Tank Regiment

RHQ (4 × A–10, 3 × Scammel Wreckers)
   3 Squadrons, each: Sqdn HQ (2 × A–10, 2 × A–9 CS)
      4 Troops, each: 3 × A–10

4th Hussars Armoured Regiment

RHQ (4 × Vickers VIC, 3 recovery trucks)
   3 Squadrons, each: Sqdn HQ (4 × Vickers VIB)
      4 Troops, each: 3 × Vickers VIB

Motor Battalion

Btn HQ (2 trucks, 1 lorry, 2 rifle secs)
   3 Companies, each: Coy HQ (1 rifle sec, 1 × 2" mortar, 1 Boys, 2 trucks)
      3 Platoons, each: 4 rifle secs, 4 Boys, 1 × 2" mortar, 3 LMG, 4 trucks
      1 Platoon: Pl HQ (1 × Carrier, 1 × Daimler Scout Car, 1 LMG)
         4 Sections, each: 3 × Carrier, 3 LMG, 1 Boys, 1 × 2" mortar, 1 rifle sec

Notes
1   Radios were in all tanks and other Coy HQs.
2   Troops had no A/T grenades.

4.2 AUSTRALIAN AND NEW ZEALAND INFANTRY DIVISIONS, MARCH–APRIL 1941, GREECE

The 6th Australian Infantry Division's main combat elements were:
   3 Infantry Brigades (16th – 2/1st, 2/2nd and 2/3rd Infantry Battalions; 17th – 2/5th, 2/6th and 2/7th Infantry
      Battalions; 19th – 2/4th, 2/8th and 2/11th Infantry Battalions)
The 2nd New Zealand Division's main combat elements were:
   3 Infantry Brigades (4th – 18th, 19th and 20th Infantry Battalions; 5th – 21st, 22nd and 23rd Infantry Battalions; 6th – 24th, 25th and 26th Infantry Battalions)
   1 Maori Battalion (28th Infantry Battalion)
   1 Divisional Recce Regiment (2nd Divisional Cavalry Regiment)
Troops are rated average training and good morale, except for the Maoris, who are rated good training and excellent morale.

SUPPORT UNITS

Divisional Support

Included:
   3 Artillery Regiments, each:
      2 Artillery Batteries, each: Battery HQ (1 radio van, 4 trucks, 4 rifle secs, 2 AALMG)

3 Troops, each: 4 × 25pdr, 4 × trucks, radio van, 1 AALMG
4 A/T Companies, each: Coy HQ (1 rifle sec, 1 truck)
3 Troops, each: 4 × 2pdr, 4 trucks
3 Engineer Companies, each: Coy HQ (1 rifle sec)
3 Platoons, each: 4 (12 man) rifle/engineer secs, 2 lorries
4 MG Companies, each: Coy HQ (1 rifle sec, 1 truck)
3 Platoons, each: 4 × MMG, 2 trucks

Brigade Support
Infantry Brigade HQ (6 rifle secs, 4 lorries, 1 Boys, 3 LMG)

MAIN COMBAT ELEMENTS

Infantry Battalion
Btn HQ (2 rifle secs)
4 Companies, each: Coy HQ (1 rifle sec)
3 Platoons, each: 4 rifle secs, 3 LMG, 1 × 2", 0–1 Boys A/T Rifle
1 Support Company: Coy HQ (1 rifle sec)
1 Platoon: 2 × 3" mortars, Assigned FC
1 Platoon: 2 rifle/engineer secs
1 Platoon: 4 × Twin AALMG
1 Platoon: Pl HQ (1 × Universal Carrier, 1 LMG)
3 Sections, each: 3 × Carrier, 3 LMG, 1 rifle sec, 1 × 2" mortar, 1 Boys

New Zealand 2nd Divisional Cavalry Regiment
RHQ (4 × Marmon-Herrington I, 1 radio van, 4 × Bren Carriers)
3 Squadrons, each: Sqdn HQ (2 × Marmon-Herrington A/C, 2 × Bren Carriers)
3 Troops, each: 4 × Marmon-Herrington A/C

Notes
1 Radios were in all AFVs and other Coy HQs. Artillery is rated Assigned FC.
2 Infantry sections had no A/T grenades.
3 This list can also be used for Australian and New Zealand divisions operating in Crete in 1941.
4 Corps-level support included some 40 AAA, at least one British Medium Artillery Regiment, 2 Blenheim bomber squadrons, 2 Gladiator fighter squadrons, and 1 mixed squadron of Blenheim fighters and bombers.

4.3 COMMONWEALTH INFANTRY DIVISIONS, 1943, SICILY

The Division's main combat elements were:
3 Infantry Brigades (each of 3 Infantry Battalions)
1 Divisional Recce Regiment
Troops are rated at average training and average morale.

SUPPORT UNITS

Divisional Support
Included:
9 Artillery Batteries, each: Battery HQ (1 radio van, 4 trucks, 4 rifle secs, 2 AALMG
2 Troops, each: 4 × 25pdr Mk.1, 4 trucks, radio van, 1 LMG
3 A/T Batteries, each: Battery HQ (1 rifle sec, 1 truck)
3 Troops, each: 4 × 2pdr or 6pdr, 4 truck portées, 2 LMG
3 Engineer Companies, each: Coy HQ (1 rifle sec, 2 × Scout Cars)
3 Platoons, each: 4 (12 man) rifle/engineer secs, 1 AALMG
1 MG Battalion:[1]
3 MG Companies, each: Coy HQ (1 rifle sec, 1 truck)
4 Platoons, each: 4 MMG, 2 trucks
3 AA Batteries, each: Battery HQ (1 rifle sec, 1 truck)
3 Troops, each: 6 × 40mm Bofors, 6 trucks
2 Beach Group "Bricks", each:[2]
Btn HQ (4 rifle secs, 2 LMG, 2 trucks)
1 Defence Company: standard Infantry Company (see below)
1 Heavy AA Battery: Battery HQ (2 rifle secs, 2 trucks)
2 Troops, each: 4 × 3.7" AA, 6 lorries
1 Light AA Battery: Battery HQ (1 rifle sec, 1 truck)
3 Troops, each: 6 × 40mm Bofors, 6 trucks
1 Field Engineer Company: see Engineer Company above
2 Engineer Support Companies, each: standard Infantry Company (see below) but equipped as Pioneers

1 Only in 5th, 44th, 50th, 4th British Infantry Divisions from 1943, and in all Commonwealth Divisions, 1941–43.
2 Assaulting Divisions were given two Beach Group "Bricks" to maintain traffic flow off the beach, provide local defence, and to unload stores from landing craft, and were temporary, battalion-sized, formations provided until ports were secured. The British 5th Division also had an attached regiment of 24 × 105mm M7 Priests. At army-level support there were a total of five RAF Servicing Commandos.

Beach Unloading Troops (1 standard Infantry Company, 1 Btn Support Company plus crews w/rifles and LMGs)
Signals units from Infantry Btn HQ, RN and RAF

Brigade Support
Infantry Brigade HQ (10 rifle secs, 3 LMG, 1 × 2") with:
  1 Support Company:[3] Coy HQ (1 rifle sec, 1 truck)
    3 Platoons, each: 4 Vickers MMG, 4 trucks, 4 rifle crew secs
    2 Platoons, each: 4 × 4.2" mortars, 4 trucks, radio truck

MAIN COMBAT ELEMENTS
Infantry Battalion
Btn HQ (5 rifle secs, 1 LMG)
  4 Companies, each: Coy HQ (1 rifle sec)
    3 Platoons, each: 4 rifle secs, 3 LMG, 1 × 2"
  1 Support Company: Coy HQ (1 rifle sec)
    1 Platoon: 4 or 6 × 3" mortars, 6 × Carriers
    1 Platoon: 2 rifle/engineer secs, 1 lorry
    1 Scout Platoon: Pl HQ (1 × Carrier, 1 × Daimler S/C, 1 LMG)
      1 Section: 3 × Carrier, 3 LMG, 1 × 2", 1 rifle sec
    2 Platoons, each: 4 × 2pdr, 4 × Carriers
    1 MG Platoon: 4 × Vickers MMG, 8 × Universal Carriers

Divisional Recce Regiment
RHQ (3 rifle secs, 3 LMG, 3 × Light Recce Car)
  3 Squadrons, each: Sqdn HQ (3 rifle secs, 1 LMG, 3 trucks, 1 Light Recce Car, 1 Jeep)
    3 Troops, each: Troop HQ (1 × Carrier, 1 LMG, 1 × 2" mortar)
      1 Section: 3 × Humber Light Recce IIIA, 2 × Humber III or Marmon-Herrington II+47mmL32
      2 Sections, each: 3 × Carrier, 3 LMG, 1 × 2", 1 rifle sec
  1 Troop: 4 rifle secs, 5 trucks, 4 LMG, 1 Jeep
    1 Mortar Battery: 6 × 3" mortars, 7 × Universal Carriers, 1 Jeep
    1 A/T Platoon: Pl HQ (1 Jeep, 4 × Lloyd Carriers)[4]
    3 Troops (1942), each: 4 × 2pdr A/T guns, 4 × Lloyd Carriers
    OR 2 Troops (1943), each: 4 × 2pdr or 6pdr A/T guns, 4 × Lloyd Carriers
    1 AA Platoon: 2 × twin AALMG on trucks

Notes
1 Radios were in all Coy HQs and AFVs. All artillery is rated as Flexible FC, with one OP team per battery in truck, Daimler S/C or turretless Marmon-Herrington.
2 Infantry sections had No.74 or No.75 Hawkins A/T grenades.
3 For wargames purposes, the Divisional Recce Regiment could have Humber IIIs mixed in, and could replace the Daimler S/C with Humber Light Recce Mk II or III. Each Recce Squadron could add one troop of 6 jeeps (unarmed).
4 2pdr A/T guns could be towed by Lloyd Carriers.

4.4 BRITISH 231ST INFANTRY BRIGADE, JULY 1943, SICILY
The Brigade's main combat elements were:
  3 Infantry Battalions
Troops are rated at average training and average morale.

SUPPORT UNITS
Brigade Support
Infantry Brigade HQ (6 rifle secs, 4 lorries) with:
  1 Support Company: Coy HQ (2 rifle secs, 1 lorry)
    1 Battery: 6 × 4.2" mortars, 7 × Carriers, OP Team
    2 Platoons, each: 4 MMG, 5 × Carriers
  1 Engineer Company: Coy HQ (1 rifle sec)
    3 Platoons, each: 4 (12man) rifle/engineer secs, 3 LMG
  3 Artillery Batteries, each:
    Battery HQ (4 rifle secs, 4 trucks, radio van, 4 AALMG, 3 OP Teams)
      2 Troops, each: 4 × 25pdr, 4 Quad Tractors, radio truck, 2 AALMG
  4 A/T Companies, each: Coy HQ (1 rifle sec, 1 truck)
    3 Platoons, each: 4 × 6pdr, 4 trucks, 2 LMG
  3 AA Companies, each: Coy HQ (1 rifle sec, 1 truck)
    3 Platoons, each: 6 × 40mmL60 Bofors, 6 trucks

---

3 Only if there was no Divisional MG Battalion.
4 For extra ammunition.

MAIN COMBAT ELEMENTS

Infantry Battalion
Btn HQ (2 rifle secs, 1 LMG)
 4 Companies, each: Coy HQ (1 rifle sec)
  3 Platoons, each: 4 rifle secs, 3 LMG, 1 × 2" mortar, 1 PIAT
 1 Support Company: Coy HQ (1 rifle sec)
  1 Platoon: 6 × 3" mortars, 7 × Carriers
  1 Platoon: 4 × Twin AALMG in 2 rifle crew secs
  1 Platoon: 2 rifle/engineer secs
  1 Platoon: Pl HQ (1 × Carrier, 1 Daimler S/C, 1 LMG)
   4 Sections, each: 3 × Carriers, 3 LMG, 1 rifle sec, 1 PIAT, 1 × 2"

Notes
1 Radios were in all Pl HQs and above.
2 Infantry sections had Hawkins 75 A/T grenades.

4.5 BRITISH 1ST AIRBORNE DIVISION, JULY 1943, SICILY

The Division's main combat elements were:
 3 Parachute Brigades (1st – 1st, 2nd and 3rd Parachute Battalions; 2nd – 4th, 5th and 6th Parachute Battalions; 4th – 10th and 156th Parachute Battalions)
 1 Air Landing Brigade (1st Border Regiment, 2nd South Staffordshire Regiment, 7th King's Own Scottish Borderers, 1 Battalion each)

Paratroops are rated at good training and excellent morale, with Pathfinders as excellent training and excellent morale.

SUPPORT UNITS

Divisional Support
Included:
 1 Pathfinder Company
 1 OP Team
 1 MP Company
 1 Defence and Employment Platoon: 4 rifle/SMG secs, 3 LMG, 1 × 2" mortar, 4 trucks
 1 Field Security Section: intelligence and rear security officers, Jeeps
 1 Engineer Stores Squadron: explosives, tools
 1 Artillery Regiment: RHQ (4 SMG secs, 2 LMG, 16 Jeeps or 6 trucks)
  3 Batteries, each: 6 × 75mm M1 pack howitzers, 12 Jeeps, 3 trailers, OP Team
 2 A/T Batteries, each: Battery HQ (1 rifle sec, 1 truck)
  3 Platoons, each: 4 × 6pdr, 4 Jeeps
 1 AA Battery: Battery HQ (1 rifle sec, 1 truck)
  1–2 Troops, each: 6 × 40mmL60 Bofors, 6 trucks
  1 Troop: 6 × 20mm Oerlikon, 6 Jeeps
 1 Recce Squadron: Scout Cars

Brigade Support
Airborne Brigade HQ (6 rifle/SMG secs, attached Naval FC Team) with:
 1 HQ Defence Platoon: 4 rifle/SMG secs, 3 LMG, 1 × 2" mortar
 1 Attached Engineer Squadron: Sqdn HQ (2 rifle/SMG secs)
  3 Platoons, each: 4 (12 man) rifle/engineer secs, 3 LMG, 4 flamethrowers
Air Landing Brigade HQ (6 rifle/SMG secs) with:
 1 HQ Defence Platoon: 4 rifle/SMG secs, 3 LMG, 1 × 2" mortar
 1 Battery: 4 × 4.2" mortars, 4 trucks, 1 radio Jeep
 1 Attached Field Engineer Company: Coy HQ (1 rifle sec)
  3 Platoons, each: 4 (12 man) rifle/engineer secs, 3 LMG, 4 flamethrowers

MAIN COMBAT ELEMENTS

Parachute Battalion
Btn HQ (4 rifle/SMG secs)
 3 Companies, each: Coy HQ (2 (8 man) rifle secs)
  3 Platoons, each: 1 (6 man) rifle/SMG Pl HQ sec, 3 rifle/SMG secs, 3 LMG, 1 × 2"
 1 Battery: 4 × 3" mortars
 1 A/T Platoon: 4 × 2pdr, 4 × Jeeps
 1 MG Platoon: 4 × Vickers MMG
 1 Pioneer Platoon: 2 rifle/SMG/engineer secs, 2 LMG

Air Landing Infantry Battalion
Btn HQ (4 rifle/SMG secs)
 4 Companies, each: Coy HQ (2 (8 man) rifle secs)
  4 Platoons, each: 1 (7 man) rifle/SMG Pl HQ sec, 3 rifle secs, 3 LMG, 1 × 2"
 1 MG Platoon: 4 × Vickers MMG, 4 Jeeps
 1 Battery: 6 × 3" mortars, 8 Jeeps

1 A/T Platoon: 4 × 6pdr A/T guns, 4 Jeeps
1 Pioneer Platoon: 2 rifle/SMG/engineer secs, 2 LMG

Notes
1 Radios were at Coy HQ and above.
2 Infantry had Type 74 or Type 75 A/T grenades.

4.6 CRETE GARRISON, NOVEMBER 1940–APRIL 1941

Troops are rated at average training and average morale unless noted otherwise. Included:
14th Infantry Brigade HQ (February 1941 onwards)
15th Coastal Artillery Regiment (poor training, average morale):
    1 Sqdn: 2 Batteries, each: 4 × 6" naval guns, 4 × Hotchkiss AAMG, 120 crew
2 Royal Marine Batteries, each: 2 × 6" Mk VII coastal guns in concrete dugouts (December 1940 onwards)
1 Heavy AA Battery: 2 Troops, each: 4 × 3.7" AA
6 further Heavy AA Batteries (arrived April 1941)
1 Light AA Battery: 3 Troops, each: 4 × 40mmL60 Bofors
3 further Light AA Batteries (arrived April 1941)
1 Engineer Company
SOE Detachment: 3 agents, Cretan guerrillas, few arms
2 British Infantry Battalions, with third arriving February 1941
2 Greek Infantry Battalions (rifles only)
Royal Marine MNBDO 1
805 Squadron, Fleet Air Arm: Gladiators, Fulmars, Buffalo
30 Squadron, RAF: 18 × Blenheim (arrived April 1941)
203 Squadron, RAF: 9 × Blenheim (arrived April 1941)
33, 80, 112 Squadrons, RAF: totalling 16 × Hurricanes, 6 × Gladiators
2–3 Sunderland flying boats

4.7 CRETE GARRISON, MAY 1941

Troops are rated at average training and good morale unless noted otherwise. Included:
15th Coastal Artillery Regiment (average morale, poor training):
    1 Sqdn: 1 Battery: 4 × 6" naval guns, 4 × Hotchkiss AAMG, 120 crew
        1 Battery: 4 × 4" naval guns, 4 × Hotchkiss AAMG, 120 crew
2 Royal Marine Batteries, each: 2 × 6" Mk VII coastal guns in concrete dugouts
2 Light AA Batteries, each: 12 × 40mmL60 Bofors
7 Heavy AA Batteries, each: 2 Troops, each: 4 × 3.7" AA
Royal Marine MNBDO 1:[5]
  HQ and Signals: 208 men
  Survey Troop: 29 men
  Z, × Coast Defence Batteries, each: 1 Troop: 2 × 4" naval guns, 92 men, Lewis MGs, Bren LMGs
  A, C AA Batteries, each: 4 Sections, each: 2 × 3" 20cwt AA, 57 crew
  23rd Light AA Battery: 4 Troops, each: 42 crew, 2–3 × 40mmL60 Bofors
  S Battery, 11th Searchlight Regiment: (450 men serving as infantry)
    HQ: 4 (9 man) rifle secs, 1 Workshop Section
      4 Sections, each: HQ (1 (6 man) rifle sec, 1 Lewis MG)
        2 Clusters, each: 3 searchlights, 3 (9 man) rifle secs, 1 (8 man) HQ sec
  Landing Company: 145 men (dock unloading)
  Transport Company: 123 men, Matador lorries
  1 ad-hoc AA Battery: 3 × 2pdr pom-pom AA guns, 3 Lewis AAMG
5 Tank Troops, each: 3 × Vickers VIB
2 Tank Troops, each: 3 × Matilda II
1 British Engineer Company
2nd New Zealand Division:
  Divisional Petrol Company: 2 Bren, 1 Lewis, 1 Boys, c.100 technicians and drivers as infantry (average morale, poor training)
  4th New Zealand Brigade: 18th and 19th Infantry Battalions, 1 Artillery Battery, 1 CS Company, 1 Transport Battalion
  10th New Zealand Brigade: 20th Infantry Battalion, 6th and 8th Greek Infantry Regiments (1 Battalion each), 1 Artillery Battery, Divisional Cavalry Regiment[6]
  5th New Zealand Brigade: 21st, 22nd, 23rd and 28th (Maori) Infantry Battalions, 1st Greek Regiment, 1 Engineer Battalion, 1 Artillery Battery, 1 AA Battery
14th Infantry Brigade:
  3 British Infantry Battalions (2nd Btn Leicestershire Regiment, 2nd Btn York and Lancaster Regiment, 2nd Btn Black Watch – best equipped of units in the Brigade)
  1 Australian Infantry Battalion (2/4th)
  1 Australian Light AA Battery: 40mm Bofors
  1 Artillery Regiment w/ 24 guns

5 Part only.
6 Reduced to 194 men in 3 squadrons serving as infantry on arrival in Crete.

       3 Greek Battalions (3rd and 7th Regiments, plus Garrison Battalion)
19th Australian Infantry Brigade:
       4 Australian Infantry Battalions (2/1st, 2/7th, 2/8th and 2/11th)
       1 MG Company: 6 MMG
       1 Artillery Regiment: 250 gunners serving as infantry
       3 Greek Battalions (4th and 5th Regiments, Gendarmerie Battalion)
6 Reserve Infantry Battalions
2 Reserve Infantry Companies
SOE Detachment: 3 agents, Cretan guerrillas, few arms
805 Squadron, Fleet Air Arm: few Gladiators, Fulmars, Buffalo
30 Squadron, RAF: 18 × Blenheim
203 Squadron, RAF: 9 × Blenheim
33, 80, 112 Squadrons, RAF: totalling 16 × Hurricanes, 6 × Gladiators
Reinforcements during the battle for Crete:
       1 Tank Troop: 3 × Matilda II
       2nd Btn Argyll and Sutherland Highlanders
       A, B and D Battalions, Layforce, each: 250 men, small arms only

Notes

1. The British battalions are the only ones that appear to have possessed a Carrier Platoon.
2. Most Battalions had only 2 × 3" mortars and a few 2" mortars; entrenching tools were scarce, and many were down to 350 men, about half-strength.
3. The Greek Battalions were armed only with rifles, carbines, knives and bayonets. They were organised into 3 Companies, each: of 3 Platoons, plus 1 MG Company of 3 Platoons, the MG crews possessing no MGs. Greek troops should be rated at poor training and average morale.
4. Radios were at Btn HQ and above only.
5. Aircraft units were quickly destroyed or withdrawn within a few days of German air attacks.
6. Artillery totalled 85 guns, including some ex-Italian light artillery without sights. It is known that 47mm/32 A/T field guns were refurbished by the British and used in the war, but whether these were sent to Crete is unknown.

PART 5
FAR EAST, AUSTRALASIAN AND INDIAN THEATRES 1939–LATE 1943

5.1 BRITISH 7TH ARMOURED BRIGADE, 1942, BURMA

The Brigade's main combat elements were:
2 Armoured Regiments (7th Queen's Own Hussars, 11th Hussars)
The Armoured Regiments are rated at average training and good morale, the remaining units average training and average morale.

SUPPORT UNITS

Brigade Support

Armoured Brigade HQ (3 × Stuart I, 3 × Humber Staff Cars, radio van) with:
    414th Artillery Battery:
        D, E Troops, each: 4 × 25pdr guns, 6 trucks, 2 LMG, 2 Boys, radio truck
    1 A/Tank Battery, 95th Anti-Tank Regiment: Battery HQ (1 rifle sec, 1 truck)
        1 Troop: 4 × 2pdr, 5 trucks

MAIN COMBAT ELEMENTS

Armoured Regiment

RHQ (3 × Stuart I, 1–3 × Humber Staff Cars)
3 Squadrons, each: Sqdn HQ (3 × Stuart I)
    4 Troops, each: 3 × Stuart I

Notes
1   Radios were in all tanks and other Pl HQs. Artillery is rated Assigned FC.

5.2 BRITISH AND COMMONWEALTH INDEPENDENT ARMOURED UNITS, 1942–43, VARIOUS THEATRES

Troops are rated at average training and average morale unless otherwise noted.

ARMY-SUPPORT LEVEL

B Squadron, King's Own Hussars, February–March 1942, Java (average training, poor morale)
    Sqdn HQ (3 × Vickers VIB)
        5 Troops, each: 3 × Vickers VIB light tanks
146th Tank Regiment, 1942–43, India[1] (average training, good morale)
    RHQ (4 × Valentine)
    3 Squadrons, each: Sqdn HQ (2 × Valentine III or V)
        2–4 Troops, each: 3 × Valentine III or V
25th Dragoon Regiment, late 1943, India, Burma
    RHQ (4 × M3A3 Lee, 1 × Carrier OP, 3 × Grant ARV Mk.2)
    3 Squadrons, each: Sqdn HQ (4 × M3 Lee)
        4 Troops, each: 3 × M3 Lee
3rd New Zealand Division Special Tank Squadron, June 1943 onwards, training in Guadalcanal[2]
    Sqdn HQ (2 × Valentine III, 2 × Valentine CS, 1 Jeep)
        5 Troops, each: 2 × Valentine III, 1 × Valentine CS
    1 Recce Troop: Troop HQ (1 × Daimler Dingo S/C, 2 Jeeps)
        3 Sections, each: 3 × Daimler S/C
    Field Park: 2 Tank Transporters, 4 × Valentine III, 2 × Valentine III CS,
        3 × Dingo Scout Car (spare vehicles)
Australian 1st Tank Battalion, July 1942–late 1943, Australia
    Btn HQ (4 × Matilda II)
    3 Squadrons, each: Sqdn HQ (3 × Matilda II)
        3 Troops, each: 3 × Matilda II
        2 Troops, each: 3 × Matilda II or (July 1943 onwards) 3 × Matilda II CS
Australian 1st Tank Battalion, late 1943 onwards, Australia, New Guinea
    Btn HQ (4 × Matilda II)
    3 Squadrons, each: Sqdn HQ (3 × Matilda II, 5 Jeeps, 1 × fitter's Carrier)
        5 Troops, each: 2 × Matilda II, 1 × Matilda IICS

---

1   2 Troops of 3 tanks and 2 Sqdn HQ tanks were used in Arakan with the 14th Indian Division, February 1943.
2   2pdr had HE, canister and AP, Valentine CS had 3" howitzer with HE.

5.3 INDIAN INFANTRY DIVISION, 1937-42, INDIA, BURMA, MALAYA

Pre-war India possessed 3 Infantry Divisions, each of 2 Infantry Brigades and 1 Divisional Cavalry Regiment. The 3rd Infantry Division also possessed a Cavalry Brigade of 3 Cavalry Regiments. There were several 'Regions' for home defence, equating to divisions of 2–5 brigades each. Infantry Brigades usually had 1 British and 2 Indian Infantry Battalions, but some varied, and contained up to 8 Battalions (never more than 1 British). About 25% of all Brigades contained a British Artillery Regiment in 1939. Massive expansion of the infantry units meant that by 1941 there tended to be 1 Field or Mountain Artillery Regiment per Division. Morale and training varied enormously, from average training and good morale in the best British units, to poor training and average or poor morale in many units tasked for internal security only. The Gurkhas were an exception to this, maintaining good training and good to excellent morale throughout the period. This list includes corps-level support units.

SUPPORT UNITS

Corps-Level Support Units
Included:
    1 Field Artillery Regiment:[3] RHQ (4 rifle secs, 6 trucks), Assigned FC
        2–3 Batteries, each: Battery HQ (4 rifle secs, 4 lorries)
            2 Troops, each: 4 × 25pdr field guns, 6 trucks, 2 LMG
    1+ Medium Artillery Regiment: RHQ (6 rifle secs, 8 lorries), Assigned FC
        1 Battery: 4 × 5" 60pdr guns, 6 trucks, 2 Lewis MG
        2 Batteries, each: 6 × 6" 26cwt howitzers, 8 trucks, 2 Lewis MG
    3 (increasing to 8 by late 1941) Construction Companies, each: Coy HQ (1 rifle sec, 1 lorry)
        3 Platoons, each: 4 rifle/engineer secs
    Multiple Animal Transport Companies, each:
        3–4 Troops, each: 14 carts, 90 horses/mules/camels
    1+ AA Regiments,[4] each:
        3 Batteries, each: Battery HQ (2 rifle secs, 1 lorry)
            2 Troops, each: 4 × 3.7" AA, 8 lorries, 2 LMG
    1+ Anti-Tank Regiments (1939 onwards):
        3 Batteries, each: Battery HQ (1 rifle sec, 2 trucks, 2 LMG)
            3 Troops, each: 4 × 2pdr, 4 trucks, 4 LMG
    1 Machine Gun Battalion (1939 onwards):
        4 Companies, each: Coy HQ (1 rifle sec, 1 LMG)
            3 Platoons, each: 4 × Vickers MMG, 1 LMG, 4 trucks or pack mules
    2–4 Coastal Artillery Batteries, each:
        2 Troops, each: 2–4 × 4" or 6" naval guns, gunpits, telephones
    1 Bridging Section (June 1941 onwards): pontoons, boats, lorries

Divisional Support
Included:
    1 Indian Mountain Artillery Regiment: RHQ (4 rifle secs, horses)
        4 Batteries, each: 4 × 3.7"pack howitzers, pack mules, 2 Lewis MG
    1 Signals Company: Coy HQ (2 rifle secs)
        1 Operating Section, 1 Cable Laying Section, 1 Pack Cable Section,
        1 Wireless Section
    1 Signals Company: Coy HQ (4 rifle secs)
        2 Infantry Brigade HQ Signals Sections
        2 Artillery HQ Signals Sections
    3 Field Engineer Companies, each: Coy HQ (4 rifle secs, 1 lorry, 2 LMG)
        3 Platoons, each: 5 (12 man) rifle/engineer secs, 1 lorry
    1 Field Park Company: Coy HQ, Workshop Section, Field Stores Section
    1 A/T Battery (1942, Malaya only): Battery HQ (1 rifle sec, 1 truck)
        3 Troops, each: 3–4 × 47/32 Bohler (ex-Italian) A/T guns, trucks, 1 LMG

Brigade Support
    Infantry Brigade HQ (5 rifle secs, horses and lorries) with:
        1 Field Artillery Regiment: RHQ (4 rifle secs, horses), Assigned FC
            2 Batteries, each: 4 × 18pdr field guns, horses, 2 Lewis MG
            2 Batteries, each: 4 × 4.5"L15 QF infantry howitzers, horses, 2 Lewis MG
        OR (new model, 1939 onwards)
        1 Field Artillery Regiment: RHQ (4 rifle squads, 6 trucks), Assigned FC
            2–3 Batteries, each: Battery HQ (4 rifle squads, 4 lorries)
                2 Troops, each: 4 × 25pdr field guns, 6 trucks, 2 LMG

MAIN COMBAT ELEMENTS

Indian Infantry Battalion
    Btn HQ (4 rifle secs)
        3 Companies, each: Coy HQ (2 rifle secs)

---

[3] 1941 onwards.
[4] First one introduced in 1939, increasing to at least 2 in 1941.

64 British and Commonwealth Armies, 1939–43

        4 Platoons, each: 1 (6 man) rifle Pl HQ sec
            1 (10 man) rifle sec with 1 × Vickers-Berthier LMG
            3 (10 man) rifle secs
    1 Machine Gun Company: Coy HQ (1 rifle sec)
        2 Platoons, each: 4 × Vickers MMG, pack horses

British Infantry Battalion
    Btn HQ (4 rifle secs)
        3 Companies, each: Coy HQ (2 rifle secs)
            4 Platoons, each: 1 (6 man) rifle Pl HQ sec,
                1 (10 man) rifle sec with 1 × Lewis LMG
                3 (10 man) rifle secs
        1 Machine Gun Company: Coy HQ (2 rifle secs)
            3 Platoons, each: 4 × Vickers MMG, pack horses

Gurkha Infantry Battalion
    Btn HQ (4 rifle secs, Kukris)
        3 Companies, each: Coy HQ (2 rifle secs, Kukris)
            3 Platoons, each: 1 (6 man) rifle Pl HQ sec, 4 (10 man) rifle secs, Kukris
            1 Platoon: 1 (6 man) rifle Pl HQ sec,
                1 (10 man) rifle sec with 1 × Vickers-Berthier LMG
                3 (10 man) rifle secs
        1 Machine Gun Company: Coy HQ (1 rifle sec)
            2 Platoons, each: 4 × Vickers MMG, pack mules

1939 Model Indian Infantry Battalion For 'Local Defence'
    Btn HQ (4 rifle secs, 1 LMG)
        4 Companies, each: Coy HQ (1 (13 man) rifle sec, 1 × 2" mortar, 1 Boys A/T rifle)
            3 Platoons, each: 1 (6 man) rifle Pl HQ sec,
                3 (10 man) rifle squads, 3 Bren LMG
        1 Support Company: Coy HQ (1 rifle sec)
            1 Platoon: 2 (6 man) rifle/engineer secs, 1 stores truck or pack mules
            1 Scout Platoon: Pl HQ (1 × Bren Carrier or light truck)
                3 Sections, each: 3 × Bren Carrier or light truck, 3 LMG

1939 Model Indian Infantry Battalion For 'External Defence'
    Btn HQ (4 rifle secs, 1 LMG, 1 Boys)
        4 Companies, each: Coy HQ (1 (13 man) rifle sec)
            3 Platoons, each: 1 (6 man) rifle Pl HQ sec, 1 × 2" mortar, 1 Boys
                3 (10 man) rifle secs, 3 Bren LMG
        1 Support Company: Coy HQ (1 rifle sec)
            1 Platoon: 4 × Bren AALMG or 2 × Lewis AAMG, pack mules or 4 trucks, 4 Boys anti-tank rifles
            1 Platoon: 2 × 3" mortars, 2 trucks or 40 pack mules, Assigned FC
            1 Platoon: 3 (6 man) rifle/engineer secs, 1 stores truck or pack mules
            1 Scout Platoon: Pl HQ (1 × Bren Carrier, 1 LMG)
                3 Sections, each: 3 × Bren Carrier, 3 LMG

Divisional Indian Cavalry Regiment
    RHQ (4 rifle secs, horses)
        1 MG Troop: 1 rifle HQ sec, 4 × Vickers MMG, pack mules
        3 Squadrons, each: Sqdn HQ (2 rifle secs, horses, sabres)
            3 Troops, each: 5 (8 man) rifle secs, horses, sabres
            1 Troop: 1 (8 man) rifle HQ sec, horses, sabres,
                4 (6 man) rifle secs, 4 LMG, horses, sabres

Notes
1   Radios were in Btn HQs and above. From 1939 could be down to Coy HQs as well, although this was rarely achieved.
2   Infantry had no A/T grenades.
3   Field Artillery Regiments tended to have 2 Batteries from 1939, with a few having 3 Batteries from November 1941.
4   Whilst most Infantry Battalions were supposed to be converted to the new standard using Brens by 1939, many still had the older organisations with Lewis or Vickers-Berthier LMGs even as late as 1942, and were used in Burma and Malaya. Very few British or Indian units reached the 'External Defence' equipment levels.
5   Cavalry Regiments were supposed to be converting to Mechanised, but a shortage of vehicles prevented this.

5.4 BRITISH INFANTRY DIVISION, 1942–43, ASIA
    The Division's main combat elements were:
        3 Infantry Brigades (each of 3 Infantry Battalions)
        1 Divisional Recce Regiment[5]
This list is typical of British Infantry Divisions that arrived in theatre from Europe after the fall of Singapore and Burma, deployed to India, and became involved in fighting in the Arakan in 1943. Troops are rated at average training and average morale.

---

5   Not present in all divisions.

British and Commonwealth Armies, 1939–43

SUPPORT UNITS

Divisional Support
Included:
- 3 Engineer Companies: Coy HQ (4 (11 man) rifle secs, 1 LMG, 1 Boys, 2 lorries)
    - 3 Platoons, each: 1 (17 man) rifle/engineer Pl HQ sec
    - 4 (12 man) rifle/engineer secs, 4 LMG, 2 lorries
- 1 Field Park Company: Coy HQ (3 rifle/engineer secs, 2 lorries
    - 1 Workshop Platoon: 4 rifle/engineer secs, workshop lorries, gantry cranes
    - 1 Stores Platoon: 3 rifle/engineer secs, explosives, tools, etc
    - 1 Bridging Platoon: 5 rifle/engineer secs, pontoon bridges, etc
- 2–3 AA Batteries, each: Battery HQ (1 rifle sec, 1 truck)
    - 3 Troops, each: 4 × 40mm Bofors, 6 trucks
- 2–3 A/T Batteries, each: Battery HQ (1 rifle sec, 1 truck)
    - 3 Troops, each: 4 × 2pdr, 4 trucks, 2 LMG
- 1 A/T Battery: Battery HQ (1 rifle sec, 1 truck)
    - 3 Troops, each: 4 × 6pdr, 4 trucks, 2 LMG
- 3 Field Artillery Regiments, each:
    - 3 Batteries, each: Battery HQ (1 radio van, 5 trucks, 4 rifle secs, 4 AALMG)
    - 2 Troops, each: 4 × 25pdr, 5 trucks, radio van, 1 Boys, 2 AALMG, OP Team
- 1 Machine Gun Battalion:
    - 4 MG Companies, each: Coy HQ (1 rifle sec)
    - 3 Platoons, each: 4 MMG, 1 Boys A/T rifle, 1 LMG, 4 rifle crew secs

Brigade Support
Infantry Brigade HQ (6 rifle secs, 4 lorries) with:
- 1 Defence Platoon: 4 rifle secs, 3 LMG, 1 × 2" mortar, 1 Boys

MAIN COMBAT ELEMENTS

Infantry Battalion
Btn HQ (5 rifle secs, 1 LMG)
- 4 Companies, each: Coy HQ (1 rifle sec)
    - 3 Platoons, each: 4 rifle secs, 3 LMG, 1 × 2" mortar, 0–1 Boys
- 1 Support Company: Coy HQ (1 rifle sec)
    - 1 Platoon: 6 × 3" mortars, 7 × Universal Carriers
    - 1 Platoon: 2 rifle/engineer secs, 2 trucks, 2 LMG
    - 1 Platoon: Pl HQ (1 × Universal Carrier, 1 × Daimler S/C, 1 LMG)
        - 4 Sections, each: 3 × Carrier, 3 LMG, 1 Boys, 1 × 2", 1 rifle sec
    - 1 Platoon: 4 × twin AALMG, 4 Boys, in 2 rifle crew secs
    - 0–1 Platoon: 4 × 2pdr A/T guns, 4 × Carriers

Divisional Recce Regiment
RHQ (3 rifle secs, 3 LMG, 2 Boys, 3 × Light Recce Car)
- 3 Squadrons, each: Sqdn HQ (3 rifle secs, 1 LMG, 3 trucks, 1 Light Recce Car)
    - 3 Troops, each: HQ (1 × Carrier, 1 LMG, 1 Boys, 1 × 2", 1 × Light Recce Car)
        - 2 Sections, each: 2 × Light Recce Car
        - 2 Sections, each: 3 × Carrier, 1 Boys, 3 LMG, 1 × 2", 1 rifle sec
    - 1 Troop: 4 rifle secs, 4 trucks, 1 Boys, 4 LMG
- 1 Mortar Battery: 6 × 3" mortars, 7 × Universal Carriers
- 1 AA Platoon: 4 × twin AALMG on trucks, 4 Boys
- 1 A/T Troop: 4 × 6pdr A/T guns, 4 × Carriers

Notes
1. Radios were in all Coy HQs and AFVs. All artillery is rated Assigned FC up to July 1942. After that is Flexible FC, with OP teams in truck or Humber S/C.
2. Infantry secs had No.74 or No.75 Hawkins A/T grenades. Boys A/T Rifle was replaced with PIAT from June 1943.
3. Divisional A/T Batteries did not have 6pdr until July 1942, with some units receiving them later than this.
4. Daimler S/C could be replaced with Humber Light Recce Mk II or III.
5. In 1942 25pdr could have AP. From May 1942 the 2pdr had APC, and APCBC from August that year.
6. Light Recce Car is Humber Mk II, III or IIIA, or Morris Light Recce Mk I or Mk II.

5.5 AUSTRALIAN MILITIA DIVISION, 1939–SEPTEMBER 1942, AUSTRALIA

The Division's main combat elements were:
- 3 Militia Brigades (each of 2–4 Militia Force Battalions)

Troops are rated poor training and average morale. There were no support units.

MAIN COMBAT ELEMENTS

Citizen's Militia Force Battalion
Btn HQ (4 rifle secs)
- 4 Companies, each: Coy HQ (1 (13 man) rifle sec)
    - 3 Platoons, each: 1 (7 man) rifle Pl HQ sec
        - 3 (10 man) rifle secs, 3 LMG
- 1 MG Company: Coy HQ (1 rifle sec)
    - 3 Platoons, each: 4 MMG

Notes
1. Infantry had no radios or A/T weapons.
2. In late 1942 many of the Militia were retrained as regular infantry for use in the Pacific theatre, with the MG Companies being stripped out to form Divisional MG Battalions.

5.6 AUSTRALIAN INFANTRY DIVISION, AUGUST 1942 ONWARDS, NEW GUINEA, NEW BRITAIN, BOUGAINVILLE, BORNEO

The Division's main combat elements were:
   3 Infantry Brigades (each of 3 Infantry Battalions)
Note that the number of battalions and brigades under command varied continuously, units being rotated in and out, and attached to non-parental units regularly. Divisional units were often attached to brigade formations. This list also includes the so-called "Jungle Divisions", which came into existence in May 1943, and were regular Infantry Divisions with a higher proportion of supplies carried by boat and air, and reduced support elements. Troops are rated average training and average morale.

SUPPORT UNITS

Divisional Support
Included:
   2 Field Artillery Regiments, each:
      3 Batteries, each: Battery HQ (2 rifle secs, 2 LMG, 4 trucks, 3 OP Teams)
         2 Troops, each: 4 × 25pdr field guns, 6 trucks, 2 LMG
   1 Tank Attack Battery: Battery HQ (1 rifle sec, 1 truck)
      3 Troops, each: 4 × 2pdr, 4 trucks, 2 LMG
   1 Divisional Carrier Company:[6] Coy HQ (3 × Universal Carrier, 1 SMG sec)
      3 Platoons, each: Pl HQ (1 × Carrier, 1 LMG)
         3 Sections, each: 3 × Carrier, 3 LMG, 1 Boys, 1 × 2" mortar, 1 rifle sec
   1 Light AA Battery: Battery HQ (2 rifle secs, 2 trucks)
      3 Troops, each: 4 or 6 × 40mmL60 Bofors
   1 Mountain Artillery Battery:[7]
      Battery HQ (2 rifle secs, 2 LMG, 4 trucks, 3 OP Teams)
      2 Troops, each: 4 × 3.7" Pack Howitzers, mules or trucks, 2 LMG
   2 Independent Companies (excellent training, excellent morale), each: Coy HQ (2 (8 man) rifle secs, 1 (5 man) Medic staff, 4 motorcycles, 1 truck)
      1 Pioneer Section: 1 (18 man) rifle/engineer sec
      3 Platoons, each: Pl HQ (1 (9 man) rifle/SMG sec)
         3 (18 man) rifle/SMG secs, 6 Bren LMG, 3 snipers
   3 Field Engineer Companies, each: Coy HQ (2 rifle secs)
      4 Platoons, each: 4 (12 man) rifle/engineer secs, 1 (17 man) rifle/Pl HQ/engineer sec, 4 LMG, 2 flame-throwers
   1 Field Park Company: stores, bridging, boat sections
   0–1 Pioneer Battalion: 4 Companies
   0–1 Tank Squadron, 1st Tank Battalion:[8]
      Sqdn HQ (3 × Matilda II, 5 Jeeps, 1 × fitter's Carrier)
      5 Troops, each: 2 × Matilda II, 1 × Matilda IICS
   0–1 Machine Gun Battalion:
      HQ Company
         4 Companies, each: Coy HQ (1 rifle sec)
            3 Platoons, each: 4 × Vickers MMG teams
   0–1 Heavy AA Battery:[9] Battery HQ (2 rifle secs, 2 lorries)
      2 Troops, each: 4 × 3.7" AA, 6 lorries

Brigade Support
   Brigade HQ (5 rifle secs, 6 trucks, 1 Jeep)

MAIN COMBAT ELEMENTS

Infantry Battalion
   Btn HQ (4 rifle secs, 1 LMG)
      4 Companies, each: Coy HQ (1 (13 man) rifle sec)
         3 Platoons, each: 1 (7 man) rifle/SMG Pl HQ sec, 1 × 2" mortar
            3 (10 man) rifle secs, 3 LMG
      1 Support Company: Coy HQ (1 rifle sec)
         1 Platoon: 6 × 3" mortars, 7 × Carriers, mules or boats
         1 Platoon: 2 rifle/engineer secs, 2 LMG, mules for stores
         1 Platoon: 4 × Vickers MMG teams, 5 × Carriers or pack mules

---

6   May 1943 onwards.
7   May 1943 onwards.
8   August 1943 onwards.
9   April 1942 onwards.

British and Commonwealth Armies, 1939–43   67

Notes
1 Radios were in all tanks and other Pl HQs.
2 Infantry had no A/T grenades.

5.7 INDIAN 50TH AIRBORNE BRIGADE, OCTOBER 1941–SEPTEMBER 1943, INDIA, BURMA

The Brigade's main combat elements were:
(1941) – 1 British, 1 Gurkha, 1 Indian Airborne Battalion
(October 1942 onwards) – 2 Gurkha, 1 Indian Airborne Battalion
The Brigade was established in October 1941, and saw service in Burma during 1943. Paratroops are rated at good training and good morale, except for the Gurkhas, who are rated at good training and excellent morale.

SUPPORT UNITS

Brigade Support
Airborne Brigade HQ (6 rifle/SMG secs) with:
  1 Engineer Section: 1 (12 man) rifle/engineer sec, 1 LMG

MAIN COMBAT ELEMENTS

Airborne Battalion
Btn HQ (2 rifle secs)
  3 Companies, each: Coy HQ (2 (8 man) rifle secs)
    3 Platoons, each: 1 (6 man) rifle/SMG Pl HQ sec, 3 rifle/SMG secs, 3 LMG, 1 × 2"
  1 Battery: 4 × 3" mortars, Assigned FC

Notes
1 Radios were at Coy HQ and above.
2 Infantry had Type 74 or Type 75 A/T grenades. Gurkhas carried kukri knives.

5.8 INDIAN CAVALRY BRIGADE, 1937–42, INDIA

The Brigade's main combat elements were:
  3 Cavalry Regiments
In addition there were three Independent Cavalry Regiments (two Mechanised), along with the Cavalry Regiments assigned to Infantry Divisions. In theory all Cavalry Regiments were to have been Mechanised in 1940–41, but in practice only two possessed AFVs, the remainder using trucks equipped with LMGs. Some were motorised, and these formed the 3rd Motorised Brigade in 1941. Troops are rated at average training and average morale.

SUPPORT UNITS

Brigade Support
Cavalry Brigade HQ (8 rifle secs, horses and lorries) with:
  1 Signals Troop: Troop HQ (2 rifle secs, 1 field car, 1 truck, horses)
    2 Sections, each: 4 rifle/signals secs, horses, telephones
  1 Royal Horse Artillery Battery (Assigned FC):
    Battery HQ (4 rifle secs, horses, 2 Lewis MG)
      3 Sections, each: 2 × 18pdr field guns, horses

MAIN COMBAT ELEMENTS

Indian Cavalry Regiment
RHQ (4 rifle secs, horses, sabres)
  1 MG Troop: 1 rifle HQ sec, 4 × Vickers MMG, pack horses
  3 Squadrons, each: Sqdn HQ (2 rifle secs, horses, sabres)
    3 Troops, each: 5 (8 man) rifle secs, horses, sabres
    1 Troop: 1 (8 man) rifle HQ sec, 4 (6 man) rifle secs, 4 LMG, horses

Mechanised Cavalry Regiment, North-West Frontier
RHQ (2 × A/C, 2 trucks w/LMG)
  1 Squadron: Sqdn HQ (2 × Vickers VIB Light Tanks, 2 trucks w/LMG)
    3 Troops, each: 4 × Vickers IV Light Tanks
  2 Squadrons, each: Sqdn HQ (2 × A/C, 2 trucks w/LMG)
    3 Troops, each: 3 × A/C

Motorised Cavalry Regiment
RHQ (4 rifle secs, 4 trucks, 4 LMG)
  3 Squadrons, each: Sqdn HQ (1 rifle sec, 1 truck, 1 LMG)
    3 Troops, each: 3 (8 man) rifle secs, 3 trucks, 3 LMG, 1 (6 man) rifle Pl HQ sec, 1 × 2" mortar

Notes
1 Radios were in all RHQ, AFV Pl HQs, and Mechanised/Motorised Sqdn HQs.
2 Troops had no A/T grenades.
3 Armoured Cars were Chevrolet, Indian Pattern, or up to 1939, Rolls-Royce M1921 (1 Squadron only) or Crossley M1923.
4 From 1941 the trucks w/LMGs were replaced with Wheeled Carrier, Indian Pattern Mk.1.

5.9 BRITISH CHINA COMMAND, 1939, HONG KONG, SHANGAI, SINGAPORE

Troops are rated at average training and average morale.

Hong Kong Garrison
8th Coastal Heavy Artillery Regiment
5th Heavy AA Regiment
1st Hong Kong Regiment (local 4x2 armoured cars)
2 Fortress Engineer Companies
Hong Kong Brigade:
    1 British Infantry Battalion (2nd Btn Royal Scots)
    1 Indian Infantry Battalion (Kumaon Rifles, 19th Hyderabad Regiment) (both of these Battalions pre-1939 TOE)
    1 British MG Battalion (1st Btn Middlesex Regiment): 4 Companies, each: 3 Platoons, each: 4 MMG

Shangai Enclave
2 British Infantry Battalions (2nd Btn East Surrey Regiment, 1st Btn Seaforth Highlanders)

Tientsin Enclave
1 British Infantry Battalion (1st Btn Durham Light Infantry)

Singapore Garrison
9 Infantry Battalions (mixed regular, volunteer and local forces)
6 RAF Squadrons with 90 bombers, recce and transports
2 RAF torpedo Bomber Squadrons, each: 12 × Wildebeest

5.10 BRITISH HONG KONG GARRISON, 1940–41

Troops are rated at average training and average morale.

Garrison
8th and 12th Coastal Heavy Artillery Regiments
5th Heavy AA Regiment
1st Hong Kong Defence Corps Medium Artillery Regiment:
    3 Medium Batteries, each: 2 Troops, each: 4 × 60pdr or 62 26cwt howitzers
    2 Mountain Batteries, each: 1 Troop: 4 × 3.7" pack howitzers, 4 trucks
    2 Fortress Engineer Companies
1 Royal Artillery Defence Battery
Hong Kong Brigade:
    1 British Infantry Battalion (2nd Btn Royal Scots)
    1 Indian Infantry Battalion (Kumaon Rifles, 19th Hyderabad Regiment) (both of these Battalions pre-1939 TOE)
    1 British MG Battalion (1st Btn Middlesex Regiment): 4 Companies, each: 3 Platoons, each: 4 MMG
    2 Canadian Infantry Battalions (Royal Rifles of Canada, Winnipeg Grenadiers)
Kowloon Brigade:
    2 Indian Infantry Battalions (5/7th Rajput and 2/14th Punjab Regiments)
    1 British Infantry Battalion (1st Durham Light Infantry)

Hong Kong Volunteer Defence Corps
7 Companies, 2 Platoons
4 Batteries, 1 Signals unit, 1 Armoured Car Platoon (local 4 x2 A/C)
1 Field Engineer Company
1 Heavy AA Battery: 2 Troops, each: 4 × 3" 20cwt AA

5.11 COMMONWEALTH UNITS IN BURMA, DECEMBER 1941–42, BURMA

Initially, the only forces in Burma were the 1st Burma Division – 1st Burma Brigade, of 2nd King's Own Yorkshire Light Infantry[10] and 3 Burma Rifles Battalions (1st, 5th and 7th); the 2nd Burma Brigade was later created – 4 Burma Rifle Battalions (2nd, 4th, 6th, 7th and 8th); 13th Indian Brigade – 1/18th Royal Garwhal Rifles, 2/7th Rajput and 5/1st Punjab Regiments, later joined by the 1st Royal Inniskilling Fusiliers, and 1st King's Own Yorkshire Light Infantry; a battalion of the Gloucesters as resident garrison at Rangoon. At Divisional level there was 1 additional Burma Rifles Battalion.

Forces subsequently sent to Burma amounted to the 17th Indian Infantry Division – 48th Brigade with 3 Gurkha Battalions; 16th Infantry Brigade with 2 Indian and 1 Gurkha battalions; 46th Brigade with 2 British (1st Cameronians, 1st West Yorks) and 2 Indian Infantry Battalions; 63rd Indian Brigade with 2 Indian and 1 Gurkha battalions). Also sent was 1 British Infantry Battalion, the 2nd Battalion Duke of Wellington's Regiment, fully equipped with Boys and mortars. This list includes formations equivalent to corps-level support units.

Gurkhas are rated average training and good morale, British infantry as average training and good morale, Indian and British garrison battalions as poor training and average morale, Burmese Rifles are rated poor training and average/poor morale, with Burma Territorials and Military Police as poor training and poor morale.

---

10   No 2" mortars, no entrenching tools or helmets, only 7 lorries instead of 52 trucks, no radios.

SUPPORT UNITS

Corps-Level Support Units
Included:
- Burmese Auxiliary Force:
  - 4 Burmese Battalions
  - 1 Heavy AA Regiment: 1 Battery: Battery HQ (1 rifle sec, 1 lorry)
  - 2 Troops, each: 4 × 3.7" AA guns, 4 lorries
  - 1 Scout unit: 8 × Rolls-Royce Indian Pattern M1921 A/C
  - 5th Field Battery: 2 Troops, each: 4 × 18pdr field guns, 6 trucks, Obsolete FC
- Burmese Frontier Force – 10 Burmese Border Police Battalions, rifles only
- Burmese Territorial Force – 3 Burma Rifle Battalions[11]
- Burmese Military Police – 3 Burmese Military Police Battalions, small arms only
- RM Commando Viper Force (see list 6.13)
  - 4 Composite Security Sections, each: 4 men, Jeep

Divisional Support
Included:
- 3 Engineer Companies, each: Coy HQ (1 rifle sec, 1 truck)
  - 3 Platoons, each: 4 (12 man) rifle/engineer secs, 2 LMG, 2 lorries
- 1 Engineer Field Park Company: explosives, tools, bridges, 1 bulldozer
- 1 Field Security Section: 14 men, 6' staves, pistols, pump action shotguns, Jeeps
- 1 AA Battery: Battery HQ (1 rifle sec, 1 truck)
  - 2 Troops, each: 4 × 40mmL60 Bofors, 6 trucks

Brigade Support
Infantry Brigade HQ (4 rifle secs, 2 staff cars or Daimler S/C, 3 lorries) with:
- 1 HQ Defence Platoon: 4 rifle secs, 3 LMG, 1 × 2", 1 Boys, 4 trucks
- 1 AA Platoon:[12] 2 × Lewis AALMG
- 1 Indian Artillery Battery: Battery HQ (1 radio van, 4 trucks, 4 rifle secs, 2 AALMG)
  - 2 Troops, each: 4 × 25pdr Mk.2, 5 Quad tractors, radio van, 2 LMG
  - OR 2 Troops, each: 4 × 3.7" Mountain guns, 6 trucks, 2 LMG

MAIN COMBAT ELEMENTS

British Infantry Battalion
Btn HQ (2 rifle secs, 1 staff car, 2 trucks, 5 motorcycles)
- 4 Companies, each: Coy HQ (1 (13 man) rifle sec, 1 lorry)
  - 3 Platoons, each: 1 (7 man) Pl HQ rifle sec, 1 Boys, 0–1 × 2" mortar
    - 3 (10 man) rifle secs, 3 LMG, 3 lorries
- 1 Support Company: Coy HQ (1 rifle sec, 1 truck)
  - 1 Platoon: 4 × 3" mortars, 2 trucks, radio truck OR 40 pack mules
  - 1 Platoon: 4 × twin AALMG, 4 trucks
  - 1 Platoon: 2 rifle/engineer secs, 1 lorry
  - 1 Platoon:[13] Pl HQ (1 × Bren Carrier, 1 LMG)
    - 3 Sections, each: 3 × Bren Carrier, 3 LMG, 1 (9 man) rifle crew sec

British Garrison Infantry Battalion
Btn HQ (4 rifle secs)
- 3 Companies, each: Coy HQ (2 rifle secs)
  - 4 Platoons, each: 1 (6 man) rifle Pl HQ sec,
    - 2 (10 man) rifle sec, each with 1 × Lewis LMG
    - 2 (10 man) rifle secs
- 1 Machine Gun Company: Coy HQ (2 rifle secs)
  - 3 Platoons, each: 4 × Vickers MMG, pack horses

Gurkha Infantry Battalion
Btn HQ (4 rifle secs, Kukris)
- 3 Companies, each: Coy HQ (2 rifle secs, Kukris)
  - 3 Platoons, each: 1 (6 man) rifle Pl HQ sec, 4 (10 man) rifle secs, Kukris, 3 LMG
- 1 Machine Gun Company: Coy HQ (1 rifle sec)
  - 2 Platoons, each: 4 × Vickers MMG, pack mules
- 1 AA Platoon: 4 × Bren AALMG

Indian Infantry Battalion
Btn HQ (4 rifle secs, 1 LMG)
- 4 Companies, each: Coy HQ (1 (13 man) rifle sec, 1 × 2" mortar, 1 Boys A/T rifle)
  - 3 Platoons, each: 1 (6 man) rifle Pl HQ sec,
    - 3 (10 man) rifle secs, 3 Bren LMG

---

11 Lines-of-communication guards.
12 Gurkha Brigade only.
13 1942 only.

1 Support Company: Coy HQ (1 rifle sec)
   1 Platoon: 2 (6 man) rifle/engineer secs, 1 stores truck or pack mules
   1 Platoon: 2 Lewis AAMG
   0–1 Platoon: 2 × 3" mortars, 1 truck, Obsolete FC
   0–1 Scout Platoon: Pl HQ (1 × Bren Carrier or light truck)
      3 Sections, each: 3 × Bren Carrier or light truck, 3 LMG

Burmese Battalion

Btn HQ (2 rifle secs, 1 truck)
   3 Companies, each: Coy HQ (1 rifle sec)
      3 Platoons, each: 3 rifle secs, 2 LMG, 0–1 × 2" mortar
   1 Battery: 0–2 × 3" mortars, pack mules, Obsolete FC
   1 MG Platoon: 4 × Vickers MMG, pack mules
   1 AA Platoon: 2 × Lewis LMG

Gloucesters Infantry Battalion, March–May 1942

Btn HQ (2 rifle secs, 1 staff car, 4 trucks, 20 motorcycles)
   4 Companies, each: Coy HQ (1 (9 man) rifle sec, 1 lorry, 1 Jeep or field car)
      3 Platoons, each: 1 (4 man) Pl HQ rifle sec, 2 × 2" mortar, 2 Boys,
         3 (7 man) rifle secs, 6 LMG, 3 lorries
   1 Support Company: Coy HQ (1 rifle sec, 1 truck)
      1 Battery: 8 × Scout Cars w/3" mortar fitted, 1 Jeep, Assigned FC
      1 Platoon: 4 × AALMG, 4 trucks
      1 Platoon: 2 rifle/engineer secs, 1 lorry, 2 launches on 3t lorries
      1 Platoon: 2 × Italian Breda guns, 2 Jeeps, trucks with 1000 rounds
      1 Platoon: Pl HQ (3 × Bren Carrier, 1 LMG, 3 crew)
         3 Sections, each: 3 × Bren Carrier, 3 LMG, 1 (9 man) rifle crew sec
         2 Scout Sections, each: 4 × Ex-Burmese Rolls-Royce Indian Pattern M1921 armoured cars

Notes
1   Radios were in Btn HQ and Battery HQ above only, and many were carried on pack mules.
2   Infantry had no A/T grenades.
3   Only the 48th and 63rd Brigades had 25pdr guns, the remainder had 3.7" mountain guns.
4   Field Security men were tasked with intelligence-gathering and rear area security.
5   The Gloucesters were organised as a normal infantry battalion but without any Carriers, few grenades and no 3" mortar ammo until 1942. Stationed in Rangoon, it was able to loot Lend-Lease stores bound for the Chinese just before evacuation of the city in March 1942, hence the separate organisation noted above. The Breda guns may be 37mm AA types or most likely ex-Italian 47mm/32 anti-tank guns sent from the Middle East.

5.12 MALAYA AND SINGAPORE GARRISONS, 1942

Most troops should be rated poor training and average to poor morale. The Australians received untrained replacements in January 1942 that diluted them to poor training and poor morale.

3rd Indian Corps HQ

1 Army Engineer Company
2 Bridging Sections, Indian Engineers: pontoon bridges
2 Indian Pioneer Battalions
80th A/T Regiment: 4 Batteries, each:
   3 Troops, each: 3–4 × 47/32 Bohler (ex-Italian), trucks, 1 LMG
1st Indian Heavy AA Regiment:
   3 Heavy AA Batteries, each: 2 Troops, each: 4 × 3" 20cwt or 3.7" AA guns
   1 Light AA Battery: 3 Troops, each: 4 × 40mmL60 Bofors
1 Australian MG Battalion: 4 MG Companies, each: 12 × MMG

9th Indian Infantry Division

88th and 5th Field Artillery Regiments, each: 3 Batteries
1 Field Park Company
1 Field Engineer Company
8th Indian Infantry Brigade:
   4 Indian Infantry Battalions (2/18th Royal Garwhal Rifles, 2/10th Baluch, 3/17th Dogra Regiments and
      10/18th Royal Garwhal Rifles
   1 Mountain Battery (1½ Troops)
   1 Engineer Company
22nd Indian Infantry Brigade:
   2 Indian Infantry Battalions (5/11th Sikh Regiment, 2/18th Royal Garwhal Rifles)
   ½ Troop, Indian Mountain Artillery
   1 Engineer Company

11th Indian Infantry Division

3rd Cavalry Recce Regiment:
   3 Squadrons, each:[14] 12 × Marmon-Herrington w/Vickers MMG

---

14   In February 1942, the unit also received some Universal Carriers.

2 British Field Artillery Regiments, each: 3 Batteries[15]
1 Indian Mountain Artillery Regiment: 3 Batteries[16]
3 Field Engineer Companies[17]
1 British MG Battalion: 4 Companies, each: 3 Platoons, each: 4 MMG
1 Field Park Company
Plymouth Argylls' Battalion:
    Btn HQ (2 rifle secs)
        2 Scottish Argylls' Companies[18]
        C, D Companies, each: Royal Marines from Rose Force, w/small number of Boys
        Support Company:
            2 × A/C, 2 × Bren Carriers, 2 × 3" mortars
            Multiple 'Tiger Patrols', each: 1 officer, 2 Marines
6th Indian Infantry Brigade:
    2 Indian Infantry Battalions 1/8th and 2/16th Punjab Regiments)
    1 British Infantry Battalion (2nd East Surrey Regiment)
    1 Engineer Company
12th Indian Infantry Brigade:
    4 Indian Infantry Battalions (5/14th Punjab, 5/2nd Punjab, 4/19th Hyderabad and 3/16th Punjab Regiments)
    1 Field Artillery Regiment: 2 Batteries
    1 Engineer Company
15th Indian Infantry Brigade:
    3 Indian Infantry Battalions (1/14th Punjab, 2.9th Jat and 3/16th Punjab Regiments)
    2 Gurkha Battalions (2/1st and 2/2nd Gurkha Rifles)
    1 Engineer Company

28th Indian Infantry Brigade
3 Gurkha Battalions (2/1st, 2/2nd, 2/9th Gurkha Rifles)
3 Indian Infantry Battalions (2/16th Punjab, 3/17th Dogra and 5/14th Punjab Regiments)

8th Australian Infantry Division
22nd and 27th Infantry Brigades, each:
    3 Infantry Battalions (22nd – 2/18th, 2/19th and 2/20th Infantry Battalions; 27th – 2/26th, 2/29th and 2/30th Infantry Battalions)
    1 Engineer Company
2 Field Arty Regiments
4th A/T Regiment:
    1 Battery: 2pdrs
    1 Battery: 26 × 75mm M1897, but no ammunition
    1 Battery: 47/32 M35 ex-Italian, sent from Middle East
    1 Engineer Park Company
Special Reserve Battalion: Service Personnel w/rifles
3rd Transport Company (good training, good morale)

1st Malay Infantry Brigade
1st Malay Regular Infantry Regiment[19] and 1 British Infantry Battalion, each:
    3 Companies, each: Coy HQ (1 rifle sec, 1 × 2" mortar)
        3 Platoons, each: 1 (6 man) rifle Pl HQ sec, 2 rifle secs, 2 Lewis MGs
    1 A/T Platoon: 1 or more Bofors 37mm ATG

2nd Malay Infantry Brigade
1 British MG Battalion (1st Manchesters)
1 British Infantry Battalion (2nd Gordon Highlanders)
1 Indian Infantry Battalion (2/17th Dogra Regiment)
Singapore Straits Settlements Volunteer Force: 4 Infantry Battalions
Federated Malay States Volunteer Force ('James Force'): 4 Battalions

Additional garrison troops
A/C Company, Federated Malay States Volunteer Force[20]
1 Light Field Battery, Federated Malay States Volunteer Force: 8 × 18pdrs
Johore Volunteer Engineer Company
1 Mobile Coastal Defence Artillery Regiment
3 Coastal Defence Artillery Regiments sharing 5 × 15" guns, 6 × 9.2" guns, 18 × 6" guns, very limited HE rounds, remainder of ammunition was AP
2 Heavy AA Regiments, HKSA
1 Independent HAA Battery, HKSA

---

15   Possibly equipped with 25pdrs.
16   Possibly equipped with 3.7" pack howitzers.
17   2 attached from corps.
18   At half-strength, and with a small number of Boys A/T rifles.
19   1 Battalion.
20   Possibly equipped with Lanchester A/C.

1 Light AA Regiment, HKSA
2 AA Regiments (airfield defence – ad hoc units)
2nd Indian AA Regiment
56th Light AA Regiment
35th Light AA Regiment: 24 × 40mm Bofors
5th Searchlight Regiment
3 Fortress Engineer Companies
8 Coast Watcher Sections, each: 3 men w/telephone
5 Indian State Frontier Infantry Battalions
1 Indian Infantry Battalion (Penang fortress)
1 British Armoured Train: 1 Platoon, 2/16th Punjab infantry, 1 Sappers and Miners section
24th New Zealand Construction Company: 160 pioneers
Dalforce – 4,000 Chinese troops recruited locally, poorly equipped
1st Indian Independent Company (Commandos): 301 men
Dutch Commando Unit: Coy HQ (1 (11 man) rifle/engineer sec)
    2 Platoons, each: 40 native jungle troops, SMG, explosives
    1 Platoon: 40 ex-convict porters
SOE Malaya, included:
    Field Security Death Squad: 5+ men, COIN tasks
44th Indian Infantry Brigade:
    3 Indian Infantry Battalions, recently raised, of poor quality (6/1st, 7/8th and 6/14th Punjab Regiments)
45th Indian Infantry Brigade:
    3 Indian Infantry Battalions, recently raised, of poor quality (7/6th Rajputana Rifles, 4/9th Jat Regiment, 5/18th Royal Garwhal Rifles)
    1 Eng Coy
18th British Infantry Division:[21]
    148th and 118th Field Artillery Regiments, each: 3 Batteries, each: 8 × 25pdrs
    135th Field Artillery Regiment: 2 Batteries, each: 8 × 25pdrs
        1 Battery: 8 × 4.5" QF infantry howitzers
    125th A/T Regt: 1 Battery: 4 × 2pdrs
        3 Batteries, each: Battery HQ (1 rifle sec)
            3 Troops, each: 4 (6 man) rifle secs
    18th Battalion Recce Corps
    3 Field Engineer Companies
    1 Field Park Company
    53rd, 54th and 55th Brigades, each: 3–4 British Infantry Battalions (53rd – 5th, 6th and 7th Royal Norfolks, 2nd Cambridgeshire Regiment; 54th – 4th Royal Norfolk, 4th and 5th Suffolks; 55th – 5th Bedfordshire and Hertfordshire Regiment, 1st and 2nd Cambridgeshire Regiment, 1/5th Foresters)
6th HAA Regiment:[22] 3rd Battery: 2 Troops, each: 4 × 3.7" AA
HQ Troop: 1 air search radar
85th A/T Regiment: 3 Batteries, each: 12 × 2pdrs
100th Independent Light Tank Squadron:
    Sqdn HQ (3 × Vickers Light Tank)
        5 Troops, each: 3 × Vickers Light Tank Mk IV and Mk VIB
        1 Reserve Troop: 5 × Vickers Light Tank Mk IV and Mk VIB

RAF support available

    2 Torpedo Bomber Squadrons, each: 12 × Wildebeest
    2 Australian Maritime Recce/Bomber Squadrons, each: 12 × Hudson II
    5 Fighter Squadrons, each: 12 × Brewster Buffalo
    4 Bomber Squadrons, each: 12 × Blenheim I
    1 MR Flight: 3 × Catalina
    Reserve: 88 aircraft
    5 air search radars
    232 Squadron, RAF[23]

Notes

1   Most Infantry Battalions had only 4 × 2" mortars and 2–6 Boys, only 1 radio per battalion, and thus followed the 1939 standard 'Local Defence' organisation. 1 Gurkha Battalion had 2 Boys plus Molotovs. Only 1 Indian Battalion had a full complement of 16 Boys. Most Indian Infantry had not even seen a tank before January 1942.

2   RAF had the following mustard gas assets by mid 1941:
300 × 500lb SCI spray tanks in converted smoke screen layers
500 × 250lb bombs, 4000 × 30lb bombs
The army had 11,800 × 25pdr mustard gas shells by September 1941

---

21   February 1942 only.
22   February 1942 only.
23   February 1942 onwards.

5.13 JAVA GARRISON, FEBRUARY–MARCH 1942

The following units were en route to Singapore when it surrendered and were diverted to Java instead.
B Squadron, 3rd Hussars: Vickers Light Tanks, from Cyprus garrison
77th Heavy AA Regiment
6th HAA Regiment: 2 Batteries, each: 12 × 3" 20cwt
21st and 48th Light AA Regiments, each: 2 Batteries, each: 12 × 40mm Bofors
RAF HQ Wing
Troops are rated at average training and average morale.

5.14 NEW ZEALAND GARRISONS, 1939–45, PACIFIC ISLANDS

Troops are rated at average training and good morale, except for Fijian Commandos, who are rated at good training and good morale.

Fanning Islands, 1939–May 1942
1 Infantry Platoon, later increased to 1 Infantry Company

Tonga
Tongan Defence Force (1 Infantry Platoon)
34th New Zealand Infantry Battalion (October 1942–March 1943)
16th New Zealand Brigade Group (April–December 1943):
   6th New Zealand Infantry Battalion
   1st and 2nd Tongan Infantry Battalions
   1 New Zealand Battery: 6 × 6" guns

Norfolk Island
September 1942–March 1943:
   36th New Zealand Infantry Battalion
   1 Engineer Detachment
   1 Battery, New Zealand Artillery: 4 × 155mm guns
   215th Composite New Zealand AA Battery: Battery HQ (1 rifle sec)
      1 Troop: 4 × 3.7" AA
      2 Troops, each: 4 × 40mmL60 Bofors
   1 New Zealand Field Artillery Troop: 4 × 25pdr field guns
April 1943 onwards:
   2nd New Zealand Infantry Battalion

Florida Island
1st Battalion, Fiji Regiment (April 1942–February 1943)
1st Fiji Commando (October–November 1943)
2nd Fiji Commando (November 1943 onwards)

Kolombangara Island
1st Battalion, Fiji Regiment (October–December 1943)

New Georgia Island
1st Fiji Commando (June–August 1943)

Solomon Islands
September–October 1943:
   British Solomon Islands Protectorate Defence Force – equivalent of 5 Platoons
   30th New Zealand Infantry Battalion
   35th and 37th New Zealand Infantry Battalion Groups:
      New Zealand Infantry Battalion
      12th New Zealand Field Artillery Battery: 2 Troops, each: 4 × 25pdrs
      1 Light AA Troop: 4 × 40mm Bofors
      1 A/T Troop: 4 × 2pdrs
      1 Engineer Detachment: 1 (12 man) rifle/engineer sec
      2–3 MMG Platoons, each: 4 × Vickers MMG

Fiji
December 1941:
   Local Fijian forces
      2nd New Zealand Expeditionary Force:
         8th New Zealand Infantry Brigade:
            3 Infantry Battalions (29th, 34th and 36th)
            1 Field Battery
            1 Field Engineer Company
January–December 1942:
   Local Fijian forces
      3rd New Zealand Division:
         8th New Zealand Infantry Brigade:
            2 Infantry Battalions
            1 Engineer Coy

1 Battery: 4 × 18pdr, 4 × 25pdr, 4 × 4.5" howitzers, 4 × 3.7" howitzers)
14th New Zealand Infantry Brigade:
3 Infantry Battalions (30th, 35th and 37th)
1 Mixed AA Battery
1 Engineer Company
1 Battery: 4 × 18pdrs, 4 × 4.5" howitzers, 4 × 3.7" howitzers

December 1942 onwards:
Local Fijian forces
New Zealand Engineers
2 mixed New Zealand AA Batteries

5.15 PACIFIC ISLANDS NATIVE FORCES, 1941–43

Troops are rated at average training and good morale, except for Fijian Commandos, who are rated at good training and good morale.

Fiji Islands Infantry Brigade 1941–42
1 Regular Infantry Battalion
1 Territorial Infantry Battalion: 4 Companies
1 Fijian Home Guard Battalion
1 Fijian Heavy Artillery Regiment: 3 Fixed Coastal Batteries

Fijian Local Forces, December 1942
1 Fijian Heavy Artillery Regiment: 3 Fixed Coastal Batteries
1 Fijian Territorial Infantry Battalion: 4 Companies
2 Fijian Labour Battalions
Fijian Home Guard
Fijian Bridge Guards
1 Fijian Infantry Brigade Group:
1 Field Battery
1 Signals Section
3 Infantry Battalions
3 Independent Commandos
1 Bearer Company, Medical Corps
Instruction School

Fijian Commando, 1943
Btn HQ (2 (11 man) rifle/SMG secs)
2 Companies, each: Coy HQ (1 (9 man) rifle/SMG sec)
3 Platoons, each: 3 (7 man) rifle/SMG secs, 3 LMG
1 (1 man) Pl HQ NCO

New Guinea
New Guinea Volunteer Rifles
Papuan Infantry Battalion

PART 6
SPECIAL FORCES, ALL THEATRES
1939-43

6.1 BRITISH INDEPENDENT COMPANIES, APRIL 1940-41, NORTH-WEST EUROPE
In April 1940 there were 10 Independent Companies, each of 289 volunteers. 5 Companies deployed in Norway, others raided France and Guernsey June–July 1941. They were organised into Platoons and Sections, armed with rifles and some Bren LMGs. At least one Company 'acquired' a 3" mortar in 1941. Troops are rated at good training and good morale.

6.2 BRITISH COMMANDO FORCES 1940-43
All are rated at good training and good morale up to late 1942, excellent training and excellent morale thereafter.

Special Service Brigade, Late 1940–March 1941
    10 Commando Battalions (good training, good morale), each:
      10 Troops, each: Troop HQ (1 (4 man) SMG sec, radio)
        2 Sections, each: 1 (3 man) SMG HQ sec
        1 (10 man) rifle sec, 1 × 2" mortar, 1 Boys
        1 (10 man) rifle sec, 1+ Bren LMG
      1–2 Boat Sections, each: 1 (6 man) SMG sec, folding boats, explosives
Details of specific units:
    3 Commando (July 1940): 150 men
    6 Commando Battalion, July 1940, Kent:
      9 Troops, each: Troop HQ (1 (4 man) SMG sec, radio)
        2 Sections, each: 1 (3 man) SMG HQ sec
          1 (10 man) rifle sec, 1 × 2" mortar, 1 Boys
          1 (10 man) rifle sec, 1+ Bren LMG, molotovs
      1 Special Boat Section:[1] 2 (10 man) SMG secs, 10 folding boats, 2 Bren LMG
      1 Troop: 1 × 4.7" gun, 50 crew
Only 4 Commandos (7, 8, 11, 12) had Boat Sections of up to 20 men with folding boats, explosives, Thompson SMG. 1 Boat Section was used in Norway in November 1940. 8 Commando had 1 SBS Section of 16 men during winter 1940, these being sent to the Middle East in February 1941.

Raid On Lofeten Islands, Norway, Early 1941
    3, 4 Commando, each: 250 men
    Attached engineers: 52 men
    Free Norwegians: 50 men
    HMS Princess Beatrix LSI (carrying LCA)
    HMS Queen Emma LSI (carrying LCA)
    5 × Destroyers
    HMS Sunfish submarine

Commandos 1-12, 1941-42
In March 1941 Commandos 1–12 were formed from the Special Service Brigade:
    12 Army Commandos, each:
      Btn HQ (1 SMG sec, radio)
        1 Boat Section:[2] 6 men, folding boats, SMGs
        5 Troops, each: Troop HQ (1 (4 man) SMG sec, radio)
          2 Sections, each: 2 (10 man) rifle/SMG secs, 3 LMG, 1 Boys, 3 × 2" mortars, 1 (3 man) rifle/SMG HQ sec
In practise at least 1 Troop at least had a 3" mortar by December 1941. In 1941 12 Commando consisted of 12 Bren LMG and 223 men

30 Commando, Special Engineering Unit, Mid 1941-43
    HQ, 2 Troops, each: wreck divers and intelligence experts tasked with recovery of military documents; used in Sicily

Raid On Vaasgo, Norway, December 1941
    3 Commando: 4 Troops, each: 50 men
      1 Troop: 50 men, 1 × 3" mortar

---

1   Renamed 101 Troop, November 1940.
2   Only in 7, 8, 11, 12 Commando.

4th Troop, 2 Commando: 50 men
Royal Engineer Section from 6 Commando
RAMC medics from 4 Commando
Intelligence officers and press team
HMS Prince Leopard
HMS Prince Charles
4 × Destroyers (inc. HMS Oribi, Onslow)
HMS Tuna (submarine)
HMS Kenya (light cruiser)
3 × Hampden bombers with smoke bombs
3 × Coastal Command Blenheim bombers with smoke bombs
Additional Blenheim IF and Beaufighters as top cover

Commando Forces Used In Raid On Dieppe, August 1942
40 RM Commando: HQ, A, B, × Companies
#1, #2, #3 RM Demolition Parties

Special Service Brigade, 1943
12 Army Commandos, each:
  Btn HQ (7 rifle/SMG secs, 35 cycles, 1 car, 6 Jeeps, 8 15cwt trucks, 3 3t trucks, 1 15cwt water tanker)
    1 Signals Platoon: 21 men
    5 Troops, each: Troop HQ (1 (6 man) SMG sec)
      2 Sections, each: 1 (2 man) rifle/SMG HQ sec,
        2 (14 man) rifle/SMG secs, 3 LMG, 2 Boys, 1 × 2" mortar
    1 Heavy Weapons Troop: 1 (6 man) rifle/SMG HQ sec, 12 Jeeps
      1 Section: 2 × 3" mortars, 17 crew
      1 Section: 2 × Vickers MMG, 16 men
Mountain and Snow Warfare Camp (Arctic training)
40, 41 RM Commandos
US 2nd Rangers (attached)
SBS
COPP
Landing Craft Obstruction Clearance Unit: Naval Commando Divers trained to clear harbours of floating obstructions. By August 1943 there were 6 units, each of 73 men
14 Commando (Arctic Circle trained): 6 men at least, including Canadians and Native American Indians, raided North Norway harbour
By July 1943 PIATs were replacing the Boys, and were used in Sicily.

Layforce, March–August 1941, Middle East
7, 8, 11 Commandos in Egypt/North Africa.
1 Troop of 60 men remained in 8th Army HQ reserve as Middle East Commando, making a raid on Rommel's HQ in November 1941.

Middle East Commandos, 1941
7 Commando was designated A Battalion, 6th Division in April 1941 for raid on Bardia
May–Sept 1941 – 11 Commando: 5 Companies, each: 2 Troops, each: 50 men. Sent to Cyprus, raided Syria in June.
7 and 8 Commando, approximately 500 men in total, were sent to Crete; remnants sent to North Africa after the fall of Crete.
50 and 52 Middle East Commandos were raised in Egypt in early 1941, as D Battalion, 6th Division; they employed camels. Disbanded summer 1941, the survivors were transferred to other Middle East-based Commando units.

Royal Marine Commandos, February 1942–43
1 Royal Marine Commando (250 men):
  HQ
  Signals Platoon
  Demolition Platoon
  Close Support Platoon
  A, B, × Companies
In August 1942 it was renamed 40 RM Commando and organised as per an Army Commando with 367 men. A second Commando was formed in October 1942:
  5 Troops, each: Troop HQ (1 man)
    2 Sections, each: HQ (1 man)
      2 Sub-sections, each: 15 men, rifles, 1 LMG, 1 Boys, 1 × 2"

Army Commandos In Tunisia, November 1942–43
3 Army Commandos (excellent training, excellent morale), each:
  Btn HQ (6 rifle/SMG secs)
    5 Troops, each: Troop HQ (1 (6 man) SMG sec)
      2 Sections, each: HQ (2 men)
        2 (14 man) rifle/SMG secs, 3 LMG, 1 × 2" mortar
    1 Signals Platoon: 21 men

10 Inter-Allied Commando, July 1942–43

1st Troop: 67 French (15 men served at Dieppe)
2nd Troop: 84 Dutch (In training until December 1943)
3rd Troop: British
4th Troop: Belgian
5th Troop: Norwegian (Raided Norway November 1942–March 1943)
6th Troop: Polish (February 1943 onwards, training in Algeria until September 1943)
7th Troop: 16 Yugoslavs (August 1942 onwards, served in the Mediterranean)
8th Troop: French (June 1943 onwards, in training)
9th Troop: British, with K-Gun Section of French
X-Troop: Germans, Austrians, Hungarians, Greeks

6.3 ROYAL MARINE UNITS

7th Royal Marine Battalion/No. 31 Brick, January–July 1943, Egypt

Restructured as No.31 Brick, used to develop the landing of supplies. Troops are rated at good training and good morale except for Baluchi Rifle Companies, who are rated at average training and good morale.

HQ: 4 rifle secs, motorcycle dispatch riders, supply trucks
Signals Platoon
HQ Defence Company:
    1 Battery: 6 × 3" mortars, 6 × Universal Carriers
3 Marine Rifle Companies (used as working parties)
3 Baluchi Rifles Companies (used as working parties)
3 other Rifle Companies (used as working parties)
1 AA Group: HQ room
1 Field Engineer Company: 1 section of bulldozer crews
RASC Transport Platoons, each: supply lorries
Recovery and Repair unit: workshop lorries, recovery vehicle
1 Provost Company (MPs): 52 Marines, 52 Army MPs

Royal Marine Boom Patrol Detachment

Also known as the 'Cockleshell Heroes': 1 or more 12 man sections in canoes or kayaks, Europe and Middle East, 1942, some equipped with 1,600km range radios for surveillance in Greek islands. Rated at excellent training and excellent morale.

Royal Marine 11th Battalion, Crete And Tobruk Raids, April–October 1942,

Organisation as a typical infantry battalion with rifles and some Bren LMG. Rated at average training and good morale.

Force Henry, April 1940, Norway

Troops are rated at good training and good morale except for the platoons of sailors, who are rated at average training and average morale.
A total of 350 men in:
    2 Cruiser Detachments, each:
        2 Seamen Platoons: sailors
        2 Royal Marine Platoons
        1 Royal Marine Machine Gun Section: Lewis MGs
        1 Naval Demolition Squad: explosives

Primrose Force, April 1940, Norway

A total of 725 Marines and Sailors in detachments from 3 Battleships, plus Royal Marine 21st LAA Battery. Troops are rated at good training and good morale.
    21st RM LAA Battery: 8 × 20mm 2pdr pom-poms
    6 Marine Platoons, each: 2 × Lewis MG, 3 rifle secs
    1 Naval ad-hoc AA Battery: 6 × 20mm Oerlikon
    1 Coastal Section: 2 × 4" naval guns – incomplete
    1 Coastal AA Section: 2 × 3" 20cwt AA – incomplete
    RM Howitzer Battery: 4 × 3.7" Pack Howitzers, 131 crew

Hook Of Holland Marine Company A, May 12th 1940, Holland

This unit briefly served to assist Dutch forces. 200 men, 2 Bren LMG, 5 Boys. Rated at good training and good morale.

Royal Marine Siege Battery, 1940–Autumn 1942, Kent, England

This unit was employed in shelling France across the Channel from Kent. Rated at average training and average morale.
    A Battery: 1 × 14" gun Mk VII 'Winnie',[3] 1 × 14" gun 'Pooh'[4]

---

[3] August 1940–Autumn 1942.
[4] December 1940–Autumn 1942.

1 Defence Company (using gun crews):
    1 Section: 1 × 75mm M1897A4 field gun, 4 rifle secs
    2 Platoons, each: 4 rifle secs, 3 × Blacker Bombards
    1 Platoon: 5 Vickers MMG, 5 rifle crew secs
    1 Battery: 6 × 3" mortars, 3 rifle crew secs
B Battery: 3 × 13.5" rail guns[5]

32nd Royal Marine Howitzer Battery, 1941, Shetlands

Rated at average training and good morale.
    4 × 3.7" pack howitzers

19th Royal Marine Battalion, May 1940–43, Scapa Flow

Rated at good training and average morale.
    5 Construction Companies (including W and D Companies)
        1 Section, W Company:[6] Boom Defence Scaffolding Unit: Sea-fire coastal defences (spreading petrol on sea in event of naval landing). In 1942 they launched 20' diameter hydrogen balloons from England with trailing wires to short-circuit German power cables or "sabotage" materials.

6.4 ROYAL MARINE NAVAL BASE DEFENCE ORGANISATION 1 (MNBD01), JUNE 1940–FEBRUARY 1941, BRITAIN

The unit's main combat elements were:
    1 Land Defence Force Marine Battalion
    1 AA Brigade (of 2 AA Regiments)
    1 Coastal Defence Artillery Brigade
Troops are rated at good training and good morale.

SUPPORT UNITS

Included:
    1 Gun Location Unit: Observers
    1 Survey Unit: 30 men
    1 MP Company
    11th RM Searchlight Regiment:
        RHQ (2 (11 man) rifle secs)
            2 Batteries, each: Battery HQ (4 (9 man) rifle secs, 1 Workshop Section)
                4 Sections, each: HQ (1 (6 man) rifle sec)
                      2 Clusters, each: 3 searchlights on Guy lorries, 3 (9 man) rifle secs, 1 (8 man) HQ sec
    1 Landing Company: ship's cutters, whalers, 145 men
    1 Boat Company: wooden LCAs
    1 Signals Company
    1 Workshop Company
    1 Transport Company
    1 RM Quick Firing Regiment[7]
        41st, 42nd, 43rd Batteries, each: 8 × 12pdr Portées (naval AA guns on lorries),
            4 × WW1 6pdr tank guns on towed mounts
            4 × 15cwt trucks, 171 crew men

MAIN COMBAT ELEMENTS

11th Royal Marine Battalion

A total of 427 men and 20 MG in 3 Companies, each including a HQ and 3 Platoons, including a Support Platoon.

1st, 2nd Royal Marine AA Regiments,

Each:
    HQ
        2 Batteries, each: Battery HQ (1 rifle sec)
            2 Troops, each: 4 × 3" 20cwt AA, 4 trucks; later 3.7" AA, with radar and predictor, 1 × Vickers MMG or 4 × twin Lewis AAMG w/shields
        1 Light AA Battery: Battery HQ (2 (8 man) rifle secs)
            2 Troops, each: 4 × 40mm 2pdr pom-poms or (1941 onwards) 40mmL60 Bofors
            2 Troops, each: 4 × 40mmL60 Bofors or 20mm Oerlikon, 52 crew

Coastal Artillery Brigade

    4 Batteries, each: Battery HQ (64 men)
        2 Sections, each: 2 × 6" naval guns, 30 crew
        Line and Maintenance Section: 21 men w/Lewis AAMG

---

5   September 1940–Autumn 1942.
6   Late 1941–42.
7   May–July 1940 only.

2 Batteries, each: 4 × 4" naval guns w/wheeled mounts, 100 crew
1st Anti-Motor Torpedo Boat Battery: 4 × 40mm 2pdr pom-poms, later 40mm Bofors

Notes
1. Radios were in all Coy HQs. Artillery is rated Obsolete FC.
2. 21st Light AA Battery, with 8 × 2pdr pom-poms, was deployed in Norway, April 1940; a 4" coastal battery was deployed in Iceland in 1940. In May 1941 part of it was re-deployed to Crete, the remainder to Egypt.
3. The 11th Battalion was deployed in Egypt for most of 1941–42, being misused as pioneers, until one company was used in a raid on Crete during April 1942.
4. Force Overt, using 1st RM Coast Regiment sent 500 men to Maldives in Jan 1942 with bulldozers, diggers, Matador lorries. Their mission was to establish roads, a watch-tower and batteries. The latter consisted of 2 Batteries, each: 2 × 4" naval guns; 1 Battery: 1 × 6" naval gun. In February 1942, 100 men left to form Force Viper in Burma.
5. Elements of MNDB01 deployed to Ceylon in early 1942, including: 1st AA Regiment: 4 Batteries, each: 8 × 3.7" AA, plus twin Lewis AAMG with shields.
6. A second MNBDO was formed in January 1941, remaining in Britain until early 1943.

6.5 ROYAL MARINE NAVAL BASE DEFENCE ORGANISATION 2 (MNBD02), APRIL 1943–44, EGYPT, SICILY

The unit's main combat elements were:
1 Land Defence Force Royal Marine Battalion
1 AA Brigade (of 2 AA Regiments)
1 Coastal Defence Artillery Brigade (of 2nd Royal Coastal Artillery Regiment)

The unit deployed in Egypt in April–May 1943, then moved to Sicily in June 1943. Troops are rated at good training and good morale.

Supply Units

Included:
    1 Landing and Maintenance Unit:
        1 Landing Company: Coy HQ (2 (14 man) rifle secs, 2 cars, 1 truck, 2 LMG)
        3 Platoons, each: 100 men, 2 Sten, rifles, 2 × 20mm Oerlikon AA, 2 LMG, 1 crane, 2 boats, 2 diving suits, 1 lorry, 2 trucks, 20 × 12lb HE charges, concrete, scaffolds, electric cables
        1 Ship Unloading Company
        1 Defence and Pioneer Company
        1 Engineer Company: 1 Construction Section, 1 Workshop Section
    1 Group Ordnance Depot – supply troops
    1 Group Supply Unit:
        Supply Section
        Field Bakeries, each: 40 men, 20mm Oerlikon for local air defence
        Motor Transport Company:
            3 Transport Platoons, 1 Special Transport Platoon
            Petrol Depot Platoon, Water Platoon, Workshop Section
    1 Boat Unit: LCM Flotilla, Motor Boat Flotilla, Workshop Section
    1 MP Company
    1 Field Security Section
    1 Survey Section
    Workshop sections
    HQ Defence Platoon: 4 rifle secs, 3 LMG, 1 PIAT, 1 × 2" mortar
    Camouflage Section
    Chemical Warfare and Decontamination Section
    3 Signals Companies
    12th Royal Marine Searchlight Regiment:
        RHQ (2 (11 man) rifle secs, 1 Workshop Section)
            2 Batteries, each: Battery HQ (4 (9 man) rifle secs, 1 Workshop Section)
                4 Sections, each: HQ (1 (6 man) rifle sec)
                      2 Clusters, each: 3 searchlights, 3 (9 man) rifle secs, 1 (8 man) HQ sec

MAIN COMBAT ELEMENTS

Royal Marine Battalion
Btn HQ (6 rifle/SMG secs, radio)
    5 Troops, each: Troop HQ (1 (6 man) SMG sec, radio)
        2 Sections, each: HQ (2 men)
            2 (14 man) rifle/SMG secs, 3 LMG, 3 × 2" mortar
    1 Troop: 2 × 3" mortars, 2 Vickers MMG
    1 Signals Platoon: 21 men

3rd Royal Marine Heavy AA Regiment
RHQ
    4 Batteries, each: 2 Troops, each: 4 × 3.7" AA guns, 8 × twin Lewis AAMG w/shields, 1 Height Finder, 1 Predictor

4th Royal Marine Light AA Regiment
RHQ

24th, 25th, 26th Batteries, each: 3 Troops, each: 6 × 40mmL60 Bofors

2nd Royal Coastal Artillery Regiment

2 Batteries, each: 4 × 6" naval guns
1 Battery: trained on 88mmL56 Flak37, 90mmL53, 4" naval guns, 20mm Breda, 40mmL60 Bofors, found 6 × Vickers 3" QF AA coastal guns in Sicily, later manned captured 155mm coastal guns.
2 Batteries, each: 4 × 4" naval guns
1 Anti-Motor Torpedo Boat Battery: 4 × 40mm Bofors

Notes
1   Radios were in all Coy HQs and Battery HQs.

6.6 ROYAL NAVY COMMANDO 1942–43

Used during beach landings to mark unit boundaries and obstacles. Rated at excellent training and excellent morale.
Pl HQ (1 man)
3 Sections, each: 20 men, with rifles and 3 SMG, plus LMG and 2" mortars as required

6.7 ROYAL NAVY COMBINED OPERATIONS ASSAULT PILOTAGE PARTIES (COPP TEAMS), 1942–43, MEDITERRANEAN

11 Teams formed by Royal Navy, each: 2 men, 1 canoe. They were used for covert beach recce in the Mediterranean (Tunisia, Sicily and Italy). Rated at excellent training and excellent morale.

6.8 BRITISH SPECIAL OPERATIONS EXECUTIVE (SOE)

SOE (Special Operations Executive) formed Sections to operate agents in occupied countries, operating independently of army units, except for ventures with 10 Commando. Rated at excellent training and excellent morale. These included:
P–Section: Poland
Scandinavian Section (including Norwegian Independent Company No.1 – Commandos who operated regular fishing boat runs from Lerwick to Norway, August 1941 onwards, and resistance units in Norway)
52 Danes, from December 1941
Small scale Raiding Force, late 1940–March 1942: 5 (9 man) SMG secs, dinghies, 1 trawler
T–Section: Belgium
Netherlands SOE 'Korps Insulinde', May 1942 onwards (operated in Ceylon, raided Sumatra 1943): 50 Dutch. Later renamed Anglo-Dutch Country Section, renamed again British Force 136
N–Section: Netherlands
RF–Section: Gaullist French
F–Section: British agents in France
Malaya Section, May 1941 onwards

6.9 LONG RANGE DESERT GROUP 1940–43

Troops are rated excellent training and excellent morale.

August 1940

The unit's first foray into Italian territory as the Long Range Patrol:
HQ (3 × Chevrolet WB 30cwt, 4 × Ford V8 01 15cwt, 15 men – Signals, Light Repair, Medic sections)
R Patrol (supply): 10 × Chevrolet WB 30cwt 4x2 trucks, 1 × Ford V8 01 Pl HQ
T, W Patrols, each: Pl HQ (1 × Ford V8 01, 2 men)
4 Combat Troops, each: 10 × Chevrolet WB 30cwt 4x2 trucks,[8] 4 (7 man) rifle secs, 10 Lewis LMG, 4 Boys, 1 × 2" mortar
Marmon-Herrington Party: 4 × 6-tonne Ford-Marmon-Herrington 6x6 supply lorries

December 1940–February 1941

HQ (3 × Chevrolet WB 30cwt, 4 × Ford V8 01 15cwt, Signals, Light Repair, Medic sections)
1 Squadron: R, T Patrols, each:
Right Half-Patrol:
HQ Troop: 1 × Ford V8 01 15cwt w/Vickers MMG, 3 crew,
1 × Chevrolet WB w/radio and navigation aids, 1 Lewis, 1 Boys, 1 × 2" mortar, 3 crew
B Troop: 3 × Chevrolet WB, 1 radio, 3 Lewis, 2 Boys, 8 crew
Left Half-Patrol:
C Troop: 3 × Chevrolet WB, 1 × 37mm Bofors ATG, 2 Lewis, 8 crew
D Troop: 3 × Chevrolet WB, 3 Lewis, 1 Boys, 8 crew
1 Squadron: G Patrol (ex-Guards):[9] 2 Half-Patrols as above
S Patrol (Rhodesians):[10] 12 × Spa AS37 trucks for training

---

8   Chevrolet WB 30cwt had a Lewis MG at front right and Boys ATR on mount in the back, or a Lewis MG on central pillar in rear, 360° traverse. Its crew had an EY rifle-grenade launcher and possibly No. 68 rifle anti-tank grenades.
9   December 1940 onwards.
10   January 1941 onwards.

Marmon-Herrington Party: 4 × 6-tonne Ford-Marmon-Herrington 6x6 supply lorries
Total of 90 vehicles, 292 men. The Bofors 37mm had 45 rounds AP and 45 rounds HE. Each Troop had 1 EY rifle-grenade launcher.

March–April 1941
GHQ (30 × Ford F30 30cwt 4x4 trucks including spares)
    Heavy Section: 4 × 10-ton White 6x4 lorries
    Royal Artillery Section: 1 × Vickers VI OP Tank, 1 × 4.5" or 25pdr Howitzer, both portéed in Mack NR4 6x6 lorries
    A Squadron:
        G Patrol (Right Half Patrol):
            A HQ Troop: 1 × Ford V8 01, 1 × Vickers MMG, 1 × Ford F30 4x4 signals truck, 1 Lewis, 1 × 2" mortar
            B Troop: 3 × Ford F30 30cwt 4x4, 1 × Vickers MMG, 2 × Lewis, 1 Boys
        Left Half Patrol:
            C Troop: 3 × Ford F30, 1 × 37mm Bofors ATG, 2 × Lewis
            D Troop: 3 × Ford F30, 2 × Lewis, 1 × Vickers MMG, 1 Boys
        Y Patrol: 12 × Spa AS37 trucks for training
    B Squadron: R, S, T Patrols, each: as above

May–June 1941
GHQ (1 × 4x2 ambulance, Fiat Spa radio, workshop, office body trucks)
    Heavy Section: 4 × 10-ton White 6x4 lorries
    Royal Artillery Section: 1 × Vickers VI OP Tank, 1 × 4.5" or 25pdr Howitzer, both portéed in Mack NR4 6x6 lorries
    A Squadron: G, Y Patrol, each:
        2 Half Patrols, each: 7 × Ford F30, 1 × Ford V8 01, 2 × Vickers MMG,
            5 × Lewis, 1 Boys or .50" Vickers HMG or 37mm/45 Bofors
    B Squadron: R, S, T Patrols, each:
        Right Half Patrol:
            A HQ Troop: 1 × Ford V8 01, 1 × Vickers MMG, 1 × Ford F30 4x4 signals truck, 1 Lewis, 1 × 2" mortar
            B Troop: 3 × Ford F30 30cwt 4x4, 1 × Vickers MMG, 2 × Lewis, 1 Boys
        Left Half Patrol:
            C Troop: 3 × Ford F30, 1 × 37mm Bofors ATG, 2 × Lewis
            D Troop: 3 × Ford F30, 2 × Lewis, 1 × Vickers MMG, 1 Boys

June–August 1941
GHQ (1 × 4x2 ambulance, Fiat Spa radio, workshop, office body trucks)
    Heavy Section: 4 × 10-ton White 6x4 lorries
    Royal Artillery Section: 1 × Vickers VI OP Tank, 1 × 4.5" or 25pdr Howitzer, both portéed in Mack NR4 6x6 lorries
    A Squadron: G, Y, H Half-Patrol, each:
        6 × Ford F30, 1 × Ford V8 01, 2 × Vickers MMG, 4 × Lewis, 1 Boys or .50" Vickers HMG or 37mm/45 Bofors
    B Squadron: R, S, T Patrols, each:
        Right Half Patrol:
            A HQ Troop: 1 × Ford V8 01, 1 × Vickers MMG, 1 × Ford F30 4x4 signals truck, 1 Lewis, 1 × 2" mortar
            B Troop: 3 × Ford F30 30cwt 4x4, 1 × Vickers MMG, 2 × Lewis, 1 Boys
        Left Half Patrol:
            C Troop: 3 × Ford F30, 1 × 37mm Bofors ATG, 2 × Lewis
            D Troop: 3 × Ford F30, 2 × Lewis, 1 × Vickers MMG, 1 Boys

September–November 1941
GHQ (1 × 4x2 ambulance, Fiat Spa office body trucks, 2 × Ford F8 8cwt 4x2 pickups/signals)
    Heavy Section: 4 × 10-ton White 6x4 lorries
    Royal Artillery Section: 1 × Vickers VI OP Tank, 1 × 25pdr Howitzer, both portéed in Mack NR4 6x6 lorries
    Light Repair Section: Fiat Spa workshop trucks
    Signals Section: Fiat Spa radio vans
    Air Section: 2 × Waco biplanes
    Survey Section: 3 × Ford F30, 5 men
    A Squadron: R, T, S Patrols, each:
        Right Half Patrol:
            A HQ Troop: 1 × Ford F8 8cwt 4x2 pickup, 1 × Vickers MMG, 1 × Ford F30 4x4 signals truck, 1 Lewis, 1 × 2" mortar
            B Troop: 3 × Ford F30 30cwt 4x4, 1 × Vickers MMG, 2 × Lewis, 1 Boys
        Left Half Patrol:
            C Troop: 3 × Ford F30, 1 × 37mm Bofors ATG, 2 × Lewis
            D Troop: 3 × Ford F30, 2 × Lewis, 1 × Vickers MMG, 1 Boys
    B Squadron (detached): H, Y, G Patrols, each: refitting in Cairo

November 1941–February 1942
GHQ (1 × 4x2 ambulance, Fiat Spa office body trucks, 2 × Ford F8 8cwt 4x2 pickups/signals)
    Heavy Section: 4 × 10-ton White 6x4 lorries, 1 × 30cwt radio truck, 1 fitters/medic truck, 2 × Lancia 3RO 6t 4x4 lorries[11]
    Signals Section: Fiat Spa radio vans
    Air Section: 2 × Waco biplanes
    Survey Section: 3 × Ford F30, 5 men
    Light Repair Squadron: Fiat Spa workshop bodies
    A Squadron: Sqdn HQ (2 × Chevrolet 15cwt 1311X3, 1 × 2" mortar)
        R, T, S Patrols, each:
            1st Half Patrol: 1 × Chevrolet 15cwt, 4 × Ford F30, 2 × Vickers MMG, 3 Lewis, 1 Boys
            2nd Half Patrol: 6 × Ford F30, 1 × 37mm Bofors, 4 Lewis, 1 × Vickers MMG, 1 Boys
    B Squadron: G, Y Patrols, each: as A Squadron
In December 1941 the Indian Long Range Squadron was added:
    Sqdn HQ (2 × Chevrolet 15cwt 1311X3)
        1st Half Patrol: 1 × Chevrolet 15cwt, 4 × Ford F30, 2 × Vickers MMG, 3 Bren, 1 Boys
        2nd Half Patrol: 6 × Ford F30, 1 × 47/32, 4 Bren, 1 × Vickers MMG, 1 Boys

March–June 1942
GHQ (1 × 4x2 ambulance, Fiat Spa office body trucks, 2 × Chevrolet 15cwt 1311X3)
    Heavy Section: 4 × Mack NR9 lorries, 2 × Lancia 3RO 6t 4x4 lorries, 2 × 30cwt trucks
    Signals Section: Fiat Spa radio vans
    Air Section: 2 × Waco biplanes
    Survey Section: 3 × Chevrolet 30cwt 1533X2, 5 men
    Light Repair Squadron: Fiat Spa workshop bodies
    A Squadron: Sqdn HQ (2 × Chevrolet 15cwt 1311X3 or Jeeps),
        R, T, S Patrols, each:
            1st Half Patrol: 6 × Chevrolet 30cwt, 1 × Vickers MMG, 2 Lewis, 1 × 20mm Breda, 2 × Vickers .50" HMG, 2 × Vickers K, 1 2" mortar
            2nd Half Patrol: 5 × Chevrolet 30cwt, 1 × 20mm Breda, 3 Lewis, 1 × Vickers K, 1 × Vickers .50" HMG
    B Squadron: G, Y Patrols, each: as A Squadron
    Indian Long Range Squadron: Sqdn HQ (2 × Chevrolet 15cwt 1311X3)
        1st Half Patrol: 1 × Chevrolet 15cwt, 4 × Ford F30, 2 × Vickers MMG, 3 Bren, 1 × Vickers .50" HMG
        2nd Half Patrol: 6 × Ford F30, 1 × 20mm Breda, 4 Bren, 1 × Vickers MMG, 1 × Vickers .50" HMG
Excluding the Indian Long Range Squadron, the LRDG consisted of 349 men and 110 vehicles.

July–August 1942
GHQ (1 × 4x2 ambulance, Fiat Spa office body trucks, 2 × Chevrolet 15cwt 1311X3)
    Heavy Section: 4 × Mack NR9 lorries, 10 × 3t CMP Ford F60 4x4 trucks, 2 × 30cwt trucks)
    Signals Section: Fiat Spa radio vans
    Air Section: 2 × Waco biplanes
    Survey Section: 3 × Chevrolet 30cwt 1533X2, 5 men
    Light Repair Squadron: Fiat Spa workshop bodies
    A Squadron: Sqdn HQ (2 × Chevrolet 15cwt 1311X3 or Jeeps)
        R, T, S Patrols, each:
            1st Half Patrol: 1 × Jeep, 5 × Chevrolet 30cwt, 1 × Vickers MMG, 2 Lewis, 1 × 20mm Breda, 2 × Vickers .50" HMG, 2 × twin Vickers K
            2nd Half Patrol: 1 × Jeep, 4 × Chevrolet 30cwt, 1 × 20mm Breda, 3 Lewis, 1 × twin Vickers K, 1 × Browning .50" HMG
    B Squadron: G, Y Patrols, each: as A Squadron
    Indian Long Range Squadron: Sqdn HQ (2 × Chevrolet 15cwt 1311X3)
        1st Half Patrol: 1 × Jeep, 4 × Chevrolet 30cwt, 2 × Vickers MMG, 3 Bren, 1 × Vickers .50" HMG
        2nd Half Patrol: 1 × Jeep, 5 × Chevrolet 30cwt, 1 × 20mm Breda, 4 Bren, 1 × Vickers MMG, 1 × Vickers .50" HMG

September 1942–March 1943
GHQ (1 × 4x2 ambulance, Fiat Spa office body trucks, 2 × Chevrolet 15cwt 1311X3)
    Heavy Section: Rear Element: 4 × Mack NR9 lorries, 2 × 30cwt trucks
    Forward Element: 10 × 3t CMP Ford F60 4x4 trucks
    Signals Troop
    Air Section: 2 × Waco biplanes
    Survey Section: 3 × Chevrolet 30cwt 1533X2, 5 men
    Light Repair Squadron: Fiat Spa workshop bodies
    'Popski's Private Army':[12] 23 men, 5 Jeeps, each: 3 × Vickers K
    A Squadron: Sqdn HQ (2 × Jeeps w/twin Vickers K MG)

---

11   Captured and used from January 1942.
12   December 1942 onwards.

R, T, S Patrols, each:
    2 Half Patrols, each: 2 × Jeeps, 4 × 30cwt trucks, each Patrol sharing 2 × Breda 20mm, 5 × Browning .50"M2, 1 × Vickers MMG, 5 × Lewis/Bren MG, 3 × Vickers K
B Squadron: G, Y Patrols, each: as A Squadron, except G Patrol reduced to one Half-Patrol by November 1942.
Indian Long Range Squadron: 4 Patrols, each: as A Squadron

6.10 SPECIAL AIR SERVICE (SAS) UNITS, 1941–43

Rated at excellent training and excellent morale.

North Africa

David Stirling L–Detachment, SAS, July 1941–43: 67 men, initially parachute-trained; more vehicles became available from November 1941. From 1942 they were equipped with Jeeps w/.30" Browning on front and twin Vickers K LMG in rear.

1st Special Air Service Regiment, December 1942–December 1943

5 Squadrons, each: 80 men
1 French SAS Squadron:[13] approx. 30 men
Greek Sacred Squadron: 140 men, Jeeps w/Vickers K MGs,
From May 1943:
    246 men in 3 Commando Units, each: Multiple 5-man Combat Teams
    1 Special Boat Section:[14] 12 men, later expanded to
    Special Boat Section: HQ (1 (18 man) rifle/SMG sec, 2 trucks)
    4 Groups, each: 1 (7 man) sec, 1 LMG, 3 canoes, 1 truck

6.11 SPECIAL BOAT SERVICE/SQUADRONS, 1940–43

Rated at excellent training and excellent morale. The first Special Boat Service squadrons were established in July 1940.

March–August 1942

HQ (1 (18 man) pistol/rifle sec, 2 trucks)
    4 Groups, each: 1 (7 man) SMG/rifle sec, 3 canoes, 1–3 LMG, 1 truck

September–December 1942

1 SBS section operated in Palestine, Aegean: 8 (6 man) teams, half Greek, half British, armed w/SMG, Brens, boats
Another SBS Troop was forming in Persia, to become M Section SBS, August 1942 – 8 men.

1943

Sqdn HQ (30 men)
    3 Detachments, each: 77 men, SMG, Brens
One Detachment served in Syria, Lebanon, another was active in the Aegean, a third in Sicily, and Italy.

6.12 SPECIAL SERVICE SQUADRONS, ROYAL ARMOURED CORPS, MID-1941–MID-1942

These units were formed to support Commando operations. C Squadron went to Freetown (Sierra Leone). 1 Squadron later participated in the invasion of Madagascar. Rated at good training and good morale.
    C Squadron (July–October 1941): Sqdn HQ (2 × Tetrarch)
        1 Troop: 4 × Tetrarch
    A, B, C Squadrons, each (October 1941–42): Sqdn HQ (2 × Valentine II)
        2 Troops, each: 3 × Valentine II
        2 Troops, each: 3 × Tetrarch

6.13 BRITISH AND COMMONWEALTH SPECIAL FORCES, 1942–43, FAR EAST

Troops are rated at good training and good morale unless otherwise noted.

Royal Marine Force Viper, February–April 1942, Burma

HQ (1 (2 man) SMG sec)
    3 Platoons, each: 1 (4 man) Pl HQ SMG sec, 1 × 2" mortar, 1 radio
        3 rifle/SMG secs, 3–5 LMG, 1 × steam launch w/Vickers MMG, 1 small motor boat, 1 × 47/32 Bohler A/T gun[15]

Burma II Commando, February–April 1942, Burma

30 troops w/SMG, explosives[16]

---

13   Until June 1943.
14   Forerunner of the Special Boat Service.
15   April 1942.
16   Commanded by Mike Calvert, R.E.

240th Mission Battalion, 1942–43, China
Btn HQ (1 British Commando SMG/rifle sec, 2 Chinese rifle secs)
2–4 Chinese Surprise Companies (poor training and poor morale), each: Coy HQ (1 rifle sec)
3 Platoons, each: 3 rifle secs, 1 LMG
1 British Commando Company (good training and good morale): Coy HQ (1 rifle/SMG sec)
2 Platoons, each: 3 rifle/SMG secs, 3 LMG, demo charges

Australian Independent Companies, Late 1941 Onwards
Rated at excellent training and excellent morale.
4 Companies, each: Coy HQ (2 (8 man) rifle secs, 1 (5 man) Medical staff, 4 motorcycles, 1 truck)
1 Pioneer Section: 1 (18 man) rifle/engineer sec
3 Platoons, each: Pl HQ (1 (9 man) rifle/SMG sec)
3 (18 man) rifle/SMG secs, 6 Bren LMG, 3 snipers

1st Indian Independent Company, April 1941 Onwards, Malaya
301 men in total. Rated at good training and good morale.
Coy HQ
5 Platoons (75% Indian personnel)
Signals Section
Motor Transport Section

1st And 2nd Fiji Commando, 1943, Pacific Islands,
Each:
Btn HQ (2 (11 man) rifle/SMG secs)
2 Companies, each: Coy HQ (1 (9 man) rifle/SMG sec)
3 Platoons, each: 3 (7 man) rifle/SMG secs, 3 LMG, 1 (1 man) Pl HQ NCO

Southern And Eastern Independent Commandos, December 1942–June 1943, Guadalcanal
New Zealand officers and NCOs, Fijian guerrillas: 1 (2 man) HQ, 4 (7 man) patrols. Later reformed as the South Pacific Scouts: 2 (15 man) patrols

Rose Force, December 28th 1941–January 1942, Malaya
A Platoon from HMS Prince of Wales, conducting boat raids, ambushes, and demolitions, during the retreat to Singapore. It later merged with the 'Plymouth Argylls' Battalion, 11th Division.

NOTES FOR WARGAMERS

The lists in this book do not include points values, and therefore can be utilised with any rules system.

If not using points values, the following method can be used to generate realistic battlegroups, particularly with regard to equipment and vehicles available. Indeed, this method could be combined with points values; the lists are designed to be flexible to the gamer's own needs.

- Agree with opponent or organiser on points limit, or on the number of 'teeth arm' or main combat element companies and support platoons to be fielded. A typical limit could be two companies and three support platoons.
- Select companies as desired from the main combat elements in the particular list, up to the limits imposed above.
- The battlegroup HQ is determined from the type of main combat element companies fielded: if one type is in the majority, then field that type's battalion HQ or equivalent; if equal numbers of 2 or 3 types are fielded then combine the battalion/equivalent HQs as the battlegroup HQ. For example, if 2 tank and 2 infantry companies are used, then the battlegroup HQ would consist of a combined tank battalion HQ and infantry battalion HQ; if a full battalion plus more than one company of another battalion is fielded, then use the full battalion's brigade or regimental HQ as the battlegroup HQ.
- Any main combat element recce or support companies can be split up so that individual platoons can be fielded as desired, being classed as support that does not need to be diced for.
- Brigade level support can be fielded as desired only if the appropriate brigade or regiment HQ is fielded, otherwise it must be diced for.
- Division, corps and army level support must be diced for. Any company at these levels can be split up and individual platoons fielded.
- Dicing for support: select the platoon or company type desired, then note the maximum number of that type of unit; multiply this by the number of main combat element companies being used; then multiply by the following number, to give the % chance of obtaining the desired unit:

Regimental/brigade level support	10
Divisional level support	5
Corps level support	1
Army level support	0.5

- Before rolling, it can be decided to split the resultant percentages, thus giving more than one chance of obtaining the unit type in question, e.g. 60% could be split into 2 rolls at 30% and so on.
- Any company HQ or battalion HQ can have two couriers attached, on foot, horse, motorcycle or jeep, as appropriate to that army list. Infantry battalions can add 2 snipers per infantry company, with morale and training one level above accompanying troops.
- Any platoon can be fielded one section or vehicle short to represent combat losses, and any company can be fielded one platoon short.

ARTILLERY FIRE CONTROL

Artillery batteries have three types of fire control noted in the lists, these being Obsolete, Assigned, and Flexible. Unless noted otherwise, the fire control of all batteries listed in this book is of the Flexible type unless stated otherwise. Descriptions are as follows:

OBSOLETE FC: The battery can only be used for pre-planned fire, on-table direct fire, or indirect fire controlled by runner or telephone. This is typical of armies without radios.

ASSIGNED FC: The battery is controlled by radio or telephone, but is assigned to a battlefield company HQ or the battlegroup HQ. It can only be controlled by that HQ, and there is no separate OP team. If the controlling HQ is lost in battle, then the battery is considered out of action for the rest of the battle. Alternatively the battery can be fielded up-front as a direct fire unit. This is typical of armies with poor training and limited radios; a commander from the artillery battalion has a vehicle at the battalion or regimental command post it is supporting.

FLEXIBLE FC: This applies to WWII German and post-July 1942 US and British armies only. The battery is allocated to the battlegroup HQ (BHQ) via an artillery rear-link (usually a radio van or armoured OP) vehicle which is fielded on-table. In addition, most batteries have one or two OP (observation post) teams, each of 3 men and a backpack radio, often in a vehicle or aircraft, who control the battery and can call down fire from other batteries in the same artillery battalion or regiment. If not in an aircraft, these OPs will also have a direct radio link to the BHQ.

In addition to the above, most corps or army batteries are used only for pre-planned or counter-battery fire, although they can be assigned or allocated to the BHQ as above.

TACTICAL DOCTRINE

To a large extent, modern mechanised combat is based around the battlegroup, in which a brigade mixes and matches its battalions to the task in hand, for example, by detaching an infantry company from its parent battalion and joining it with a tank battalion, or by attaching a tank company to an infantry battalion. British and Commonwealth units were notoriously bad at forming task-orientated battlegroups until after mid-1944, and even after this date their abilities were limited. Most forces would consist of a main combat element's battalion or regiment, with artillery assigned as required; other main combat element units would also be present, remaining under their parent command, even if assigned to support a particular unit. This was especially evident in North Africa, where armoured brigades repeatedly fought without their infantry support. It was only after 1944 that improvised battlegroups became common, more so in Italy and the Far East, where combined arms groups could be formed down to company level.

For the period covered by this book no mixed battalions were formed, and if two different battalions/regiments were tasked to attack the same target, they would often act virtually independently. Initial planning may have specified that they support one other, but this was little trained for, and so rarely happened effectively. The only exceptions to this were the tank brigades, which were designed to be split and assigned at the ratio of one troop per infantry company or one squadron per infantry battalion. However, again, cross-training was in limited in practise, and the tank brigades tended to be used as heavy armoured brigades for assault work.

After about July 1942 the British restructured their artillery support, such that it became the best in the war. Adopting the 'Flexible Fire Control' system described earlier in this appendix, British OP teams (or Forward Observation Officers) could order the fire of their own battery/troop, and given time could *order*, not *request*, the fire of all batteries up the chain of command. For example, once one troop was firing, the rest of the battery could then be ordered onto the same target, then the whole regiment (so-called 'Mike Target'), then all the divisional regiments ('Uncle Target'), and then all corps batteries ('Victor Target'), and army level batteries ('William Target'). Fire could be restrained and timed so that all shells landed together – Time On Target firing, but this was rarely done. British OP teams were highly trained and had good initiative in deciding the level of fire required for a certain target type – they would not request a corps heavy artillery regiment to destroy one A/T gun platoon holding up a tank advance, when one battery could do the job, but on the other hand, they could request everything up to offshore battleships when a Panzer corps presented itself, as happened in Normandy. However, British artillery prior to mid-1942, despite the fact that it had possessed separate OP teams as far back as 1940, did not have the training and radio support required to be rated 'Flexible Fire Control', so instead should be treated as 'Assigned Fire Control'.

BIBLIOGRAPHY

Atkin, Ronald *Pillar of Fire, Dunkirk 1940* (London: Sidgwick & Jackson, 1990)
Bellis, Malcolm A. *Divisions of the British Army 1939–1945* (Crewe: Malcolm A. Bellis, 2000, 2nd ed.)
Bellis, Malcolm A. *Commonwealth Divisions 1939–1945* (Crewe: Malcolm A. Bellis, 1999)
Bijl, Nick van der *The Royal Marines 1939–1993* (London: Osprey, 1994)
Command Post/Command Post Quarterly – various issues, 1993–2000
Draper, Alfred *Dawns like Thunder – the Retreat from Burma* (London: Leo Cooper, 1987)
Elphick, Peter *Singapore, the impregnable fortress* (London: Hodder & Stoughton, 1995)
Farran, Roy *Adventures on Special Service* (London: Arms & Armour Press, 1986)
Forty, George and John Duncan *The Fall of France* (London: Guild Publishing, 1990)
Gregory, Barry *British Airborne Troops* (London: Macdonald & Jane's, 1974)
Hughes, David, James Broshot and Alan Philson *The British Armies in World War Two, an Organisational History Volume One – British Armoured and Cavalry Divisions* (West Chester, Ohio: George F. Nafziger, 1999)
Hughes, David, James Broshot and Alan Philson *The British Armies in World War Two, an Organisational History Volume Two – Polish, Australian, Canadian, South African and Indian Armoured and Cavalry Divisions, British Regular Infantry Divisions* (West Chester, Ohio: George F. Nafziger, 2000)
Hughes, David, James Broshot and David A. Ryan *The British Armies in World War Two, an Organisational History Volume Three – British Infantry, Mountain, Reserve and County Divisions, Independent Infantry Brigade Groups, Deception Divisions and Dummy Brigades* (West Chester, Ohio: George F. Nafziger, 2001)
Hughes, David, James Broshot and David A. Ryan *The British Armies in World War Two, an Organisational History Supplement One – Orders of Battle 1939–1941* (West Chester, Ohio: George F. Nafziger, 2001)
Jenner, Robin and David List *The Long Range Desert Group 1940–1945* (London: Osprey, 1999)
Kersaudy, Francois *Norway 1940* (London: Arrow Books, 1990)
Ladd, James *Commandos and Rangers of WW2* (London: BCA, 1978)
Ladd, James *The Royal Marines 1919–1980* (London: Jane's, 1980)
Leasor, James *The Marine from Mandalay* (London: Leo Cooper, 1988)
Lord, Cliff and David Birtles *The Armed Forces of Aden 1839–1967* (Solihull: Helion, 2000)
Mains, Tony *The Retreat from Burma* (London: W. Foulsham, 1973)
MacDonald, Callum *The Lost Battle, Crete 1941* (London: Macmillan, 1993)
Parish, Michael Woodbine *Aegean Adventures 1940–1943* (Lewes: Book Guild, 1993)
Perrett, Bryan *British Tanks in North Africa 1940–1942* (London: Osprey, 1981)
Perrett, Bryan *The Churchill Tank* (London: Osprey Publishing, 1980)
Pitt, Barrie *Special Boat Squadron. The Story of the SBS in the Mediterranean* (London: Century Publishing, 1983)
Plowman, Jeffrey *Armoured Fighting Vehicles of New Zealand 1939–1959* (Christchurch: JEP Publications, 1985)
Rutherford, Bill *The Gamer's Guide to WW2 Small Unit Organisations and TOEs* (Alexandria, Virginia: Quality Castings Inc., n.d.)
Tank TV – the World of Fighting Vehicles – various issues, 1993–2000
Thomas, Nigel *Foreign Volunteers of the Allied Forces 1939–1945* (London: Osprey, 1991)

It must be acknowledged that David A. Ryan has given permission to use much of his material on British and Commonwealth orders of battle that he has collected over the years, and he has graciously supplied many notes on individual unit organisations. Amongst others, David kindly supplied notes on the following formations:

    Middle East orders of battle, February 1943
    Expansion of the Armed Forces and Defence Organisations, Plosad, Orient
    Indian Army order of battle, December 1941
    9th Army in Palestine
    10th Army in Persia
    Malaya Garrisons November 1941, January 1942
    New Zealand garrisons
    Gary Kennedy kindly supplied notes on the following:
    1940 and 1943 Motor Battalion War Establishments
    British Air Landing Battalions

Also available from Helion & Company

The Armed Forces of Aden 1839–1967
Cliff Lord and David Birtles
120pp., 8pp. colour plates, 102 b/w photos, maps
Hardback, limited edition of 500 numbered copies   ISBN 1-874622-40-X

In a Raging Inferno: Combat Units of the Hitler Youth 1944–45
Hans Holzträger
148pp., 4pp. colour plates, 100+ b/w photos, maps
Hardback   ISBN 1-874622-60-4

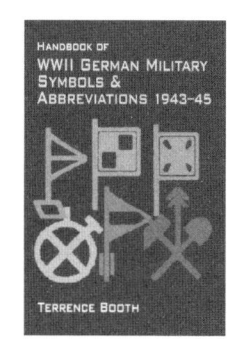

Handbook of WWII German Military Symbols and Abbreviations 1943–45
Terrence Booth
128pp., 800 b/w symbols, over 1,200 German military terms translated
Paperback   ISBN 1-874622-85-X

A SELECTION OF FORTHCOMING TITLES:

British and Commonwealth Armies 1944–45 (Helion Order of Battle volume 2)
Mark Bevis   ISBN 1-874622-90-6

Imperial German Army 1914–18 – Organisation, Structure, Orders of Battle
Hermann Cron and Duncan Rogers   ISBN 1-874622-70-1

US Army Infantry Divisions 1943–45 Volume 1 – Organisation, Doctrine, Equipment
Yves J. Bellanger   ISBN 1-874622-95-7

Rays of the Rising Sun. Japan's Asian Allies 1931–45 Volume 1 – China and Manchukuo
Philip S. Jowett and John Berger   ISBN 1-874622-21-3

SOME ADDITIONAL SERVICES FROM HELION & COMPANY ...

BOOKSELLERS
- over 20,000 military books available.
- four 100-page catalogues issued every year.
- unrivalled stock of foreign language material, particularly German.

BOOKSEARCH
- free professional booksearch service – no search fees, no obligation to buy.

Want to find out more? Visit our website

Our website is the best place to learn more about Helion & Co. It features online book catalogues, special offers, complete information about our own books (including features on in-print and forthcoming titles, sample extracts and reviews), a shopping cart system and a secure server for credit card transactions, plus much more besides!

HELION & COMPANY
26 Willow Road, Solihull, West Midlands, B91 1UE, England
Tel 0121 705 3393   Fax 0121 711 4075
Email: publishing@helion.co.uk   Website: http://www.helion.co.uk